PLAYING THE PERCENTAGES

PLAYING THE PERCENTAGES

*How Film Distribution Made
the Hollywood Studio System*

Derek Long

University of Texas Press   *Austin*

Requests for permission to reproduce material from this work should be sent to:
    Permissions
    University of Texas Press
    P.O. Box 7819
    Austin, TX 78713-7819
    utpress.utexas.edu

♾ The paper used in this book meets the minimum requirements of ANSI/NISO
Z39.48-1992 (R1997) (Permanence of Paper).

Library of Congress Cataloging-in-Publication Data

Names: Long, Derek, Ph. D., author.
Title: Playing the percentages : how film distribution made the Hollywood stu-
dio system / Derek Long.
Description: First edition. | Austin : University of Texas Press, 2024. | Includes
bibliographical references and index.
Identifiers: LCCN 2023035286 (print) | LCCN 2023035287 (ebook)
    ISBN 978-1-4773-2894-1 (hardback)
    ISBN 978-1-4773-2895-8 (pdf)
    ISBN 978-1-4773-2896-5 (epub)
Subjects: LCSH: Motion pictures—United States—Distribution—History—20th
century. | Motion picture studios—United States—History—20th century. |
Motion picture industry—United States—History—20th century.
Classification: LCC PN1993.5.U6 L595 2024 (print) | LCC PN1993.5.U6
(ebook) | DDC 384/.809730904—dc23/eng/20231023
LC record available at https://lccn.loc.gov/2023035286
LC ebook record available at https://lccn.loc.gov/2023035287

doi:10.7560/328941

For my father, who taught me to love "the show"

Contents

Illustrations

PLAYING THE PERCENTAGES

Introduction

Between 1910 and 1930, the American film industry underwent profound changes in its corporate organization and the product it sold. In the early 1910s, dozens of production companies contracted with one of three national distributors that rented films to more than eighteen thousand independent theaters. This industry was geared toward the production of short films, sold as part of a variety program that most theaters changed every day. By the beginning of the 1930s, that industry had transformed into an oligopoly of eight distributors producing in-house, five of which collectively owned the most lucrative theaters in practically every American city. These distributors released individual sound features, sold and packaged as part of a block program but marketed and priced as individual units. This was what Tino Balio has termed the "mature oligopoly"—the Hollywood studio system—and elements of its basic corporate and sales structure remain in place even in the multimedia conglomerates of today.[1]

Film studies certainly has no shortage of books about this system and its origins. Some of these books conceive of Hollywood as fundamentally an industry of film production—a factory system for the movies that chafed against the creativity of individual artists while simultaneously creating great art through the "genius of the system."[2] Others examine the studio system as an institution of cultural production, highlighting its racism, sexism, and poor treatment of workers, or the ways it interfaced with broader cultural phenomena of the twentieth century. Still others have considered the studio system through its retail side, as an industry of exhibition and reception in both theatrical and nontheatrical settings. Few book-length works on Hollywood, however, have focused on the sector that built and sustained it as an *economic* system rather than a creative or cultural one: distribution.

As an economic engine, distribution situated the nascent film industry within the existing system of entertainment in the early twentieth century. It also allowed the industry to control its product according to the logics of contemporary capitalism and to dominate exhibitors. Yet most accounts of the studio system either ignore the distribution sector entirely or conceptualize it as an adjunct of film exhibition or vertical integration. What if we were to examine film distribution as an active and contested set of practices? What if we attended to the conventions of early twentieth-century marketing, sales culture, and show business that influenced it? Or to distribution's role in structuring both the production of films and their exhibition to audiences? How would a history of film distribution reframe our understanding of the other historical developments that forged the Hollywood studio system?

This book is the story of how Hollywood's vertically integrated studio system came to be, told not as a "golden age" narrative of films, stars, or individual studios, but as an economic history of the industry's film distribution practices. It examines a twenty-year campaign waged by various distributors to package, circulate, and price their product to theater-retailers with a degree of flexibility and control matched by few other businesses in early twentieth-century industrial capitalism. Through a combination of archival research, critical surveys of the film industry trade press, and approaches from business history, theater history, and economic analysis, this book locates precursors to Hollywood's distribution practice in live-theatrical industries and examines the role of local distribution concerns in the industry's drive for control. It examines the effect of changing distribution practices on production organization at the scale of the individual release season. It also illustrates the importance of power struggles between distributors and exhibitors over booking, pricing, and playing time and highlights the crucial changes in film distribution brought about by the transition to sound.

The book's central argument is this: Over the course of the 1910s and 1920s, the marketing and sales practices that governed the commercial distribution of films to theatrical venues in the United States developed in a nonlinear way. The distribution industry, faced with the problem of profitably marketing multireel feature films to tens of thousands of individual theaters across the country, experimented with a variety of practices for packaging and pricing films while spatially and temporally controlling their circulation. This was a development of fits and starts, governed by several proximate contexts but ultimately driven by the distributors' goal of maximizing the profitability of each film playing in each theater, however marginal. Distributors initially sought this maximization by maintaining rigid distinctions within film distribution, with specially marketable feature films released through a completely separate channel from regular program films. These distinctions mirrored both the structure and the practice of distribution in legitimate theater and vaudeville. However, beginning in the mid-1910s, distribution companies began to merge these bifurcated channels into a single system, modeled on mass-market merchandising, that gave them maximum logistical flexibility and pricing power over their films' circulation. They did so by creating booking, pricing, and contracting practices unique to cinema and forcing exhibitors to adopt them.

Distributors honed these practices through continuous experimentation and adjustment based on previous experience. Like a baseball manager putting a right-handed batter up against a left-handed pitcher, the studios used distribution practices to create a favorable set of conditions for the economic success of their films. As in baseball, this process was not always successful in individual instances or even across a single release season. But applied in the long run and on an industry-wide scale, it yielded a powerful engine for control over producers and exhibitors. This book examines how the studios learned to play the percentages of film distribution by deploying specific industrial practices in the 1910s and 1920s.

This history also draws attention to a somewhat underexamined period in the history of the American film industry: "Early Hollywood," from 1915 to about 1925. These years coincided with Hollywood's vertical integration and its emergence as a heavily capitalized industry financed by Wall Street, yet they tend to get short shrift compared to the transition to sound and the "Golden Age" of the 1930s and 1940s. To be sure, the period has been mapped extensively by work on such industry-related issues as the development of classical film style and technology,[3] Hollywood's dominance of overseas markets,[4] women's changing roles in the industry,[5] and the intersections between cinema and theater.[6] The historiography of this period has likewise detailed the "theater wars" between Paramount and First National, the rise of United Artists, the Arbuckle and William Desmond Taylor scandals, and the creation of the Motion Picture Producers and Distributors of America (MPPDA). Nevertheless, nestled as it is between two canonical transitions—first to multireel feature films, then to sound—the history of the industry in the late 1910s and early 1920s is sometimes reduced to a linear narrative charting the rise of vertical integration, theater acquisition, and corporate consolidation. While most scholars would acknowledge the dynamic changes in industry structure occurring in this period, film historians have barely begun to articulate the relationship of those changes to distribution, let alone their specific implications for film production, style, and culture.

In an age when digital technology has upended traditional distribution models for audiovisual media, why do we need a book about distribution in the "old medium" of cinema? A distribution-centered history of the early studio system is necessary for several reasons: First, distribution remains the least understood sector of the American film industry, and media industry studies in general have tended to neglect it relative to production, exhibition, and reception. Work that does attend to distribution tends to examine it as a phenomenon of media *circulation* rather than as a set of industrial *practices*. Put another way, distribution tends to be thought of first and foremost as a circulatory structure or conduit for getting media from producers to exhibitors. As a result, studies of it have tended to emphasize questions of cultural circulation and power: who saw and did not see particular films, how films moved geographically, how particular distribution models gave certain films and audiences cultural cachet, and so forth. These questions are important, and the scholars who have addressed them have made this work possible. However, attending to the material, operational specifics of film distribution *practice*—such as booking, dating, pricing, packaging, programs, quotas, exhibition valuation, and sales drives—highlights distribution not as a linking system or mere context for other questions, but as itself an active site of dynamic struggle between studios and exhibitors for control over the product that made them both money. Such an approach allows us to situate exhibitors' resistance to distributor control, which in the late 1910s and early 1920s was widespread and more effective than is often acknowledged, as a crucial factor in the making of the studio system.

Second, film historians have tended to reduce the somewhat complicated history of film distribution in these years to a single poorly understood term: "block booking." As a general description of the studios' mandate that exhibitors rent a group of films as a unit, block booking has been used as a shorthand to encapsulate a variety of distributor practices during a period when those practices shifted significantly in form, even between individual release seasons. Although the contemporary definition of the term did not widely appear in trade circulation until 1921, historians have used it unsystematically to describe essentially any form of distribution that organized films into group sales from the 1910s on. The details of these practices matter, and this book recovers them. While most film historians assume that exhibitors hated and resisted block booking, as well as the related practice of blind selling, historical evidence points to a more complicated picture. Most exhibitors changed their bills every day or two in the 1910s, and it was economically impossible, both for them and for distributors, to individually buy or view every film they played. In the late 1910s and 1920s, many such exhibitors actually preferred block sales to individual booking, which they viewed as an attempt by distributors to raise their prices to cover exorbitant production costs and star salaries. *Playing the Percentages* nuances our understanding of block booking by pointing out the diversity of uses to which the studios put it in an extremely heterogeneous exhibition market.

Third, most histories of Hollywood have tended to reduce the entire period between the rise of features in the mid-1910s and the transition to sound to a linear narrative of increasing vertical integration, picture palace construction, and capital investment from Wall Street. However, as this book shows, this period was not one of uninterrupted industry consolidation, and the eventual form that the Hollywood oligopoly took was not inevitable. Distribution practices from other forms of industrial entertainment provided potential strategies of economic domination that did not hinge on producing product in-house or directly owning massive theater chains. Indeed, histories of the industry during the 1920s have tended to ignore a curious delay in capital markets' investment in Hollywood. After an initial investment in the industry in 1919–1920 (as detailed by Janet Wasko, Lee Grieveson, and others), Wall Street interests did not systematically provide the studios with capital for the purchase of theater chains until the second half of the 1920s and especially after 1927, when studio purchases of exhibition chains accelerated substantially.[7] This delay may have been a result of significant problems and uncertainties in the film distribution market throughout the late 1910s and early 1920s, problems that the studios successfully quashed through specific practices, including uniform exhibition contracts, arbitration boards, prerelease distribution, and reorganized production slates. These practices were variously rolled out between 1921 and 1924—before the massive capital investments of the second half of the 1920s.

As a distribution-centered history, *Playing the Percentages* makes the case that as a particular media industry structure, the entire Golden Age period of the vertically integrated studio system should be understood as a historical aberration rather than as a norm. The structure of distributor-dominated independent production that obtained in the late 1910s and early 1920s and was replaced by the "mature" studio system over the course of the 1920s reappeared after that system's collapse in the 1950s. What truly measured the power of the distributors over the film industry during these years was as much the aggressive and exploitative trade practices they wielded to control distribution as their outright ownership of theaters. *Playing the Percentages* shows how distribution became the central locus of power relations in the media industries of the twentieth century, and how it fashioned the Hollywood studio system in the process.

Beyond Networks, Circulation, and Block Booking: Film Distribution as Practice

Media distribution studies is a rich and growing field of inquiry, but there remains much fundamental work to be done if we are to better understand the historical importance of film distribution during the early years of the Hollywood studio system. Certain unchallenged assumptions about distribution during this period have informed scholarship to this day, not only in studies of classical Hollywood but in media industry studies more broadly. To test these assumptions, we must think about distribution not only as a mechanism of cultural exchange or a network of power relations, but also as a set of specific industrial practices that are themselves historically grounded.

Business history, which as a field has tended to emphasize the historical importance of active managerial practices across different industry sectors (i.e., production, distribution, and consumption), provides some guidance. In his influential study of the development of managerial capitalism in the late nineteenth and early twentieth centuries, Alfred Chandler highlights the degree to which that development began with technologies of distribution. Railroads, in particular, required extensive logistical management practices. These fostered the development of professional management hierarchies that in turn reshaped other industries. This book marshals one of Chandler's basic ideas: that "the requirements of maintaining a high-volume, high-velocity flow of business forced the rapid growth of the multiunit managerial enterprise."[8] The film industry of the 1910s and 1920s underwent this growth in microcosm while implementing shifts in distribution strategy in reaction to shocks such as World War I and the recession of 1920–1921. My approach in this book is in part an application of what economic historians call the conduct model of industrial analysis, whereby distributors' conduct—their "observable economic behavior"—encompasses interrelated practices of production, distribution, and exhibition.[9]

This book also appeals to scholarly traditions from both within and outside of media studies. The historiographical revisionism of Robert Allen, Douglas Gomery, David Bordwell, Kristin Thompson, Janet Staiger, and others, which posits the idea of "generative mechanisms" in history, informs the consideration of specific distribution practices not simply as a conduit, circuit, or network between the production and consumption of specific media texts, but as themselves historically generative on an industry-wide scale. The emphasis on archival research in this tradition ties into what Eric Smoodin has termed "film history without films," as does scholarship on entertainment distribution outside of film in this period—most notably vaudeville and "legitimate" theater.[10] Since the 1930s, theater historians have written accounts of live-theatrical booking practice and its importance to the development of the theatrical industries in the nineteenth and twentieth centuries. Much as the film industry took live-theatrical distribution as a useful model, I take their work as a useful model for film studies.

Of course, film distribution has by no means been ignored within media or cinema studies. Robert Allen's foundational work on the interaction between vaudeville and film, as well as Charles Musser's work on early cinema's exhibition contexts, are vital starting points for considering the practices of the 1910s and 1920s. Michael Quinn's dissertation "Early Feature Distribution and the Development of the Motion Picture Industry" is a major influence on this book in its close attention to distribution as a set of discrete industrial practices. However, Quinn's account ends in 1921—just when troubles in the distribution market were coming to a head, and well before the important changes brought about by the transition to sound cinema. Furthermore, Quinn's work concentrates on one distributor, Paramount. This book takes a more expansive view, acknowledging Paramount's importance as an innovating firm and looking closely at some of its practices while also emphasizing that its model was not the only one with influence in the industry. Casting our historical gaze beyond Paramount is essential to a full account of distribution practice in this period, helping us to avoid what Mark Lynn Anderson has called the "Zukor myth."[11] Triangle, First National, Selznick, Fox, and other firms had different strategies, even if they were linked by similar goals.

Other works have attended to film distribution's broader role in transforming the American film industry in the 1910s. In his book on the career of film distributor George Kleine, Joel Frykholm makes the crucial point that "motion pictures began to be made, traded and widely regarded as qualitatively differentiated products rather than as piece goods" in the mid-1910s.[12] Frykholm emphasizes Kleine's advocacy for a qualitatively differentiated cinema by tracing his role in introducing multireel features to the American market and his criticism of one-reel program cinema. The bifurcation Frykholm notes is an important one for this book, which traces a similar distinction between "programmatic" and "idiosyncratic" strategies of film distribution. Rather than casting these two conceptions of cinema as separate and irreconcilable, however, this book shows how the distribution industry fused the separate models of differentiated features and more programmatic fare into a single, flexible system.

Lee Grieveson's *Cinema and the Wealth of Nations* details the role of finance capital firms, national governments, and other institutions in using cinema to expand the liberal capitalist system in the years between the world wars. His book has a broad and transnational focus and attends to distribution as an important factor in solidifying the "world machinery" and "infrastructural power" of the cinema industry.[13] However, Grieveson's examination of distribution, like Gerben Bakker's in *Entertainment Industrialized*, operates at a relatively high level of historical analysis that emphasizes its status as a network or circulation system for power relations.[14] *Playing the Percentages* is a more mid-level account that emphasizes the operational practices that upheld distribution as a working system of power.

Kia Afra's *The Hollywood Trust* attends to the role of Hollywood's trade associations in forging the industry's oligopoly across a periodization similar to the one discussed in this book. It covers distribution as one of many issues on which the MPPDA and other trade associations worked, alongside censorship, government regulation, and exhibitor relations. Afra's work provides crucial context and draws from sources similar to mine, but, like Grieveson's work, its discussion of distribution practices is limited to the standard catchalll of "block booking," defined broadly. Janet Wasko's *Movies and Money* deals with a similar institutional history in its attention to Hollywood's relationship with Wall Street, but focuses on distribution's importance for securing production financing for individual films.

Many scholarly books and other works cover the intersections between film and other show business industries, but none examine film distribution as an outgrowth of equivalent theatrical practice in detail. Robert Allen's study *Vaudeville and Film* emphasizes vaudeville's role as one of the earliest release and exhibition platforms for cinema, but his work focuses on broader economic interrelationships rather than distribution specifically.[15] William Paul's brilliant *When Movies Were Theater* includes important findings about distribution practice that go beyond the usual circulatory approach. While Paul's primary focus is the architecture of cinema exhibition spaces and its impacts on film style, business practice, and technology, his work highlights the practical distinctions studios made between theaters as channels for film distribution that served specific economic goals.

Aside from Quinn's and Frykholm's, the above-mentioned book-length works examine film distribution relatively briefly, and in relation to some other institutional aspect of cinema. Studies that attend to film distribution in a more sustained way tend to be article length, but even then usually as a means to illuminate some aspect of film production or (more commonly) exhibition. Indeed, one of the reasons film distribution has received less attention within scholarly literature is that it is surprisingly difficult to define. I would argue that this is due to a conceptual slippage—or at least a lack of distinction—between specific practices of film distribution and a broader concept that might be termed "exhibition patterning," or simply "film circulation."

Consider the introduction to the edited collection *Networks of Entertainment*, in which Frank Kessler systematically lays out three functions of distribution prompted by Jean Giraud's definition of the term in *Lexique française du cinéma des origines à 1930*: (1) a "relay function" involving the linking of film production and film exhibition; (2) a "placing" of prints "for exhibition purposes" and any physical processes, networks, or other forces attendant to that placing; and (3) the local, national, and international networks linking the "geographic areas in which distribution takes place."[16] Kessler's definition of distribution's functions, via Giraud, is a useful delineation of how film distribution's functioning has traditionally been conceived: as a network of circulation linking the making of films with their showing.

Despite its utility as a preliminary starting point, this definition and the functions it comprises remain unsatisfying. The idea of distribution as having a "relay function" or acting as an "intermediate stage" between production and distribution seems straightforward enough, but it is less a positive definition of distribution than a negatively defined assertion of in-betweenness, the unspecified filling of a conceptual lacuna. Certainly, characterizing distribution as a missing link opens several possible conceptualizations. Implicit in the notion of a "relay" are functions of both transportation and communication, for instance, and the physical and logistical aspects of film circulation are an important part of distribution that this book will examine. But the distinction between those implicit functions and the second function of the "placing of prints" remains somewhat unclear. Additionally, the idea of a relay, with its connotations of "passing something along," threatens to restrict our thinking about distribution to the notion of a top-down, one-way conduit for films.

Much of the most compelling recent scholarship on film distribution, from scholars such as Richard Maltby, Deb Verhoeven, Ramon Lobato, Paul S. Moore, Jeffrey Klenotic, Julia Hallam, Daniël Biltereyst, and many others, has tended to go in the direction of Kessler's third notional function: distribution as a geographical or cultural network of circulation. This work, which has emerged in large part thanks to computational tools and approaches within the fields of digital and spatial humanities, tends to offer fine-grained analyses and visualizations, broadly conceptualizing cinema distribution as it is instantiated by various forms of movement through space and time.[17] This scholarship's emphasis on circulation often comes out of methodological foundations in New Cinema History, which Richard Maltby defines as a multidisciplinary tradition that "has shifted its focus away from the content of films to consider their circulation and consumption, and to examine the cinema as a site of social and cultural exchange."[18] The multidimensionality implied by the terms "circulation" and "network" is useful because it conceptualizes cinema distribution as a set of two-way relationships existing not only *from* commercial producers *to* commercial exhibitors and vice versa, but also *among* and *between* other potential agents of exchange (audiences, itinerant projectionists, film pirates, etc.). This helps us to think about distribution beyond the simple top-down notion of cinema as a product that corporate producers "shipped out" for consumption. Visualizing that circulation also helps us to understand distribution as a network of power relations between those who make, move, and consume cinema.

However, given distribution's status as a site of power relations, visualizations of networks and analyses of circulation, whether close or distant, can only meaningfully describe those relations if they are accompanied by an understanding of the institutional and cultural practices that enforce them. Given the sheer volume of scholarship on the classical Hollywood studio system, there is often an implicit assumption that we already understand these practices. Some we certainly do, even within the domain of film distribution. Historians of the studio system are generally familiar with the importance of the first-run theater that served as a "show window" for its wares, its systematic and hierarchical division of exhibitors according to a run/zone/clearance model, and the wholesaling of films both desirable and undesirable into tied packages via block booking. However, cinema historians have barely scratched the surface of these practices. This goes for their role during the studio system's height in the 1930s and 1940s, and certainly in terms of their development in the 1910s and 1920s.

Block booking is a perfect example of a practice that has been oversimplified in previous accounts of film distribution. This is in part due to the work of Mae D. Huettig, whose 1944 book *Economic Control of the Motion Picture Industry: A Study in Industrial Organization* served as the foundation for nearly all subsequent industrially focused scholarship on the studio system.[19] Though a seminal achievement, Huettig's work relied heavily on somewhat unreliable historical accounts of the industry and contemporary framings of film distribution as an oligopolistic practice from the Federal Trade Commission (FTC) in the 1920s, as well as 1939 House and Senate hearings on block booking and blind selling.[20] While film distribution was and is an oligopolistic practice, Huettig's work elevated norms and assumptions about those practices as they stood specifically in the late 1930s—such as the assumption that most exhibitors resented block booking—to the level of a more general historical record. Later historians, working backward from Huettig in the absence of any alternative, subsequently wrote accounts of the development of block booking that anticipated the system specifically as it stood in the 1930s. Consider the following passage from Huettig: "In few other industries . . . does the distributor have such complete and detailed power as he has in the motion picture industry. The distributor of films may designate the admission price, the days in the week on which the film may be exhibited, the nature of the accompanying program, the amount and kind of advertising, and a host of related matters."[21] While distributors may have had these powers over exhibitors in the late 1930s—at the very height of the studio oligopoly—this had not always been the case. As I show later in this book, many exhibitors in the 1920s accepted block booking and related policies as the price of doing business, and some even saw them as welcome alternatives to the practices they replaced.

Huettig's emphasis on vertical integration into exhibition as the source of economic control in the movie industry has also tended to focus studies of distribution specifically around first-run exhibition in key cities. This has arguably marginalized other strategies of control the industry used, such as circuit booking, uniform contracting, and trade associations, within subsequent histories. As with her account of block booking, Huettig's account of distribution emphasizes the structure of the industry circa 1939. Though Huettig included a survey history of the industry, her book was not primarily a work of history but an economic study of contemporary Hollywood, conducted under the auspices of the Carnegie-financed Motion Picture Research Project. In that sense it was, as Wyatt Phillips has written, "an explication of the federal government's antimonopoly perspective."[22] Indeed, as Aimee-Marie Dorsten has shown, Huettig worked closely with attorneys and government officials who were associated with the case for *United States v. Paramount Pictures* (1948), and she may have provided research to or served as a witness for the government.[23]

For historians, Huettig's work provides an excellent synchronic view of one moment in the larger development of film distribution in the United States, but as a historiographical starting point for writing that history, we should be critical about its utility. Huettig's foundational work introduced several linear assumptions about block booking and first-run theaters into film distribution studies, assumptions that subsequent scholars have not fully interrogated. The received teleological narrative about film distribution in these years continues to emphasize the innovations of Adolph Zukor and Paramount while characterizing block booking as effectively an adjunct to the primary goal of controlling first-run theaters through vertical integration.

If historians are to accurately narrate the development of film distribution practice, they must work forward from the origins and contexts of that practice, not teleologically backward from its most developed form. Ultimately, I argue that distribution, rather than vertical integration, was the primary instrument most studios used to exert domination over the national film market before 1925. The film industry had to refine its distribution practices to a considerable extent before integration into exhibition at a national scale even became possible in the second half of the 1920s. There was little consensus about the exact form those practices should take before around 1922, and studios relied on a variety of distribution strategies—many of which looked to other industries as models, and some of which appealed to decentralized models of distribution.

Of Kessler's three functions of distribution, the second is closest to my own, as it accounts for "economic, political, legal, etc. forces" that "had an impact on the circulation of films."[24] Film distribution is a set of active practices governing the production and exhibition of cinema, with the goal of optimizing both according to some regime of economic or cultural valuation. Ultimately, this is why its history has remained underresearched. Distribution's practices tend to make sense only in relation to production- or exhibition-related norms of valuation, so studying it, paradoxically, tends to lead the researcher away from its specifics and toward those other contexts. There's also the fact that the study of distribution as such sometimes calls for a deep dive into primary material that seems far removed from aesthetic, technological, and cultural questions, such as accounting documents, booking forms, and legal contracts. The operational practices of distribution are often simply less conceptually compelling for scholars of audiovisual media and culture, which perhaps explains the impulse to approach it through maps and other forms of visualization. Having worked on this project in one form or another for ten years, I understand why no one has yet written a book solely dedicated to the history of film distribution in the United States!

This book attends to the development of commercial American domestic film distribution—defined both historically and contemporarily within the industry as encompassing the United States and Canada. The history of Hollywood's distribution practices in international markets merits a monograph of its own, and the present volume is already long enough. However, I would be remiss not to offer some thoughts on the relevance of this history to the development of Hollywood's international distribution practice.

As Ross Melnick has shown in *Hollywood's Embassies*, the major studios exported the "shop window" model of exhibition to every corner of the world.[25] This exhibition model anchored an accompanying model in domestic film distribution: the run/zone/clearance system, which became standard around 1914 and reached its zenith in the 1930s. This system is familiar to cinema historians. By proving the value of their films in major-market, first-run cinemas that they controlled themselves, the studios initiated each film's journey through a structure of successive distribution networks. According to the "typical" model (which, as we will see, was never typical, but a constant work in progress), a film premiered in major urban markets first—its "first run"—as a way of both testing its value in exhibition and drumming up business for subsequent-run bookings. The film was then temporarily removed from circulation to encourage cinemagoers to see it during its run, a practice known as "protection" before the term's mob connotations prompted its redesignation as "clearance."[26] After its clearance period, the film reappeared in a different subsequent-run theater in the same distributor-defined geographic area, or "zone." This system established a hierarchy of theaters within each zone—first-run, second-run, and so on—that ensured the maximization of revenue to the distributor at every step.

Hollywood conceptualized the entire world according to this model. International distribution essentially amounted to another set of subsequent runs defined by economic criteria—which, under the logic of capitalism, also meant national, racial, and ethnic criteria. The specific practices that turned this conceptualization into reality, such as the manufacture of multiple negatives and the logistics of international exchange networks, will have to wait for another book. However, chapter 4's discussion of how early distributors managed both logistical and marketing problems on a national scale through franchising is relevant to the question of international distribution. American distributors had foreign sales agents, and some of them also operated as contracted franchisees. In 1915, the Triangle Film Corporation contracted its distribution in Canada to franchisee Ernest Fenton, whose contract required him to pay Triangle 50 percent of all rental profits plus a flat rate per foot of positive for each film he released.[27] Given the geographic distances, political contexts, and cultural differences that international distribution needed to account for, Hollywood doubtless relied on many "ambassadors" of distribution like Fenton (to continue Melnick's metaphor).

I should also acknowledge this work's relative lack of attention to the question of how race houses, ethnic theaters, and other sectors of exhibition conceived of by the industry as "marginal"—that is, not white or middle-class—fit into film distribution during this period. This is a direct function of the work's goals and scope. In part, a full account of these spaces would require a deep dive into film exhibition, and for the reasons outlined above I felt that an account too rooted in exhibition would dilute its focus on distribution. The diverse quality of film exhibition in this period is a running theme that carries through the book, however, and the form that film distribution took by the 1930s was engineered around the explicit hierarchization of theaters. In an era before modern consumer marketing, theaters were the primary way that distributors understood their audiences.[28] Considered from the standpoint of distribution, theaters that primarily served audiences of color were not outside of the distribution system, but they were at the bottom of a market hierarchy that conceptualized a national and global system with a totalized reach. As a result, they aligned with sectors in production and distribution that were excluded from consistent circulation and thus marginalized in the industry.

In chapter 2, I offer a potential way to conceptualize these sectors of the industry through the notion of idiosyncratic releasing. Idiosyncratic releasing treats individual films as special in some way, and thus to some extent as separate from the "normal" programmatic channels of distribution. For films made specifically for Black, Yiddish-speaking, Spanish-speaking, Chinese, and other "specialty" audiences in the United States during the studio system period, idiosyncratic releasing tended to be the norm, through either specialist companies, state rights firms, or even the filmmakers themselves (Oscar Micheaux being the most famous example). One of the goals of this work is to offer a historical framework and descriptive vocabulary for distribution that highlights how both roadshowed super-features and race films were, to varying extents, "outside" of programmatic systems geared toward the constant and temporally predictable circulation of films. The primary difference was that the former was eventually integrated into that system because of one omnipresent feature of American life (capitalism), and the latter was not because of another (racism).

Before proceeding to a breakdown of the chapters, a word on the overall approach of this work, which is rooted in archival research. In general, studios and archives did not prioritize saving distribution records to the same extent as other types of material. Archival records of distribution are not particularly rare, but they are geographically dispersed and often quite fragmentary. Primary documents that paint a *clear* picture of the practices of film distribution are especially hard to come by. As a result, the research for this book has required visits to several repositories both physical and digital, including the Wisconsin Historical Society and the Wisconsin Center for Film and Theater Research, the Margaret Herrick Library, the Harry Ransom Center, the Library of Congress, the New York Public Library, the Shubert Archives, the MPPDA Digital Archive, and the Internet Archive. While only some of these archives are represented by direct citation in the book, all contributed to its overall direction. The most fundamental resource for this work, however, was the Media History Digital Library (MHDL) and its search engine, Lantern. The trade papers, yearbooks, and other materials it made easily accessible allowed a view of Hollywood's distribution practice at a fuller scale, and the book would not have come together either conceptually or practically without it. Essentially, every trade paper and yearbook cited in this volume was accessed via Lantern or the MHDL.

Chapter Overview

This book presents a mostly chronological account, structured according to the specific marketing and sales practices that film distributors adopted in their quest for a flexible system of control: precursor practices from live theater (chapter 1), packaging as it relates to groups of films (chapter 2) and individual films (chapter 3), space (chapter 4), time (chapter 5), and pricing (chapter 6). Because these practices developed in a largely ad hoc way, this book's narration cannot help but give form to some of the false starts and double-backs of a nonlinear process. The period 1917–1923 was an especially turbulent and complicated one for film distribution; thus, there is significant temporal overlap between chapters 3, 4, and 5. I have done my best to narrate these shifts.

Chapter 1 examines a broad set of precursor practices from entertainment distribution that the American film industry took up in its earliest years. The main theatrical industries of the late nineteenth century—vaudeville and legitimate theater—introduced many of the practices and models that would situate the distribution policies of the film industry in the 1910s and 1920s. Although cinema's need to distribute mechanically reproduced entertainments rather than live ones introduced unique problems, these earlier forms structured the relationship between the provider of an entertainment and the theatrical venue in ways that proved useful for the nascent cinema industry. This chapter presents three heuristic categories for thinking through how the practices of live-theatrical industries in the nineteenth and early twentieth centuries eventually became dominant models for cinema: booking, circuiting, and packaging.

Live-theatrical distribution provided paradigmatic options for the film industry as it developed its own distribution practice, and they help to reframe that development not as a teleology leading toward a "mature oligopoly" but through the context of established practices in other culture industries. As a case study of these intersections, the chapter concludes with an account of the distribution of *The Life of Our Saviour*, a 1914 passion-play film. As the booking correspondence covering the film reveals, the Shubert theatrical organization's motion picture division distributed the film to legitimate theaters according to a fundamentally live-theatrical model. The release's resulting problems highlight both the continuity and the increasing unsuitability of theatrically based strategies of feature film distribution in the mid-1910s.

Chapters 2 and 3 explore the development of the film industry's *packaging* practices, which specified the sales formats in which cinema might be sold for circulation. Chapter 2 concentrates on film packaging from its origins in the 1890s to the rise of feature programs in the mid-1910s, a period when the dominant models of film releasing sharply distinguished between the distribution of multiple-film programs and that of individual films. From the earliest days of the American film industry, the packaging of film as a product had been bifurcated between what might be called programmatic releasing—the sale of film product in tied bundles comprising multiple titles—and idiosyncratic releasing, an individually tailored approach reserved for those singularly marketable titles that warranted special handling. In the early 1910s, this bifurcation defined entirely separate distribution systems, but these separate systems began to merge starting around 1914 with the advent of the multireel feature program system.

Chapter 3 picks up in 1916, when the multireel feature program began to give way to other forms, marketed by the industry as "open booking," that ostensibly packaged films into smaller units of sale centered on various elements of differentiation. Though it took different forms, open booking reflected the differentiating power of individual stars and films as literal brands of distribution. In practice, however, its higher price compared to the earlier feature program effectively forced theaters to rent multiple packages of films from distributors for volume discounts. These packaging strategies provided distributors with a more flexible means of marketing their product individually while pricing it in bulk, and by the early 1920s major studio distribution accommodated both programmatic and specialized approaches for all their titles in a single flexible system. This system also helped to organize film production in a way that accounted more directly for distribution.

Whereas chapters 2 and 3 detail the history of film packaging, chapter 4 covers distributors' spatial strategies for managing national feature distribution. Received scholarship tells us that film distributors, from the General Film Company to Paramount, constantly sought to centralize a national system of releasing out of a patchwork of independent exchanges; this chapter, however, complicates that view. Major feature distributors in the mid-1910s, most notably Triangle and First National, risked significant capital on the assumption that a more decentralized system of distribution, one based on franchises controlled by local theater and exchange magnates, was the most effective way to sell, market, and ensure higher rental prices for expensive feature programs. At the same time, more centrally minded distributors nuanced film merchandising strategies in their New York home offices in an attempt to account for local preferences. By the early 1920s, the franchise system had been marginalized in favor of more centralized approaches, but the story of that marginalization, supported here by evidence covering Triangle and Paramount, reveals that there was little consensus in the industry about the optimal form of organization and integration before then. Ever more intricate systems for recording data on individual theaters and towns enabled this more centralized form of national feature distribution. This chapter concludes with case studies of that system based on surviving issues of *The Brain Exchange*, the internal house publication for distribution workers at the Selznick Organization in the early 1920s. I argue that *The Brain Exchange* itself served as a crucial instrument of the New York home office's centralized control over local exchanges, enabling it to conduct its distribution business as one of mass-market merchandising rather than wholesaling or franchising.

Chapter 5 covers film distribution as a strategy of temporal management. Despite the transformation of film packaging by the early 1920s, the distribution market remained an unsettled, unwieldy mess. Postwar inflation, increased production costs, economic recession, and the smaller units used to package films had resulted in overbooking, overselling, and large numbers of signed exhibition contracts that went unplayed. As distributors increasingly recognized the importance of granular, national-scale control over packaging, pricing, and runs to consistent profitability, they adopted various strategies that exerted closer control over the playdates of their films, including a Uniform Exhibition Contract for industry-wide use. As a case study of the implementation of these new strategies, the chapter looks closely at four consecutive release seasons at Paramount from 1920 to 1924. Across this period, the company rolled out block booking, instituted new policies for determining films' playdates, adopted the Uniform Contract, and introduced new extended-run release models for promising titles. By the 1924–1925 season, Paramount's release strategies enabled the distributor to sell its films to exhibitors in a small number of packaged blocks while at the same time pricing and scheduling the playdates of those films individually for maximum profit. The combination of selling films in bulk while scheduling them individually became standard practice by the mid-1920s.

Chapter 6 details the impact of the transition to sound in solidifying Hollywood's distribution practices. Since the rise of features and throughout most of the 1920s, most distributor contracts charged exhibitors flat fees for the right to rent films. While contracts charging exhibitors a percentage of their actual ticket sales were not unheard of, even among small-town theaters, before the mid-1920s they were reserved for the biggest and most marketable productions. By the end of the transition to sound in 1930, however, percentage rentals were a standard part of nearly all block-booked exhibition contracts. Citing trade press discourse and material from the MPPDA Digital Archive, this chapter argues that the transition to sound provided an opportunity for distributors to accelerate an ongoing industry shift toward percentage contracts through the mechanism of the MPPDA. The uncertainty around sound cinema in the industry between 1927 and 1929 gave distributors a powerful point of both rhetorical and economic leverage over exhibitors. By creating a National Board of Adjustment that took advantage of that leverage through various incentives for exhibitors to switch their contracts from flat fees to percentages, the MPPDA led a successful campaign to cut distributors in, decisively and permanently, on the American box office.

The Legacy of the Studio System: Distribution as Media Consolidation

Distributors undertook the distribution strategies detailed in this book—bulk packaging, centralized booking, and percentage pricing—in the context of numerous political and legal challenges. These challenges reached a zenith in the late 1920s, with resistance to block booking and the now renamed Standard Exhibition Contract from both exhibitor organizations and federal authorities. These included the Federal Trade Commission's case against Paramount, Iowa senator Smith Brookhart's 1927 anti–block-booking bill, and a 1929 US district court ruling, in *United States v. Paramount Famous Lasky* (the "Thacher Decree"), that neutered the compulsory arbitration clause of the distributors' Standard Exhibition Contract.

However, these challenges were almost completely ineffective in loosening the major distributors' control of the national market. Paramount effectively ignored the findings of the FTC case, the Brookhart bill went nowhere in Congress, and the Thacher Decree, upheld by the Supreme Court in 1930, did nothing against the other provisions of the Standard Contract. By the beginning of the 1930s, the major studios' control over the booking, dating, and pricing of films in the United States was overwhelming. Even with the 1940 consent decree and its limitation of the size of distribution blocks to five pictures, the temporal and pricing flexibility that the major studios had successfully built into the system in the 1920s remained, maintaining the distributors' power until the 1948 *Paramount* decision.

The "rationalized" distribution system that the major studios developed in the 1910s and 1920s has remained with us in modified forms to this day. As the first mass-distributed form of mechanically reproduced audiovisual entertainment, cinema adopted precursor practices from show business and set the stage for distribution policies in other media. From radio and television to Netflix and Disney+, careful spatial and temporal control over the availability and unavailability of individual media texts, combined with strategic packaging and pricing of those texts both individually and in groups, has enabled a handful of media distributors to exert dominance over markets. This has been the case whether or not distributors directly controlled the production or retail end of the industry through vertical integration; even the *Paramount* decision's forced divestiture of theaters and banning of block booking did not end the distributor oligopoly in Hollywood. It was likewise true in the days of vaudeville and the Theatrical Syndicate.

Recognizing that distribution, rather than vertical integration, is the fundamental mechanism of anticompetitive control in the media industries forces us to reconsider the role of the studio system in media historiography. Film historians, pointing first and foremost to the studios' ownership of first-run theaters as its defining characteristic, have characterized the studio system using various deterministic languages of culmination and decline: a "golden age," a "classical era," or a "mature oligopoly." But for the major studios, vertical integration was not a fundamental instrument of control; it was the icing on distribution's cake. Integration was arguably not even *possible* on any kind of scale before distributors had mastered the circulation of eight hundred films every year to eighteen thousand exhibitors.

Thus, the studio system of the 1930s and 1940s was not an inevitability, no matter how much the General Film Company and Adolph Zukor seemed to anticipate it in the 1910s, but an aberration within a longer-term pattern of distributor domination over otherwise independent production and exhibition sectors. Strategies deployed in the 1910s and 1920s in an industry struggling over the packaging, circulation, and pricing of cinema created this domination by the mid-1920s, even before large-scale vertical integration, and enabled it to continue after the *Paramount* decision of 1948 ended that integration. Given the continued dominance of half a dozen media conglomerates and the termination of the *Paramount* decrees in 2020, the story of Hollywood's rise to dominance through distribution continues to be relevant for historians, media critics, and regulators.

1 PRECURSORS

The Circuits of Show Business

*Vaudeville, Legitimate Theater, and the Origins of
American Entertainment Distribution, 1800–1920*

Hollywood was not the first American entertainment industry to face
the problem of efficiently circulating cultural performance at a national
scale. In the late nineteenth century, the two most important industries
of live-theatrical performance—legitimate theater and vaudeville—
introduced many of the distribution practices that would become standard for the film industry in the 1910s and 1920s. While cinema's distribution of mechanically reproduced attractions rather than live ones
posed unique problems, practices in live theater proved particularly
useful for the nascent film industry. By offering preexisting models for
structuring the relationship between entertainment providers and theatrical venues, these practices tended to serve film distributors in the same
way they had served live-theatrical interests: as instruments for market
control framed within a seemingly neutral discourse of efficient, "rationalized" management.

The circulation practices that the film industry imported from live
theater—a term that, along with the adjective "live-theatrical," I use
to encompass both vaudeville and legitimate theater—can be divided
into three broad categories: *booking*, *circuiting*, and *packaging*. It is

important to emphasize that these distinctions should not be considered especially useful as historical trade terms. The live-theatrical industries of the time tended to reduce all circulation practices to a single catchall term—"booking"—and rarely distinguished between the varied functions these practices fulfilled. The three categories offered here are useful primarily as a heuristic, and specific practices might fall into one or more of them. They help us to consider live-theatrical distribution as a specific market control model *for cinema* across separate, if related, conceptual domains (space, time, pricing, packaging, and the like).

These categories, which will be discussed in more detail later in this chapter, help to bridge an apparent difference between the respective products being distributed in theater and cinema. It seems obvious that theater, as an individual live performance, cannot be "distributed" in the same way that cinema can. Although performers might present the same show multiple times at multiple venues, they can only do so within a singular space and time. In strict economic terms, at the level of distribution, theater is not a tangible product at all, but an ephemeral service. Cinema, on the other hand, sells a mechanically reproduced physical product—the positive film print—that can be distributed simultaneously, repeatedly, and en masse. Because of this major difference, it can be tempting to downplay live theater as a model for film distribution practice in the early twentieth century, useful as it might be for production or exhibition.

Historically, however, the distinction between the respective distribution of live theater and cinema in this period was less clear than we might assume. From cinema's origins, live-theatrical bookers and film distributors served many of the same venues. The rise of storefront Nickelodeons after 1905 and more luxurious permanent theaters in the 1910s and 1920s did create a dedicated exhibition sector for the burgeoning film industry, and with it an accompanying set of cinema-specific distribution practices. But throughout this period and into the 1940s, established vaudeville and legitimate houses regularly booked both live performance and cinema, often within a single bill. As a result, the latter picked up several of the former's established distribution practices. These practices are the main subject of this chapter. As we will see, they continued to be used by the film industry well into the 1910s, even as their unsuitability for cinema distribution became obvious.

Histories of the institutional links between theater and cinema have tended to focus on theater's influence on movie exhibition specifically. As historians have noted, early cinema's exposure to mass audiences in the United States came primarily through its placement as an act on vaudeville bills in the 1900s and 1910s.[1] Later film industry magnates, such as Marcus Loew and William Fox, started out as owners of small-time vaudeville circuits, booking both film and live variety theater in that same period. Any casual fan of *Footlight Parade* (Lloyd Bacon, Warner Bros., 1933) knows that moviegoers went to theaters for more than just films, and that the booking of prologue shows and other live stage entertainments alongside shorts and features was widespread, particularly before sound. However, theater's influence on cinema was not just as an incubating venue or as an adjunct to a full evening's entertainment. The live-theatrical industry offered direct models of distribution practice.

Perhaps because of the troubled status of live-theatrical "distribution" already discussed, theater historians have rarely treated booking as a third sector of the industry, as distinct from the production and the venue. Theater historian Alfred Bernheim, writing in 1932, recognized only two essential "factors" of theatrical presentation: "On the one hand there is the production; on the other, there is the theatre."[2] In Bernheim's conception, booking and its attendant institutions and practices are defined as instruments of control only insofar as they were marshaled by theatrical magnates such as Edward Albee or the Shuberts. This is a specific feature of American theater historiography; distribution has rarely been considered the self-standing industry in theater that it is in cinema. Instead, it is theorized primarily as an outgrowth of venue owners or managers. This impaction may seem to trouble any argument that film distribution took inspiration from a preexisting live-theatrical "distribution industry," particularly when the more obvious connections between the two industries—live-theatrical production and the theater spaces themselves—have played such an important role in the historiography of the studio system. Nevertheless, linking film and theater historically while carefully distinguishing between them is a productive exercise for understanding the development of film distribution.

What follows is a theatrically focused prehistory of entertainment distribution practices. I have separated those practices according to the live-theatrical industries that employed them (legitimate theater and vaudeville) and organized them into the heuristic categories of booking, circuiting, and packaging. However, this discussion of specific practices is also integrated into a more holistic account of the history of those industries, with particular attention to how they anticipated and influenced Hollywood's strategies of distribution control. As the case study at the end of this chapter shows, these theatrical precursors to film distribution practice continued to be highly influential even through the early 1910s as multireel feature distribution came to the fore.

Stars, Benefits, and Runs: Preindustrial Distribution Practices in Live-Theatrical Entertainment

Perhaps the most important distribution practices Hollywood adopted from the theatrical industries of the late nineteenth century were those of *booking*: the arrangement of scheduling and payment surrounding a specific performance or set of performances in a specific venue. As an exercise in logistics, it is no accident that booking emerged as a standardized practice in the United States along with national railroad networks in the 1870s. Before the railroad, there was no way to reliably organize the circulation of live entertainment from afar, at least at the level of the individual performance.

As a result, live-theatrical entertainment before the 1870s tended toward localized models of organization. In legitimate theater, this took the form of the resident stock company system. Under the stock system, theater production centered around individual self-sufficient venues, each with its own company of actors performing plays three to five nights a week for their local communities. The specific bill typically changed with every performance.[3] The local theater manager often owned or leased the theater building and handled the major aspects of production, including the hiring and firing of actors, casting, and directing.[4] As an economic model of live-theatrical production, the stock company system was essentially preindustrial; it emphasized the permanence of the company and of theater itself as a ritual enacted by the local community. In that sense, it contributed to antebellum theater's function as what historian Rosemarie Bank has termed a "universal space" of performance—not just of the literal performance of the actors on stage, but of the cultural performance of audiences and communities enacting the social relationships of a changing America.[5]

The increasing importance of stars in American theater would eventually lead to more conventionalized (if not entirely rigorous) approaches to theatrical booking, even as the stock company system remained the norm through most of the nineteenth century. As an economic phenomenon, the "star system" in theater—whereby star actors recognizably drew audiences more than individual plays—was evident in England as early as the seventeenth century. In the United States, theatrical stars from Europe began to appear more frequently in resident stock company productions beginning in the 1820s, following several very lucrative tours organized by Stephen Price, the shrewd manager of New York's Park Theatre.[6] By the mid-1820s, most stock companies supported a star for at least part of their season, and a decade later, stars were central to the business of American theater.[7]

Theater historians working with the booking material that survives from the "stock era" have shown that the arrangements theaters used to book traveling stars in the first half of the nineteenth century could vary widely.[8] Managers who wanted visiting stars to perform in their theater engaged them either by direct correspondence or in person, typically on a visit to London or New York. Bringing a star to a theater in the early nineteenth century was a hope-and-pray affair, but even if a star failed to appear as scheduled, stars were not yet so essential that any night without them could not be covered by regular stock company performances, which also filled in the days or weeks between star engagements. As a result, the nonindustrialized booking processes of correspondence and direct visits sufficed. Stars' engagements might be as short as a single performance or stretch to three months, though a week or two was most common.[9] Regardless of the length of the engagement, a change of bill with each new performance remained customary; the emphasis was on the star rather than any specific play.

Stars were paid either through a flat salary or, more commonly, via "benefit" performances. A benefit was an arrangement by which the star (or the stock company, which also enjoyed occasional benefit nights) earned some substantial proportion of ticket sales at a particular performance. This was usually half of the evening's proceeds, with any remainder going to the theater manager. Benefits could be very lucrative for actors; the yield from a single benefit night might equal several weeks or even months of flat salaried income.[10] Benefit income was typically calculated after deducting the house's expenses, but so-called clear benefits, with the actor(s) taking every penny of ticket sales, were also common.[11]

The benefit performance—which stretches back at least to Britain in the 1680s—might seem far removed from film distribution. But in it lay the roots of the percentage pricing that would become standard in the film industry after the 1920s, and that still underpins theatrical releasing today.[12] The increasing use of benefits as the standard method of paying traveling stars also marked an important shift in the economic history of the live-theatrical industry in the United States, as it separated the formerly insular interests of the individual venue from those of an outside agent, the star, who might have different incentives. As historian Douglas McDermott has argued, the star system succeeded because "traveling stars were an economically more efficient way to supply constant variety to new audiences spread across a vast territory."[13] A century after the rise of the star system in theater, the film industry would again marshal stars and percentage arrangements to optimize the distribution and profitability of their product across a geographically immense area.

Even before theatrical booking emerged as a more systematized practice in the 1870s, the stock system was under an obvious threat from the increasing dominance of traveling stars. By the 1840s, theatrical periodicals and other publications frequently railed against what they perceived as the evils of the star system, or, as one 1849 history of theater in New Orleans referred to it, the "starving system."[14] The crux of the critique against stars was both economic and artistic. While some stars could indeed generate large sums for theater managers in the short term, critics argued that the use of stars ultimately degraded the stock company system. As stars' share of companies' expenses grew, managers had an incentive to spend less on the salaries of the stock players, who at the same time were now encouraged to modulate their performances in favor of that of the star.

Stars also changed the theatrical industry by helping to increase the continuous duration of a particular play's place on theater bills. This created a new practice: the theatrical "long run." Before the 1830s, the total number of theatergoers was generally not large enough to support a weeklong run of a single play, even in the biggest cities. By midcentury, however, Saturday matinees and Sunday evening performances became more popular, and continuous runs of a week and sometimes longer were more common.[15] While Bank has shown that the long run stretches back at least to the Bowery Theatre in New York in the 1830s, it was not until the success of *Uncle Tom's Cabin* on Broadway in 1852 (one hundred performances), and again in 1853–1854 (three hundred performances), that longer runs were decisively acknowledged to be both desirable and consistently possible.[16] By the end of the Civil War, runs of four hundred or five hundred performances for the most successful plays were not uncommon.[17] A similar pattern of increasing run lengths would apply to cinema between 1915 and 1930.

Before moving to an account of the rapid industrialization of legitimate theater in America in the 1870s, it is worth taking a moment to reemphasize the importance of these various antebellum developments to the origins of film distribution. Put in film-centric terms: the rise of the visiting star and the benefit arrangements used to pay them bifurcated theater into separate sectors of production and exhibition, each with somewhat diverging economic interests. A major element of that divergence was the fact that stars, as units of idiosyncratic economic value, offered the promise of greater returns to management while displacing the programmatic stock company. In the practice of the benefit performance, we see the origins of the percentage split of box-office receipts as an attempt to align these two sectors.

Finally, the rise of long runs for single attractions marks the beginning of systematic temporal management in distribution. By "temporal management" I mean practices that specifically organize playing time as a strategy of both risk management and profit-making in the distribution of cultural performance. Under the repertory system, theaters managed risk by encouraging constant variety and turnover of bills within the stability of the stock company. The emergence of the long run, however, presented managers with evidence that continuous playing time for popular plays could generate revenue much more efficiently than a repertory approach. At the same time, it was also quite risky, as the hope for long runs encouraged managers to invest more in advertising, publicity, lavish staging, and untested material.[18] The decline of the stock company, the rise of the star, and long runs made the temporal questions of when to arrange engagements, and how much time to leave between them, much more critical, presenting challenges of temporal management similar to the ones that would confront the film industry after it reconfigured itself around multireel films in the mid-1910s.

Enter the Combination: Booking, Circuiting, and Syndicates in the Age of Industrial Theater

The 1870s saw major changes to the way that legitimate theater was produced and booked in the United States. A new practice, the combination company, quickly became standard in the theater industry and replaced the repertory stock company by the end of that decade. The combination company transformed booking and constituted the single most important theatrical influence on feature film distribution as it coalesced in the 1910s. Several assumptions baked into the combination would translate into the development of feature film distribution strategies, including the notion of a continuous run of a single attraction having economic value over frequent changes of bill, the pattern of "the star" as a unit of idiosyncratic economic attraction displacing the programmatic stock company, and the idea of shared percentage stakes between the production and the venue.

Combinations emerged as a corollary to the increasing popularity of traveling stars, who by the 1850s were beginning to bring their own supporting players, costumes, scenery, and even stagehands with them to engagements rather than relying on the stock companies and resources of local theaters.[19] The national railroad network made this model economically viable by lowering the cost and increasing the speed at which such companies could be booked into venues. The total mileage of railroad track in the United States increased fivefold in the antebellum years, from less than six thousand in 1849 to more than thirty thousand by 1860. This growing interconnectedness meant that it was much easier and more profitable to distribute theater centrally, as traveling companies could be booked more reliably and spent less time in transit. The growth of the combination company in the 1870s was reflected in the collapse of the stock company system. In the 1871–1872 season, fifty permanent companies existed in major cities; by 1880 this number was less than ten. Those stock companies that were able to survive in the biggest markets also disappeared by 1900.[20]

By combining the essential assets of a rehearsed production into a single package, the combination company transformed American theater into an industrial product. The stock company had been a singularly local enterprise; the combination, in contrast, encouraged the centralization of all booking in the largest, richest, and most prestigious market of the nation's theatrical industry: New York. Although the combination replaced the stock company relatively quickly, the specific practices used to book combinations in New York developed more gradually. In the early days of the combination in the 1860s and 1870s, booking was conducted between individual theater managers and representatives for each individual attraction in an open-air market centered on Manhattan's Union Square. This environment was often referred to in racist theatrical parlance as the "slave market," a name that reflected the informal, ethically dubious, and rather haphazard quality that characterized the booking of attractions there. By the mid-1880s, however, this process had become more efficient.

By packaging theatrical attractions so that they could be circulated centrally and simultaneously, the combination company served as an important originating model for feature film distribution. This is certainly true in the case of the film roadshow, which, as William Paul notes, is essentially the combination system applied to cinema.[21] But it should be emphasized that the combination company *also* influenced the basic model of centralized film distribution with its simultaneous, coordinated release of duplicate performances (i.e., prints) of a single attraction on a national scale. This release method was used as early as the 1880s, when theatrical producers began touring multiple combination companies of the same production simultaneously. In the 1882–1883 season, playwright-actor-producer Steele MacKaye's 1880 hit *Hazel Kirke* sent fourteen companies on the road, all centrally managed from New York.[22] Though the duplicate company strategy was not entirely analogous to later models of feature film program distribution, it served as an organizational starting point for those models as they developed. As Marlis Schweitzer argues, the practice of duplicate companies "anticipat[ed] the nationalizing power of radio, film, and television" and "participated in the transformation of heterogenous local audiences into a more cohesive if not homogenized national audience."[23]

The combination company's influence on film distribution extended beyond simply the bifurcation of production and venue, or the model of simultaneously distributing multiple units of the same attraction. By creating the possibility of complex and centrally managed forms of circulation, combinations anticipated basic practices that would govern the logistics of film distribution. The most fundamental of these circulatory practices was *circuiting*: the efficient routing of attractions from venue to venue that served as the primary mechanism of booking power in both legitimate theater and vaudeville. Some terminological clarification is warranted here. Film historians often think of the "circuit" as a term of exhibition synonymous with "chain," as in a theater circuit. However, in this live-theatrical context, a circuit referred not only to a chain of theaters, but also to a literal route of circulation. Vaudeville artists playing the "Orpheum circuit" appeared not only in those theaters directly owned by the Orpheum chain, but also in those independently owned theaters *booked* by the Orpheum's central booking office. Circuits were not just groups of theaters, but also travel itineraries that formed the basic logistical structure of theatrical distribution. If booking describes those distribution practices covering appearance and payment arrangements between an attraction and a single venue, then circuiting describes a different (if related) set of practices covering spatial and temporal arrangements with and across multiple venues.

Circuits also grew alongside the railroad. However, while transcontinental rail networks made the centralized booking of combination companies *possible*, circuiting made it *economical*. Because of the significant expense in railroad fares, food, and hotel accommodations involved in moving an entire company to various bookings, planning that company's route such that it was kept constantly working was a key factor in a show's profitability. A specific routing strategy was typically employed to achieve this. First, a show was booked in larger, more profitable city venues for multiple-night engagements—"stands," in theatrical parlance—that provided the bulk of a show's income. The goal was to fill as much time as possible with these longer stands and avoid gaps between such bookings, but gaps inevitably emerged, often owing to factors such as venue availability or the need to transport the company to the next venue. Long railroad journeys between bookings were avoided if possible, as such travel represented a pure loss to the company. If a company's overall route necessitated such a journey, bookers sought to mitigate its financial impact by scheduling as many "one-night stands" as possible— short stints in the cities and towns that lay along the route between the longer engagements.[24] Circuiting was thus an exercise in both temporal and spatial management that structured the distribution of live theater according to networked relationships between venues.

Circuits were fundamental to the power of the theatrical booking industry as it coalesced in the late nineteenth century. In the 1870s and 1880s, as the combination model took over legitimate theater, the informal booking arrangements between venues and attractions undertaken via correspondence or at Union Square proved insufficient to the task of organizing the movement of companies on a national scale. Individual combination managers generally arranged their companies' routes in this period, and in theory, they booked a continuous and organized route across the venues of a particular territory well ahead of time. In practice, however, bookings were rarely ironclad, particularly in the case of one-night stands. It was not uncommon for attraction managers to simply cancel a one-night stand if an opportunity at a more profitable venue presented itself. Anticipating last-minute cancellations, venue managers sometimes double-booked to protect themselves, creating an awkward situation if both attractions showed up. Theaters were the most common victims of unsystematic booking, but the haphazard character of circuiting practice as it existed before the mid-1880s presented problems for company managers as well. Beyond having to account for double-booking and other logistical issues with theaters, managers needed to carefully monitor the movement of other combinations in the same territory. Otherwise, a company might unwittingly put on a show too similar to a rival's that had just played the same house, severely limiting their box-office income.[25] The film industry would confront similar problems with overbooking in the early 1920s.

Both theatrical producers and venues thus had strong incentives to further systematize the booking of attractions, and their respective strategies for doing so would form the basis of a more centralized circuiting practice. Venues along the most common routes, particularly those that lay geographically in between major markets, began negotiating with attractions as a group. Organized circuits gave the theaters bargaining power they lacked individually. Companies were much less likely to cancel a booking at an individual theater in a circuit, as they risked being blacklisted by all the other theaters on that circuit. Circuits also offered combination managers a preconstructed route that vastly reduced the logistical complications of theater distribution. Instead of negotiating with many individual theaters one stand at a time, a manager could build the route for an entire season out of just a handful of deals with circuits. Circuits promised a similar kind of economizing for venues, as a single representative could visit New York on behalf of the entire circuit to arrange its bookings.[26]

Theatrical circuits thus proliferated across the country during the 1870s and 1880s. Increasingly, they ceased being cooperatives of separately managed theaters and began to be taken over by dominant managing interests, typically the owners of the most powerful theater in the circuit.[27] By acquiring stakes in other houses on the circuit and privileging bookings for their own theaters, these owners became local magnates and held outsized power representing the circuit in New York. Figures such as John D. Mishler in eastern Pennsylvania (whose 1873 circuit was one of the earliest to organize), Harry Greenwall in Texas, and Charles Frohman in New York were among the first moguls of truly industrialized entertainment distribution.[28]

Another more systematized approach to circuiting came in the early

1880s with the rise of booking agencies in New York. Booking agencies consolidated the circuiting labor of combination companies (much as circuits did for venues) by taking on the work of planning the routes of the combination and contracting with circuits on its behalf. They grew out of the theatrical talent agencies of the 1860s, which initially served as little more than clearinghouses for actors and stars looking for work. These agencies evolved as stars began hiring them to handle their business arrangements, including their routes, with some agents even taking a commission on a star's salary or benefit. One of the earliest true booking agencies was C. R. Gardiner's Managers' and Stars' Agency, founded in 1878. According to Alfred Bernheim, Gardiner's agency innovated the principle of theatrical exclusivity. In theory, stars who wanted the agency's services not only had to use the agency exclusively, but also could only play the specific theaters or circuits with which the agency had booking relationships.[29] Other booking agencies followed in Gardiner's wake, adopting similar policies at a grander scale.

Booking agencies have been characterized as a major factor in the centralization of American theater, and some of that influence derived from their relationships with the most prestigious venues in New York. The primary source of their power, however, was their relationships with theaters and circuits on "the road."[30] Agencies offered combinations an economical way to access the national market for live theater and granted circuits access to New York–quality attractions. By the 1890s, individual theater and company managers no longer flocked to the Union Square "slave market" every May to cobble together routes. Booking and circuiting were now the province of agencies in New York, led by the two biggest concerns: Marc Klaw and Abraham Erlanger (K&E), who booked some two hundred houses in the South, and Charles Frohman, who represented more than three hundred theaters in New York, New England, and the mid-Atlantic. Along with roughly forty other agencies, K&E and Frohman collected combinations under their exclusive control and charged a flat fee on the order of $25 to $250 for every engagement they booked.[31]

The emergence of the booking agency supercharged the consolidation of power in legitimate theater and ensured that the basis of that power lay in control over distribution. Even the best-positioned circuits had to accept being subject to the whims of booking agencies if they wanted the stars and productions they represented. In the market for the still substantial proportion of talent not controlled exclusively by a booker, the circuits and the agencies were effectively in competition, as circuits continued to contract with any companies not using an intermediary. It did not take long for powerful theatrical interests to realize that a cooperative arrangement between booking agencies and circuits amounted to control over the entire industry. This was the driving principle of the famous Theatrical Syndicate, formed in 1896 from the booking interests and combinations represented by Charles Frohman and K&E, Al Hayman's circuits in the West, and the Pennsylvania and Ohio theaters of Samuel Nixon and Frederick Zimmerman.

At its height in the mid-1900s, the Syndicate controlled as many as seven hundred houses—nearly all the first-class theaters in the United States.[32] It was essentially conceived as one nationwide booking agency; its primary instrument of theatrical domination was not the outright ownership of theaters, but control over the booking and circuiting of those theaters' attractions. Consequently, the Syndicate required exclusivity of all the combinations and stars who booked with them as well as of the circuits it represented. Syndicate-affiliated theaters could not book talent directly; they had to work through Klaw and Erlanger and accept the agency's booking, pricing, and circuiting arrangements.[33] In return for ceding control over their bookings, plus a 5 percent cut of the box office, theaters got reliable access to a full season's worth of world-class theatrical attractions without having to double-book or negotiate with company managers in New York. Stars and combinations, for their part, got efficient and profitable routing from coast to coast in the best venues in the country.

As it grew, the Syndicate took geographical advantage of circuit routing. By targeting the circuits situated *between* major cities, it could exert de facto control over the key stands in those cities. Unless a particular combination was able to book the circuit of smaller theaters along, for example, the north-south route between Seattle and San Francisco—that is, Tacoma, Portland, Chico, and Sacramento—it was very unlikely to play one or the other of those major cities. By controlling the apparatus of booking in circuits of one-night stands, the Syndicate could threaten to deny the most profitable urban theaters top-drawing attractions. As a result, the influence of the Syndicate grew to the point where even these powerful theaters were effectively obliged to book with the organization.[34]

Legitimate theater taught early Hollywood distributors something fundamental about the role of theaters in controlling an entertainment industry. For the Syndicate, directly owning or renting retail outlets for the entertainment product being distributed was certainly an advantage, but it was never strictly necessary. The key to controlling theaters was to make them dependent on the distributor's supply of product. For the Syndicate, this took the form of booking exclusivity and a chokehold on circuit routing, but any number of strategies could accomplish similar goals, including packaging deals, contract practices, price discrimination, temporal scale, spatial dominance, and good old-fashioned intimidation. This basic relationship between the distributor/booker and the individual theaters it contracted with—not as a vertically integrated *owner* but as a spatial and temporal *manager* and *supplier* of the product—was thought to be the most appropriate and effective model of oligopolistic organization among film distributors before the 1920s. To a large extent, that model continues in media distribution today.

Vaudeville and the Industrial Packaging of Entertainment

If legitimate theater provided the nascent film industry with a model for distributing individual films, vaudeville served as its model for groups of films. The basic logistical problems posed by booking and circuiting in vaudeville resembled those of legitimate theater, particularly as the raucous concert saloon version of the form, "variety," evolved into the more respectable, middle-class, and family-oriented "vaudeville" in the 1880s and 1890s. Of the two terms, "variety" better describes the fundamental structure of the tradition: a series of dissimilar acts, including comedic routines, musical performances, magic, juggling, contortionists, animal acts, and others, united into a single program. Like legitimate combinations, vaudeville attractions also depended on continuous, logical routing that avoided long railroad jumps and extended hotel stays between stands. In many ways, vaudevillians (referred to in the industry as "artists") were even more dependent on routes than legitimate companies were. They were all independent performers and as a rule were therefore responsible for their own traveling expenses.[35] To budget for their routes, artists relied on published guides, such as Herbert Lloyd's *Vaudeville Trails through the West*, that contained information about local stands, such as lodging costs, railroad times and prices, and theater policies.[36] As a result, the vaudeville industry developed a system of centralized booking similar to that of legitimate theater. However, variety theater also presented unique complications, most of which required even more intricate systems of spatial and temporal management. These systems would shape the development of industrialized film distribution even more directly than those of legitimate theater.

The most obvious problem vaudeville presented in terms of booking was its programmatic multiple-attraction format: a two- to three-hour show of between seven and fifteen acts, referred to within the context of the larger program as "turns." In general, each turn was a relatively small unit, independently booked and circuited. Turns were often just one or two performers, as in the case of monologists or duo acts, but they could feature groups as large as a small theater company or a full-sized band of twenty or more musicians. As vaudeville industrialized, the most common show format became the nine-act program of individually booked turns. Compared to legitimate theater, vaudeville presented a whole new question of scale in booking. During the era of monopoly distribution in legitimate theater, the number of road companies simultaneously booked by those concerns at any one time numbered at most in the hundreds, and many of these were duplicates of the same production.[37] At the height of vaudeville's popularity in the years just before World War I, in contrast, as many as 20,000 separate acts competed for bookings in some 1,600 variety-exclusive theaters and many more mixed vaudeville-and-film "pop" (popular) houses.[38] Variety theater thus presented distributors with a booking and circuiting problem more complicated by an order of magnitude than that of the legitimate stage.

This problem was not simply one of larger numbers. Putting together a successful vaudeville program required the booker to prioritize variety when selecting individual acts. Each bill needed to be organized with something for everyone—within the narrow limits of late nineteenth-century white middle-class morality, of course. Thus, vaudeville bills frequently included a mix of "dumb" acts (jugglers, animal acts, contortionists, and other nonspeaking attractions), verbal and physical comedy, vocal and instrumental music, theater, and dance. Ideally, no two acts performing on a given date would be even remotely similar, and the resulting modular nature of the vaudeville bill had ramifications for film distribution that would not be realized until cinema's mechanical reproducibility brought them to the fore. Even though vaudeville acts were booked through individual contracts between venue and performer for each stand, vaudeville bookers could not simply ignore the bill as a totality. Every booking was implicitly structured by the needs of the wider program. What vaudeville theaters were ideally buying by using a booking office was not a collection of random acts thrown together, but a complete package of attractions that could work in concert with each other across the duration of the evening's bill. Indeed, one of the basic premises of vaudeville—and its economic advantage as a form of live entertainment—was that the program as a whole would please audiences even if they disliked some of the individual acts.

Vaudeville distribution thus had to account for the art of *packaging* acts together. As with the other heuristic terms offered in this chapter, I use packaging in a broad sense, in this case to refer to distribution practices that combine individual entertainments together as a unit for the venue, either explicitly through contract or implicitly as a matter of planning. In business and economics scholarship, the explicit packaging together of separate products for a single sale is technically referred to as *bundling* or *tying*.[39] However, for the purposes of entertainment distribution history, it is helpful to draw a distinction between tying and packaging. Tying is essentially a strategy of bulk sales, but I define the concept of packaging as also occurring at every stage of distribution, from distribution planning to marketing through to the final sale to the customer. This approach allows us to conceptualize different forms of live-theater distribution as having to account for packaging to a greater or lesser extent and at different levels of the supply chain.

A comparison of packaging in legitimate theater and vaudeville may be illustrative. In legitimate theater, the combination model essentially sold live theater as a complete package. A star, full cast, crew, and scenery were combined for the purposes of performing a specific production. The work of packaging in this case was essentially that of the producer; booking agencies simply marketed an already-made show. In the early years of vaudeville, before the rise of standardized booking practices, packaging was done by individual theater managers or a single manager for the whole circuit. This work required careful attention to the packaging together of disparate acts, and centralized booking agencies would eventually take on the not insignificant work of putting together a variety show that would work for an individual theater.

Vaudeville bookers packaged theater bills according to an almost mechanical set of criteria. The makeup of the bill was designed first and foremost to create a sense of rhythm by building tension and astonishment and then releasing it, often through comedy. However, bills also had to account for more concrete aspects of audience behavior. For example, to create a nonverbal buffer for audience members arriving late to the show or trying to beat the departing crowd, dumb acts were almost always scheduled as the first and last ("chaser") turns on the program.[40] Two "feature" acts—those that served as the biggest audience draws— were scheduled strategically. The first feature got the fifth slot, just before intermission, to climax the first half of the show and encourage the audience to stay for the second. The second got the headlining second-to-last slot: the most desirable of all for vaudeville artists.[41]

However, variety, audience behavior, and dramatic flow were not the only criteria of packaging in vaudeville. The variety format imposed very specific physical constraints on the kinds of turns that could be mixed within the program and the order in which they could be presented. Vaudeville publicity agent (and later Hollywood screenwriter) Marian Spitzer described some of these constraints in a 1924 article:

> It is not enough to have a bill that will afford the audience as great a variety of entertainment as possible. It must at the same time work into the backstage arrangements. Obviously in a vaudeville theatre the scenery for one act must be set while another act is on the stage. Consequently there must not be too many full-stage acts. As a rule the booker tries to have the acts alternate so that a full-stage act follows one played down in front of the olio [a curtain serving as a backdrop for the smaller acts, a practice known as performing "in one"].[42]

Spitzer provided an example of a hypothetical nine-act bill:

THE NINE-ACT BILL:
1 - Acrobats—full stage
2 - Song-and-dance team—in 1
3 - Flash act—revue, girl show, etc.—full stage
4 - Smart comedy talking act—in 1
5 - A jazz band—full stage
    Intermission and News
6 - Good musician—in 1
7 - Sketch with a big name—full stage
8 - Strong comedy single—in 1
9 - Animal act—full stage[43]

From the standpoint of distribution, the physical constraints of the vaudeville bill thus encouraged a modularity defined by various categories of performance and prestige: music / song & dance / comedy; full stage / in one; headliner / filler; dumb / speaking; unknown / name, etc. This modularity determined the starting point for bookers' negotiations with individual acts.

An array of theater-specific concerns structured the packaging of vaudeville acts, but the most important for the artists themselves was the relative prestige of the venue. The toniest stands were undoubtedly those owned by the showmen Benjamin Franklin (B. F.) Keith in Boston and Fred Proctor in New York. Early on, Keith regularized the practice of "continuous" vaudeville at his theaters, whereby performances ran from 10:00 a.m. to 10:00 p.m. without set showtimes. Bills simply restarted after the last turn, and audience members could come and go as they pleased.[44] This policy was well suited to Keith's Bijou Theatre, located in a busy shopping district on Washington Street that had a high possibility for customer turnover. Proctor brought the continuous policy to his 23rd Street Theatre in New York in 1889 ("After Breakfast Go to Proctor's, After Proctor's Go to Bed"), but abandoned it a few years later in favor of a three-shows-a-day schedule.[45] This allowed him to attract more in-demand acts uninterested in performing six times every day, in turn justifying higher admission prices and attracting audiences with higher socioeconomic status. It also better suited his theaters, which were mostly located in residential neighborhoods. This arrangement encouraged repeat attendance by nearby locals rather than casual drop-ins, which tended to be driven solely by foot traffic or sheer urban density. As a result, continuous performance gradually became a practice associated with the lower strata of vaudeville venues; Keith would hold on to it until 1909, when, at the urging of his general manager, Edward Albee, he too abandoned it.[46]

Historian David Monod argues that through this stratifying of theaters' performance policies and locations, Keith and Proctor were essentially "designing an amusement that could be taken casually, without planning or forethought, at a time or in a place that suited the consumers' lifestyles."[47] Vaudeville's early capitalists conceptualized a broad middle-class audience that sought the "popular prices" unavailable in legitimate theater, while nevertheless creating the distinctions *within* that audience necessary for entertainment to be distributed as widely, frequently, and profitably as possible. This possibility, embedded in vaudeville's modular performance structure, oriented the growing film industry's distribution and exhibition practices around the model of the diverse program rather than the singular attraction of legitimate theater.

By 1910, vaudeville theaters were generally classified as either "big time" or "small time." The roughly eighty big-time theaters were urban houses with high salaries and relatively good working conditions. Their admission prices were generally between 25 cents and $1.50, and they were exclusively booked by either the Keith-Albee or the Orpheum circuit. Artists could typically expect to play only two or three shows a day at big-time houses. All other theaters were small time, also known as "family time." Small-time theaters charged less than 25 cents for admission, and sometimes as little as a dime or nickel.[48] Their conditions and policies varied widely, particularly if they were outside of the Keith-Orpheum empire. The Midwest houses of the independent Gus Sun circuit, for example, were generally well appointed, even if vaudeville performers could expect to play four or five shows a day for split (half) weeks.[49] The Theatre Owners Booking Association, known as T.O.B.A., or the Toby Time, strung together a well-traveled circuit of Black vaudeville theaters from New York to Chicago to the South that paid very low salaries for continuous performances. Performers famously joked that T.O.B.A. stood for Tough on Black Acts (or Asses).[50] Comedian Benny Rubin described the bottom of the small-time barrel: the Butterfield time, where managers paid artists "in the dark, with old programs and baked apples," and the Crescent circuit, whose houses looked as if "somebody stuck a name on some toilets."[51]

Bookers thus had to reckon with an incredible diversity of acts, theaters, playing policies, and other constraints when conducting the business of vaudeville packaging. Consequently, the mechanics of that business developed to a much more intricate degree than in legitimate theater. From the 1870s to the 1890s, when it was still a relatively small industry, vaudeville was booked essentially the same way that legitimate theater was in the earliest days of the combination—in an open-air market in Union Square or through correspondence. Booking manager Daniel F. Hennessy related a common saying about these early years: "A man did business in his hat."[52] Although some acts booked directly with venues, most outsourced their booking to agents in New York, who arranged routes in exchange for a cut of the act's salary (typically 5 or 10 percent).[53] There were between fifteen and twenty such agencies in New York in the 1890s.[54] As the variety industry grew, vaudeville houses banded together into circuits to protect themselves and create profitable routes for performers, also as in legitimate theater. However, while the Theatrical Syndicate had emerged as a partnership between the most powerful booking agencies and circuits, the move to centralize vaudeville booking came mostly from the circuits themselves—most importantly, the Orpheum and Keith, which consolidated out of various smaller vaudeville circuits through the 1890s. These two circuits would come to dominate vaudeville as it developed an intricate system of national distribution around 1900—just in time for the earliest film exchanges to look over their shoulders.

Models for Centralized National Distribution: The VMA and the UBO

In 1900, inspired by the model of the Syndicate, Keith manager Edward Albee brought together all the leading theater circuits—but primarily Keith and Orpheum—into a single alliance: the Vaudeville Managers Association (VMA).[55] The VMA sought (among other things) to simplify and rationalize vaudeville distribution by creating a single large pool of theaters available for continuous booking. And it did just that; two years after its founding, the VMA represented sixty-two theaters total, including the entirety of the Keith and Orpheum circuits and major houses in Canada. For performers, combining all of these circuits offered an unprecedented opportunity: anywhere from thirty weeks' to a full year's itinerary of virtually ironclad bookings, efficiently routed from coast to coast, without having to spend any time negotiating individual stands.[56]

For access to these bookings, artists paid 5 percent of their salary to the VMA. More importantly, however, they ceded control and negotiating power to the combine over the terms of their individual stands. The VMA was simply a middleman at the booking stage, and artists still signed individual payment contracts with all the theaters where they appeared. But the VMA negotiated the salary terms of those contracts across an artist's entire route, which might be lower on a per-appearance basis than an artist or their agent might have been able to get individually. Artists who booked through the VMA effectively traded control over their booking and salaries for longer routes in better theaters—a trade they were generally happy to make, as a longer route easily yielded more money than a marginally higher salary at any one stand.[57] Theaters and circuits had a strong incentive to align with the VMA for the same broad reasons that the artists did: the association offered substantial financial stability and booking predictability. The sheer scale of the association's booking "time" attracted the top acts in vaudeville, and its pay-or-play contract policy discouraged double-booking and ensured that those acts would appear.[58] Finally, the VMA offered what film historians would call an "exclusive zone." Theaters who booked an artist though the VMA had a territorial monopoly on that artist and did not need to worry about getting into a bidding war with a rival house, which kept salary expenses in check.[59]

In its overall design, the VMA was thus a wholesale adaptation of the structure of the Syndicate to the specific practices of vaudeville. It offered booking efficiency, both through genuine economies of scale and through its implicit power as a cartel to muscle out theaters or artists who did not cooperate with it. Functionally, however, the VMA was less powerful than the Syndicate in its early years and operated more like a close-knit trade association of two dominant circuits. The organization's initial formation was set to last only five years, and instead of a single centralized national booking office, the VMA had two: one for the Orpheum and its affiliates in Chicago, and one for Keith in New York. As the 1905 dissolution date of the VMA approached and passed, the Keith and Orpheum circuits increasingly behaved like competitors at the level of booking. Both continued to expand their booking empires; the Orpheum doubled its theaters, while Keith added the Poli and Proctor circuits, enabling it to offer routes as long as seventy-five weeks by 1906.[60]

In 1906, after much negotiation between the Keith, the Orpheum, and their affiliated circuits, the VMA was essentially re-formed, this time with explicit agreements surrounding territory and new venue-establishment policies designed to prevent circuits from destructively competing with each other.[61] Even after the formation of this new combine, however, powerful theater owners continued to operate outside of it, offering top artists more than the VMA and working with independent firms, such as the William Morris Agency, for their booking. By 1906, Morris controlled its own fifty-week circuit. This competition was good for the vaudeville artists, who were offered ever higher salaries, and it was arguably good for the industry, as the number of theaters, circuits, and acts exploded. Film historians have long studied the Nickelodeon boom of the second half of the 1900s, but the growth in storefront movie theaters that began in 1905 should be understood in the context of a wider growth in programmatic media exhibition. According to David Monod, the number of big-time vaudeville theaters at least doubled in the period 1905–1912, while the number of small-time theaters grew even more quickly.[62] It was almost as easy (and sometimes easier) for an aspiring impresario to set up a small-time vaudeville house in a storefront as it was to set up a movie house. Vaudeville's flexible, modular format meant that programs could be tailored to individual houses if booked thoughtfully. Journalist Hartley Davis, writing in 1907, emphasized that while vaudeville theater management involved continuously high expenses and slim profit margins, "of all branches of amusements, an established vaudeville theatre is the most stable. It is more of a business and less of a gamble than any other kind of show."[63]

Vaudeville's explosive growth required an even more intricate booking system, as bookers contended with the increasing importance of the small-time. In 1907, VMA members signed another agreement to establish the United Booking Offices of America (UBO), which centralized booking for all eastern VMA managers and prevented them from working with independent agents directly. Through a combination of exclusive territory agreements and threats to build or buy competing theaters, Keith was able to get most of the powerful independents in vaudeville to leave the William Morris Agency and sign with the UBO.[64] Though initially separate, the UBO and Orpheum created a combined booking apparatus in 1913, when both organizations began sharing Times Square offices.[65]

The systematized booking practices used at the UBO in the 1910s were by no means completely new, having been developed at Keith and Orpheum's individual offices as those circuits grew in the 1890s, and from the earlier practices of theatrical booking agencies. However, the linking of the Keith and Orpheum booking offices meant that the UBO represented the first truly national theatrical distribution firm; its booking practices had to account for the movement of acts through routes at a national scale. The primary hub of activity where these functions of vaudeville distribution were arranged was the sixth floor of the Palace Theater, centered on Edward Albee's executive offices.

A close look at the workings of the UBO helps us to understand how the film industry's distribution practices in the 1910s and 1920s took shape. In the UBO, film distributors saw the extent to which flexible and profitable management of packaging, pricing, routing, and time of attractions was possible. Though the film industry never established a single industry-wide distribution office, the UBO did serve as a model for particular practices, including uniform exhibition contracts, geographically defined exchanges, variety-centered packaging, and sub-franchised booking. For our purposes, we can divide the complicated machinery of negotiation taking place in the UBO offices into the three heuristic categories suggested above—booking, circuiting, and packaging—and the three categories of workers directly involved in the process—artist agents, circuit bookers, and theater managers. Marian Spitzer likened the activity of workers engaged in the business of national vaudeville distribution to a noisy stock exchange, with "a great deal of excited gesticulation."[66] This apparent disorder belied an inherent interest in organizing the functions of distribution. Booking, circuiting, and packaging were compartmentalized into separate rooms, and the work was structured by both official policies and unofficial norms of behavior.

The process started with the artist's agent. The UBO tightly controlled which agents could deal directly with their bookers. To even enter the booking office of the UBO, an agent needed a special franchise from the UBO's executive board—a personal license from Edward Albee, essentially—making him a "floor man." While it was possible for non-sanctioned agents or the vaudevillians themselves to book with the UBO, they would have to wait, usually for hours, outside the booking office in the hopes of seeing a booker who needed to fill any remaining empty slots on his assigned theaters' bills.[67] Thus, as a practical matter, any artist who wanted easy access to the UBO's routes and time needed to deal with an agent who had floor privileges. Additionally, for the purposes of efficient booking, agents generally represented multiple artists. This made the work of booking talent in the first place, which at its heart was a series of negotiations between agents and UBO bookers, much more flexible and efficient. A booker's need to fill holes in any individual theater's bill could be answered by multiple options from the agent, with varying act types, prices, and levels of prestige.

This was essentially when the work of packaging was done, as bookers announced their needs to agents—a chaser act starting this particular week, an opener for this circuit, and so forth—and agents with the privilege of the floor responded with appropriate acts. These negotiations between agents and bookers settled the appearance dates of each act. A separate room was available for any extended negotiations between the bookers and agents, typically over salary.[68] Systematic arrangement of routes was made possible by the very layout of the booking floor. Each of the thirty-five or so bookers had a separate desk and was responsible for a particular geographically defined market.[69] UBO booking manager Samuel K. Hodgdon described one desk as encompassing Keith theaters in Midwest cities across at least five states. New York, Boston, and Washington, DC, were likewise handled by a single booker, and the rest of the United States and Canada was similarly divided.[70] By subdividing the national distribution of entertainment into local geographic structures, vaudeville bookers did the same work that film exchanges did.

Bookers had power of attorney for the theaters and circuits they represented and communicated frequently with managers, who sent along requests for particular kinds of turns and reports about the popularity of individual acts. Depending on the area, some bookers might have an entire staff to deal with correspondence from theaters, while some circuits had direct representatives onsite, in an office on the sixth floor.[71] Some of the bookers were themselves personal representatives of powerful managers within the Keith and Orpheum orbits. James "Jimmie" Moore, the owner of two important stands for routes headed toward Toronto, had such a representative, with his own desk, for just those theaters.[72]

The organization of the booking floor was thus not simply a structuring of space and time for the purposes of "systematized" distribution. It was also a manifestation of the relative power of individual circuits in the Keith and Orpheum empires. Powerful interests got not only representation but also direct power on the floor, even if it made little sense within the logics of temporal management or as an economy of scale. This often conflicting organizational logic was reinforced by the physical separation of big-time and small-time booking. While big-time theaters were booked on the sixth floor, the small-time was booked on the fifth floor, which completely duplicated the big-time's setup and had an entirely separate manager.[73] This separation reflected the rigid distinction in distribution between the big-time and the small-time with regard to both acts and theaters. However, the separation was also not absolute, and particularly important small-time circuits could have influence on both booking floors.[74] Film distribution would eventually inherit and modify these distinctions in its hierarchized run system. As we will see in chapter 4, it would also adopt models that gave powerful local interests outsized influence over the circulation and marketing of film.

Gender also structured the different work phases of vaudeville distribution at the UBO. Bookers were almost all men and presided over the first step of negotiating with (usually male) agents over an artist's route and salary, as well as haggling with each other over popular acts. After settling on these details, the booker confirmed them by writing them on a booking slip, stamping the slip with a time clock, and sending it through a slot to the clerical department. There, a bookkeeper verified the logistics of the booking against existing records, seeing whether an act already had dates at the venues written on the slip and making sure it had not already been booked elsewhere, relying on the timestamp to determine the priority of individual slips. After this verification, the slip was passed along to a stenographer, who typed up contracts in triplicate for each individual stand at a theater. These stenographers were almost all women, in keeping with the gendered conventions of office spaces in the early twentieth century. The bookkeepers, by contrast, were of mixed genders, with women more likely to be working in the small-time clerical department. Hodgdon, who managed the big-time, spoke of "the boys in the clerical department," while Daniel Hennessy, the small-time manager, referred to booking slips being "brought back to *her* to be checked off" (emphasis added).[75]

This gendered distinction between negotiatory, logistical, and clerical work in vaudeville distribution, which would carry over to the film industry, neatly reflected both a division of labor and the relative value and prestige associated with each type of labor. The initial booking of artists was thought to require a certain hard-nosed, aggressive, and stereotypically male back-and-forth akin to stock trading. The more analytical work of circuiting and logistical verification performed by the bookkeepers was akin to that of the human "computers" in contemporary scientific fields, a job that skewed female. At the end of the process, the repetitive clerical drudgery of typing contracts was performed almost exclusively by women. Erin Hill situates the importance of the low-paid women who worked as "steno-typists" in late nineteenth- and early twentieth-century office settings within a developing economy of information: "The operator became a conduit through which information passed—unaltered—from sender to receiver."[76] The reliable recording of information about booking, circuiting, and packaging was an undervalued but fundamental practice of the United Booking Office, curtailing practices such as double-booking and last-minute cancellations that in the 1870s and 1880s had essentially been accepted as the cost of doing business.

Indeed, while this last step of the preparation and dispersal of contracts could easily be dismissed as a routine formality, or a mere "conduit" within the workings of vaudeville distribution, it was essential to the consistent dispersal of agreed-upon terms of performance and payment. The very form of the contracts themselves was crucial to the standardization of the entire system, particularly once the UBO made vaudeville booking possible at a national scale. Every big-time UBO contract contained identical covenants and agreements, including the pay-or-play provisions and a cancellation clause. Small-time contracts also came in standardized (if less monolithic) versions.[77] The contract, as the only legally enforceable manifestation of the VMA's policies, thus served as the primary means by which those policies were standardized across hundreds of theaters and thousands of individual acts. At the same time, through its clerical practices, the UBO built in possibilities for variation according to an act or theater's place within the distribution hierarchy. As we will see in chapter 5, film distributors enacted the exact same strategy in establishing uniform exhibition contracts with theaters. There, as at the UBO, the distributors' goal was not complete uniformity, but highly structured flexibility.

As Samuel Backer emphasizes, vaudeville was not the only live-theatrical industry to employ a centralized system of distribution management, but its complexity "required the development of a particularly flexible system built to enable the flow of information." This flow of information was a way for the UBO to exert power over artists. Such power was exemplified most clearly by the famous reports that VMA-affiliated theater managers sent in with reviews of the performance of individual acts. As Backer notes, these reports, situated within the modular and highly stratified framework that made acts easily replaceable, tended to stabilize the salaries paid to artists. This stabilization through information was so important to the system that an act's price—the weekly salary it conventionally garnered—came to stand in as a crucial shorthand for its place within the entire hierarchy. One of the key functions of bookkeepers in the UBO was to prevent collusion between artists and theaters by checking the proposed salary of an act against its previous stands and to immediately flag it with the booker if it was significantly higher than before.[78] This convention of indexing entertainments primarily by price would be directly imported into the practices of the first national film distributor, the General Film Company.

However, the scale of the information management required in vaudeville was not just about distributing artists. It was also, in one sense, about distributing theaters' *time*, the one truly limited economic commodity they offered. The main appeal of a booking with the UBO was its ability to offer an individual artist as many as eighty weeks' worth of work on the big-time—two full forty-week theatrical seasons—at a single stroke.[79] It was no coincidence that vaudeville circuits were widely referred to as "times": the Orpheum time, the Gus Sun time, the Sheedy time. The convention reflected the degree to which twentieth-century vaudeville was an industry of temporal management. A vaudeville house with a forty-week season running a standard nine-act bill required 360 acts every year, while continuous houses or small-time theaters with split weeks might need even more. Aside from the handful of exceptionally popular artists who justified repeat bookings, most of these acts needed to be new year to year Given these time requirements and the additional material constraints of individual houses, the systematized management of information about theaters was as essential a function in vaudeville and film distribution as the booking of attractions.

These functions and practices—and in many cases, the literal theaters themselves—would be modified to serve the purposes of film distribution beginning in the second half of the 1900s. Throughout the 1910s, feature distributors would take up strategies from live theater in hybrid and haphazard ways. One of the major arguments of this book is that Hollywood did not begin to successfully synthesize the multiple strains of live-theatrical circulation practice for cinema until after World War I. Thus, we will return to booking, circuiting, and packaging later in this book, as the film industry worked through its own variations of these live-theatrical strategies in its distribution practice.

As we will see in the following chapter, certain vaudeville-originated practices were adopted relatively quickly for shorts-oriented film distributors starting around 1905. Feature distributors, by contrast, tended to look to legitimate theater as a model. Before 1914, when regular features began to overtake shorts as the production focus of the film industry, shorts and feature distribution were largely separate sectors governed by very different practices. To conclude this chapter, we turn to a case study of how distribution practices from legitimate theater were taken up by the film industry for the purpose of selling multireel feature films. While these live-theatrical models were useful and widely adopted early on, by the mid-1910s feature distributors would discover that on their own, they were untenable as a model for marketing films consistently and repeatedly.

Theater Distribution Meets Film Distribution: Feature Roadshowing at the Shubert Organization's Motion Picture Department

In the early 1910s, multireel feature film distribution had much more in common with legitimate theater booking than it did with short film distribution. Both sold an individuated product rather than a program, both relied on individually negotiated contracts rather than standing orders, and both generally conceived of their audience as middle class. The imbrication of distribution practice in the feature film and legitimate theater industries was arguably at its zenith between 1910 and 1915. This relationship went both ways: while film distributors were adopting live-theatrical models, the legitimate theater industry was making its own forays into motion picture distribution.

Perhaps no theatrical firm made more inroads into film production, distribution, and exhibition in the 1910s than the Shubert Organization. The Shuberts might be thought of as "the independents" of legitimate theater, in that they challenged an established cartel, the Theatrical Syndicate, only to adopt its methods in an essentially identical attempt to dominate the industry. The Shubert brothers, Lee and Jacob (J. J.)—a third brother, Sam, died in 1905—ran one of the most powerful theatrical production, management, and booking organizations in the United States in 1914. After managing a chain of theaters in upstate New York in the 1890s, the Shuberts controlled fifteen houses in Manhattan, London, Chicago, Boston, St. Louis, and other eastern cities by 1905. As theatrical producers, they also acquired the rights to multiple plays, including *Old Heidelberg* and *A Chinese Honeymoon*.[80]

The extent of these theatrical holdings drew the attention of the Syndicate, which the Shuberts had been using to book their houses via Klaw and Erlanger. Tensions over booking and production soon erupted into an outright break, and in July 1905 the Shuberts left the Syndicate completely, allying instead with the theatrical stars David Belasco, Harrison Grey Fiske, and Minnie Maddern Fiske, who were also fed up with the Syndicate's control over their theaters and productions. After famously announcing an "open-door" policy for their theaters, whereby all Shubert houses would ostensibly be open to any attraction regardless of affiliation, the Shuberts embarked on an expanded campaign of theater acquisition. Unlike the largely self-funding Syndicate, the Shuberts incorporated and marshaled the power of modern capital markets, funding their theater acquisitions with the aid of wealthy Wall Street firms and Cincinnati bankers. Though they posed as liberators of American theater from the tyranny of the Syndicate, the Shuberts would effectively supplant the Syndicate as the nation's major booking firm by around 1913, having lured hundreds of theaters and producers away from the Syndicate while enforcing identical exclusive booking policies.[81] They would continue to be a dominant force in American legitimate theater through the 1920s and 1930s even as the relative size of the industry shrank considerably. They remain a working theatrical organization.

The Shuberts' forays into film began as early as 1908, when they backed Marcus Loew as he began to develop his small-time vaudeville chain into a film exhibition behemoth.[82] Most of the organization's early film investments were as partners in production as stage plays were increasingly adapted into motion pictures. The feature film industry of the early and mid-1910s saw several such partnerships, such as the Frohmans and Famous Players, Klaw & Erlanger and Biograph, and David Belasco and Lasky. This was as much a result of the declining receipts of "the road" as of motion pictures' emergence as a dominant form of entertainment. The average number of combination companies touring during the theatrical season declined precipitously in the 1910s, from 236 in 1910 to just 39 in 1920.[83] As more and more theaters converted to vaudeville and motion pictures, exhibition outlets for legitimate theater outside of New York became ever scarcer. Movie adaptations offered a new market for theatrical production and distribution, and the Shuberts—Lee in particular—sought to take full advantage of that shift.

While most of the film-theatrical partnerships of the 1910s were based around adapting known properties, showcasing famous actors, or capitalizing on theater chains for exhibition, the Shuberts made several forays into feature film distribution, even before their well-known partnership with the World Film Corporation began in the summer of 1914.[84] Like most contemporary feature distributors, the Shuberts and their collaborators were uncertain about the optimal way to release longer and more prestigious motion pictures. In 1911, Adolph Zukor (yet to team up with the Frohmans to form Famous Players) corresponded with Lee Shubert about adapting successful plays from the Shubert catalog. He explained his distribution plans: "I intend to play on percentage in the large cities wherever a theatre has open dates, and in the smaller towns I would lease the picture on a rental or percentage basis, or we may sell state rights—in other words, we may sell a reel to a party which he can use in certain states for a lump sum of money. We may be able to adopt all of the above plans in each and every instance."[85]

Zukor's throw-spaghetti-at-the-wall strategy for distributing his proposed Shubert adaptations suggests that the theatrical industry did not quite know how to release "picturizations" of its plays nationally in the early 1910s. The strategy is also revelatory in the distribution option Zukor did *not* list: releasing the film through an exchange. This was not an oversight but reflected a fundamental assumption within the theater industry, even among those with motion picture experience: film adaptations of theatrical product should play primarily in legitimate houses via live-theatrical distribution models, rather than being released through the shorts-oriented film exchange system.

The Shubert Motion Picture Department (renamed the Shubert Feature Film Booking Company after mid-April 1914) grew out of this assumption. The department existed for less than a year during the run-up to the partnership with World, but it was no minor office; it had its own letterhead, and its manager reported directly to J. J. Shubert. A company promotional pamphlet intended for both exhibitors and "Feature-Owners" promised a national scale of distribution: "The film booked by us will travel from ocean to ocean—in our houses and yours."[86] The distribution model of the Motion Picture Department was fundamentally based on the booking, circuiting, and packaging practices of legitimate theater. Prints were circulated as individual "companies," complete with an advance manager who collaborated with individual theater managers to ensure a successful "performance," even including "rehearsals" of screenings. This distribution model emphasized the idiosyncratic qualities of the individual production and the spectacle of performance. Films played only once or twice a day, primarily in legitimate houses, at prices higher than would be typical for ordinary "picture theaters." It was no accident that the manager of the department, Robert W. Priest, was also the publicity director of the Shubert-owned New York Hippodrome theater. Priest had come up through the world of theatrical publicity, having promoted DeWolf Hopper, William Faversham, and other actors, but also had film distribution experience from positions at Gaumont and Pathé Exchange.[87] He would later go on to manage the roadshow companies for Thomas Ince's *Civilization* in 1916.[88]

The Shubert Motion Picture Department's distribution practices, and Priest's management of them, offer a synchronic view of the legitimate theater industry's approach to feature films during a period of dynamic change. While the department distributed several features, including *Traffic in Souls* (George Loane Tucker, 1913) and a filmed version of the spectacular Hippodrome revue *America* (Lawrence B. McGill, 1914), the release with the most surviving documentation is *The Life of Our Saviour* in March and April 1914. The film itself was a Pathé production directed by Maurice-André Maître, a hand-colored shot-for-shot remake of Ferdinand Zecca's *La Passion de Notre-Seigneur Jésus-Christ* from 1907.[89] Sources vary about the exact length of the film, but *The Life of Our Saviour* was at least twice as long as *La Passion*. In modular American terms, the 1907 film was a three-reeler (3,114 feet, or 950 meters) and the 1914 version at least an eight-reeler (about 8,000 feet, or 2,400 meters), though the Shubert roadshow released the film in versions of seven or six reels as well.[90] While Shubert handled the 1914 roadshow release of the film in the United States, Pathé Exchange itself would distribute the film in its many seasonal rereleases, typically around Christmas or Easter. This happened nearly every year until 1921, when Pathé released an expanded version of the film titled *Behold the Man*, with a modern frame story directed by Spencer Gordon Bennet.[91]

The film's 1914 roadshow involved nineteen separate combination companies, all supervised by Priest. Each company had a single print of the film as well as a manager who reported directly to Priest and Shubert Booking Department manager Jules Murry.[92] These company managers were not salaried Shubert employees but were hired on a weekly basis at the union scale of forty dollars per week set by the International Alliance of Theatrical Stage Employees (IATSE) for road workers.[93] The company managers were an integral part of *Saviour*'s distribution strategy, which was centered on exploiting Holy Week interest in the film leading up to Easter Sunday, which in 1914 would be April 12. The film's premiere presentation run in New York at the Manhattan Opera House began on March 30. This showing generated publicity for the nineteen companies booked for weeklong runs the following week—Holy Week—from April 6 to April 11, primarily in Shubert houses in larger markets east of the Mississippi. The road managers' job was twofold. First, they were supposed to make all necessary arrangements for successful performances of the film in booked venues, most of which were not equipped for film exhibition. Second, they were responsible for drumming up shorter, one- or two-day bookings for their print of the film—one-night stands, effectively—before that print had to move on to another booking in a different market. This circuit-routing strategy, which was not entirely out of place, given the ongoing expenses incurred by road managers, was an important marker of the intermediate status of the Shuberts' distribution of *Saviour* between theatrical booking and film distribution.

The road managers' jobs were quite tenuous and depended wholly on the performance of their company. Managers who built a route with insufficient small bookings between cities might be asked to "lay off" the intervening days without pay, as happened to Company #9 between the April 11 conclusion of a St. Louis booking and an April 17 premiere in Minneapolis.[94] If the film performed poorly enough in their market, or they were unable to find suitable bookings, they might find their company abruptly recalled and their employment ended—a circumstance that befell many of the managers on the film. This temporary hiring of road managers was a routine affair; there are many examples in the Priest correspondence of managers or ex-managers asking him to "keep them in mind" for any future company work. Some of the managers Priest hired for *Saviour* had experience with other film roadshows, such as *Quo Vadis* (Enrico Guazzoni, 1913), having been recommended by a correspondent who worked for George Kleine, while others seem to have worked only with theater companies.[95] Much of Priest's job was hiring, firing, and communicating with these road managers, though he also corresponded extensively with the theater managers, most of them Shubert affiliated, who had booked the film.

Although the company managers had some discretion in initially setting up their bookings, the exact form that each company's presentation of *Saviour* took was ultimately controlled and approved from New York by Priest personally. The booking process took a standardized pattern: after being contacted by the company manager, interested theaters signed an exhibition contract. It specified that the theater paid for local newspaper advertising and provided the projector and operator, organ and organist, and a "booth, calcimined screen, and everything else in accordance with the laws prevailing" in the city of exhibition.[96] The local company, for its part, provided the film itself and all advertising material, complete with the dates of the performance, and arranged for a lecturer and choir to accompany the film.

Underpinning the basic strategy for *Saviour*'s roadshow was the idea of tying in with local church groups, and a major responsibility of the road managers was to promote the film with local clergy. This was

in part in the hope that they might lecture alongside the film and provide choirs or organists to accompany it. But the managers also directly
marketed the film to clergy, schools, and religious organizations, such as
local YMCA chapters, by allowing them to sell so-called exchange tickets
to their members. These were discounted tickets that effectively cut local
institutions in on the film's grosses—sometimes as much as 25 percent of
the price of the ticket. The idea was to make money on volume by filling
theaters as close to capacity as possible. While the typical undiscounted
ticket price at the legitimate theaters where the film played was between
twenty-five and fifty cents, about on par for a feature film in 1914, it was
still significantly lower than the typical admission for a live-theatrical
performance in the same venue, which would have typically been
one dollar or more. A major advantage of having a local company manager was to ensure advantageous ticket price scales—not too low, such
that the company would not make money, but also not higher than was
typical locally for feature films.

Appealing to religious groups through reduced ticket pricing and a
general sense of Holy Week reverence was a key aspect of Priest's roadshow strategy for *Saviour*. These were audiences for whom the local
theater was not generally held in high regard, and the Motion Picture
Department pitched the roadshow to theater owners as being able to
bring in a new type of patron that did not typically attend theatrical
performances. Priest described the overall strategy to Joseph Weimer,
manager of the Auditorium Theater in Toledo, Ohio, in March 1914:
"Our main endeavour is to relegate the air of the theatre, and supersede
it by the air of a great religious revival. . . . Make the bait as strong
as possible to appeal to the religiously inclined. We do not intend to
cater to theatre-goers, but to cater almost exclusively to church-goers."[97]
A letter Priest sent to theaters with suggestions for advertising the film
repeated this message, suggested paying local clergy fifty dollars for their
involvement, and emphasized hiring a church organist wherever possible
to accompany both the film itself and the singing of hymns during reel
changes.[98] The fact that blue laws prohibited cinema exhibition on Sundays in some markets may have been another factor in motivating cooperation with clergy, though Priest's correspondence provides no explicit
evidence for this.

This focused appeal would seem at first to suggest that the Shubert
roadshow of *The Life of Our Saviour* was a one-off example of Holy

Week seasonal distribution, totally separate from more standard models and practices of film circulation in the 1910s. Indeed, scholars tend to describe the roadshow as an exceptional practice reserved for the largest productions, with other models, such as the state rights system or the variety program, ultimately becoming more influential in the development of feature film distribution as a standardized practice.[99] But we should not ignore the role of *Saviour* and other roadshows that evince crucial continuities between the distribution practices of legitimate theater and those of the growing feature film industry. In a period when many legitimate houses were being forced to convert at least part-time to motion picture exhibition, specially presented roadshows allowed such theaters to remain solvent while differentiating themselves from the so-called picture houses that played exclusively film. Live-theatrical language suffused the correspondence between Priest and his managers as well as the contracts with theaters. Managers were expected to conduct a "rehearsal" of the film before its local premiere "performance," and runs of a particular print constituted its "season."[100] As a rhetorical strategy, the film itself and its framing as a price-friendly roadshow positioned the Shuberts' foray into film distribution as both elevated and accessible.

For the Shuberts and other distributors, classifying film releases as theatrical roadshows could also have financial benefits, as IATSE rules specified standard wage scales for roadshows. For the kinds of theaters that played *Saviour*, most of which did not have their own projectors or booths, these rules required that attending operators set up and take down film-related equipment as part of their flat forty-dollar salary for the week.[101] This was true even if the operator traveled with the company to multiple venues, so it represented a manageable cost even for shorter runs. Though the Shuberts' contracts for the film specified that theaters were to provide their own projectors and operators, it is likely that in practice, some companies did have an operator that traveled with them, owing to shortages of skilled projectionists. Road company manager W. Fred Mason, writing to Priest from Albany, complained, "We will have more or less trouble in finding operators in the combination houses that we are to play, as about all these men have been discharged for incompetant [sic] work in the small picture houses. These men are unfit to handle any reels and especially ones like ours, and I would suggest that we carry an operator with us to protect our pictures, and specify in contracts that the local [theater] Manager is to pay for same at the Union scale $40 per week."[102] Mason's proposal was probably sound, given that theaters were used to paying such expenses for stagehands and other workers under the combination system. However, union rules complicated the roadshow's music strategy. Because theaters were often obliged to pay their house orchestras whether they played or not, many dispensed with Priest's plan to hire separate organists to accompany each screening.[103]

The release of *Saviour* differed in several ways from both the typical combination company run in live theater and the feature roadshow. For one, the only actual "combination" on tour in this case was the film print and its road manager (and sometimes a projectionist), rather than a whole company complete with projector, organist, and commentator—in every case, the theater had to pay for those separately, with the assistance of the company manager. Given that the film's distribution was by necessity organized around a specific Holy Week release date, it resembled a standard program feature release more than a typical roadshow, in the sense that the film's value decreased significantly just a few weeks after its release. This differed from most film roadshow releases of the period, in which the timing of a film's distribution across a territory was generally of lower priority than the quality of the presentation. The usual roadshow strategy was to generate extended runs in prestigious venues that would justify higher ticket prices, not to book the film to as many venues as possible.

Saviour's roadshow was also geographically limited. The Shuberts' distribution of the film in the United States was hardly national—it was certainly not of the scale of *Quo Vadis*, which George Kleine had been roadshowing across the entire country for the previous year (in some cases using the same road managers that the Shuberts would hire).[104] Nearly all of the film's companies toured east of the Mississippi, with several concentrated in New York State and Ohio, and very few in the South. This geographic pattern essentially represented the Shuberts' theater holdings, suggesting that the company was not very successful in booking the film outside of houses it did not already control.

All of this added up to the film's failure in distribution. While the local managers did pick up a few one- or two-day bookings for the film the week after Easter, by the end of that week it was clear that the film was a dud. In his correspondence with Priest, St. Louis company manager Henry Pierson attributed this failure primarily to the lack of cooperation from local clergy, who were generally too busy during Holy Week to assist in the presentations of the film.[105] Despite the use of exchange tickets, attendance was not up to the Shuberts' expectations, even in New York. There were also problems with the physical distribution of the film prints. Pathé sent at least two companies prints with mixed-up reels, and one company received the film without any reels at all.[106] The humidor boxes carried by each company to preserve the hand-coloring of the prints could not accommodate Pathé's twelve-inch reels, so each road company had to recut and rewind their print onto ten-inch reels once they received it.[107] These issues revealed the Shuberts' relative inexperience with the logistical and technical side of film distribution, highlighting the advantage held by distributors with a local exchange system. *Variety* reported, probably hyperbolically, that the Shuberts stood to lose almost $1 million on *Saviour*.[108]

The fundamental problem with the roadshow of *The Life of Our Saviour* was the Motion Picture Department's assumption that the live-theatrical logics of the combination company would continue to translate to film distribution in an era when multireel features were beginning to dominate the screen. Certainly, passion plays had been successfully distributed via a roadshow model in the United States since as early as 1897, when Klaw and Erlanger distributed *The Horitz Passion Play*.[109] Part of the appeal of such films had been their length relative to other films. But by 1914, the novelty of the filmed passion play had worn off, and a faithful remake of the seven-year-old *La Passion* needed careful film-specific distribution to turn a profit.

Priest did seem to realize this to an extent, given his strategy of focusing on churchgoers rather than a more general theatrical audience. But the distribution of the film relied on Shubert-controlled theaters in large and midsize cities and the sales capabilities of its road managers. There was simply no "Shubert exchange," apart from Priest himself, where exhibitors could seek out the film. Some theater owners and state rights companies did write Priest directly to inquire about separate distribution rights for the film, but Priest flatly refused, insisting that the film was not available as a "regular feature release" for "picture theaters."[110] This may have been a differentiation strategy, but it was more likely because Pathé had reserved the right to distribute *Saviour* as a regular feature for itself. Pathé would seasonally release the film through its own exchange system throughout the second half of the 1910s, and much more successfully. This tension between two incipient models of feature releasing—the combination-company-influenced theatrical roadshow and Paramount-style regular program releasing—would continue through the 1910s, as film distributors attempted to successfully combine the income potential of the roadshow and state rights systems with the reliability and efficiency of the program system.

The Shuberts' failure to effectively distribute *The Life of Our Saviour* demonstrates the influence of live-theatrical thinking among feature distributors into the mid-1910s. Before the rise of feature programs in late 1914, which suggested the viability of feature distribution within the framework of the variety shorts program, roadshows, combination companies, and state rights releasing continued to serve as default models for feature distribution. This was largely because they enabled a kind of cost-effective marketing to local venues and audiences that promised higher returns than could be expected by catering only to the "picture houses." However, locally tailored, theatrically modeled feature marketing in the absence of prearranged runs and zones and (relatively) reliable physical distribution—both hallmarks of the exchange networks of program distributors, such as the General Film Company—was risky for distributors who attempted it for film. Throughout the late 1910s and early 1920s, Hollywood distributors would adopt block booking, standard exhibition contracts, and other practices that allowed them to integrate specialized, theatrically influenced distribution models with standardized program releasing in a single, flexible system. The example of *Saviour* shows how the development of that system was often marked by failures, fits, and false starts.

However, it is worth emphasizing that the Shuberts' management of the film's distribution was by no means incompetent. By attending to the performance of Christian reverence—as evinced not only by an explicit appeal to churchgoing audiences but also by road managers' work in corralling clerical commentary, organists, and choirs—Robert Priest clearly had a cogent strategy for selling *Saviour* as a religious theatrical spectacle. Despite this, the Motion Picture Department (in contrast to Pathé's own exchange) failed to attend fully to *Saviour*'s distribution *as a film*, with needs arising from its mechanically reproduced nature and the possibility inherent in film distribution for flexible and cheap circulation.

Indeed, the live-theatrical models and strategies described in this chapter served as paradigmatic options for the film industry as it developed its own distribution practice. The 1900s and 1910s were a period of trial and error as distributors worked out not only how to adapt live-theatrical practices of booking, circuiting, and packaging to motion pictures, but also how to adapt the movies to established strategies for distributing entertainment profitably. Thinking through this double determination helps us to reframe the development of film distribution not as a teleology leading toward a "mature oligopoly," but through the context of established practices in other entertainment industries.

2 THE PACKAGE, PART I

Programming the Studio System
Packaging in Film Distribution, 1896–1917

As a mechanically reproduced form of theatrical entertainment, cinema presented a novel question of packaging: How, if at all, should individual films be grouped as units of sale to a venue? Was the attraction of cinema its novelty, multiplicity, and variety, as in vaudeville? Or was it something more sustained and singular, like a legitimate stage spectacular? Even before there was a recognizable film distribution industry in the United States, strategies for packaging cinema generally followed one of two models with different answers to these questions. The first was a model that we might call *programmatic*, with multiple titles sold as a bundled unit and released with some regularity. The second we might call *idiosyncratic*, with a singularly marketable attraction or collection of attractions given individually tailored handling. In this chapter, we will see how the film distribution industry began to build a system that flexibly incorporated both models for marketing cinema.

Film historian Charles Musser, in his study with Carol Nelson of the earliest American itinerant exhibitors, describes two forms of projection-based cinema exhibition in the 1890s—the exhibition service and the traveling exhibitor—that map neatly onto these models. According to Musser, exhibition services provided a projector, an operator, and films on a continuing basis, changing the bill of attractions every week to keep audiences interested. By contrast, traveling exhibitors toured the countryside one stand at a time with the same complete show, including not only the items necessary for projection but also a lecturer, actors, an advance promoter, and advertising materials. These two forms served different audiences. Exhibition services provided vaudeville houses with their twenty-minute film turns, and itinerant exhibitors traveled to small cities and towns to perform at the local "opera house" theater or a meeting hall, or simply under a pitched tent.[1] Even the pricing of each form was appropriate to its corresponding live-theatrical distribution outlet; exhibition services were paid a weekly fee, just as a vaudeville artist would be, while traveling exhibitors usually shared ticket receipts with the venue according to some percentage.

It is little surprise that these two early formats of cinema exhibition deployed the most important models of live-theatrical booking: the vaudeville program (exhibition services) and the touring combination company (traveling exhibition). It would be teleological to suggest that this correspondence was simply a result of entrepreneurs having to package moving pictures by any means necessary in the absence of a specific apparatus for film distribution. Rather, live-theatrical booking systems proved useful for early American film entrepreneurs because the live experience of the film screening was such a fantastically novel attraction—not just the images themselves, but the whirring of the projector, the thrilling display of electric light, the performance of the accompanying lecturers, actors, and musicians, and the delighted reactions of viewers. Even after the immediate novelty of cinema passed and permanent firms dedicated to regular film distribution began to emerge, exhibition services and itinerant exhibitors continued to develop along lines similar to those of their live-theatrical counterparts. Lyman Howe's itinerant exhibition organization eventually grew to encompass multiple companies (five touring simultaneously in 1909) and new touring circuits. Many of his rivals, including Archie Shepard and D. W. Robertson, saw similar growth. Howe's show became so successful by 1909 that it was considered a draw on the legitimate stage, playing three Sunday shows at the New York Hippodrome and multiple weeks at other Shubert houses. Exhibition services, which urban vaudeville theaters had previously been hiring repeatedly on a week-to-week basis, started signing long-term contracts with local vaudeville theaters in 1899.[2] Thus, the bifurcation between programmatic and idiosyncratic releasing, inherited from live-theatrical traditions, was built into the institutions of American cinema from the very beginning.

It is worth pausing for a moment to further illuminate what I mean by programmatic and idiosyncratic distribution. As with the heuristics of "booking," "circuiting," and "packaging" discussed in the previous chapter, "programmatic" and "idiosyncratic" are not terms with any particularly rigorous meaning in the fields of film studies, economics, or business history. They were not used in contemporary historical discourse, nor, to my knowledge, have they previously been applied to any kind of work on the economics of distribution. Rather, I present them as poles of a useful dichotomy that help us to think through film distribution's development out of live-theatrical models and into a form specific to the concerns of the film industry and to those of media distribution more generally.

Fundamental to the distinction between programmatic and idiosyncratic distribution is the way that individual, self-contained films are sold to exhibitors. Programmatic film distribution sells individual titles as just one example among others within some larger package. That package might be a purely economic unit of sale, such as a booking contract covering the rental of multiple films. It could also be a more coherent group of films linked by some inherent characteristic: films starring Gladys Brockwell, for example, or a series of Colonel Heeza Liar cartoons. The package might be defined temporally: the new films released by Mutual this week, or Paramount's first available distribution block of twenty-six films for the 1920–1921 season. Whatever logic is used to construct the package of sale—and a wide variety of logics were employed during this period—programmatic releasing links individual films according to a recurring economic, generic, or temporal relationship and structures the release and sales strategy for the package containing those films accordingly.

Idiosyncratic releasing, by contrast, treats individual films (or, commonly in early cinema, packages of very short films, as in Howe's show) as *singularly* marketable and worthy of specialized handling. The state rights system, the roadshow, and prerelease exploitation, all distribution models examined in this book, are idiosyncratic. In using the term "idiosyncratic," I do not wish to imply that there was no consistent strategy for distributing these specially marketable films. Quite the opposite, in fact: the film industry used a common set of strategies for handling films that emphasized their ostensibly distinctive and differentiated qualities, categorizing them, for example, according to the amount of money spent on them, the presence of particular stars or directors, film lengths, their status as adaptations of well-known novels or plays, or their topicality. *The Birth of a Nation* would be the best-known example of an idiosyncratically distributed American film during this period, but something like the Shuberts' handling of *The Life of Our Saviour* also qualifies.

Also fundamental to the distinction between programmatic and idiosyncratic distribution is a set of expectations about time. Programmatic distribution is periodic; the films within a particular package are released in regular temporal intervals, or at least sold with the expectation that they will be released or exhibited that way. As a result, programmatic distribution is generally offered up as the regular, reliable "backbone" of an exhibitor's overall booking calendar. Idiosyncratic distribution is, while not necessarily sporadic, less predictable. This approach is necessary by definition—idiosyncratically released films are differentiated from others partially by the fact that they may only be offered to certain exhibitors at a particular time (otherwise their distribution would be programmatic and regular). Idiosyncratically released "specials," as the most potentially lucrative films on the overall distribution slate, were also the most likely to play for extended runs. As a result, idiosyncratic distribution strategies necessarily built in a certain temporal flexibility, and programmatic distribution was more rigid.

It is common in the media industries of today to correlate distribution strategies with certain types of individual productions according to budget or genre. In the 2020s, theatrical distribution is associated with big-budget superhero and sci-fi franchises or low-budget horror, and more adult-oriented, mid-budget fare is assumed to premiere on streaming services. Similar kinds of correlations between film characteristics and distribution obtained in the first decades of the film industry. Although programmatic and idiosyncratic distribution did not *automatically* articulate to characteristics of individual films such as length, genre, budget, or stars during this period, certain types of films did tend to correlate with one or the other category. Long, expensive films with big stars tended to be distributed idiosyncratically, and shorter, cheaper films with lesser-known personalities programmatically (length and expense being relative and highly variable during this period). Thus, a mutually determined relationship structured distribution and planning in production, with films being made with a particular distribution strategy in mind while a studio's available production output shaped releasing practices.[3] However, the relationship between a film's production qualities and its distribution became more and more flexible as the studio system developed.

The role of exhibition within distribution strategy complicates these ideas significantly, and programmatic distribution is particularly troublesome in this respect. The history and format of the "film program"—in the sense of the exhibition of multiple films that cohere to form a whole evening's entertainment—have been effectively defined by Nico de Klerk and Richard Abel.[4] Their definition is related to the idea of programmatic distribution, but programs in distribution are not synonymous with or strictly articulated to "the program" in exhibition. In other words, a film distributed programmatically need not *play* alongside other films in exhibition (though it often will); it need only be *sold* along with other films as part of the same distribution bundle. This issue is further complicated by the fact that the term "program film" is often incorrectly taken to be synonymous with the program *short*—films of one or two reels that played on frequently changed program bills and made up the bulk of American film production from 1905 to 1915. As we will see, not all program films were shorts, and there were strong continuities in distribution between the one- or two-reel program film and the early four- or five-reel program feature as the latter began to appear in 1914. Despite the potential terminological confusion, I believe using the terms "program" and "programmatic" to describe distribution is both useful and historically appropriate. Putting aside their associations with a specific model of short film exhibition, both words connote the idea of scheduled, nearly automatic regularity—a notion within media distribution practice that would stretch beyond the early years of the studio system into broadcasting and digital media.

Of course, just because a film was sold or packaged according to a programmatic or idiosyncratic strategy does not mean that it was shown according to distributors' assumptions. Motion pictures have been released to and shown in a diverse array of venues and contexts throughout history, after all—Don't the terms outlined above threaten to reduce our thinking about distribution to a simple binary? And if we consider exhibition an inseparable part of distribution, isn't *all* distribution idiosyncratic to some extent? The answer to these questions is yes. But given how distribution has tended to be subsumed within scholarship focusing on production or exhibition, this binary is useful as a heuristic to delineate how distributors framed their practices. Finally, even though the actual situation when it came to film distribution in the 1910s and 1920s better resembled a spectrum than discrete poles—as is the case with any binary—this situation *arose* out of a historically accountable binary. Indeed, my argument in this chapter is that by merging programmatic and idiosyncratic distribution, film distributors turned a mostly rigid industrial binary into a spatially and temporally flexible spectrum.

This chapter and the next offer an account of how distributors created this flexible system of film packaging from the origins of the industry, through the rise of national shorts cinema distribution in 1910, and into the early 1920s. From the earliest days of the American film industry, the packaging of cinema as a product was bifurcated between programmatic and idiosyncratic (or "special") releasing. In the early 1910s, this bifurcation defined entirely separate distribution systems. Around 1914, however, these separate systems began to merge, and by the mid-1920s, major studio distribution accommodated both programmatic and idiosyncratic approaches for all of their titles in a single flexible system. This system allowed programmatic films to be affordably sold to exhibitors in tied groups while at the same time enabling them to be elevated to special release if they turned out to be unexpectedly popular. This chapter traces the causes and contexts of the industry's innovation, implementation, and revision of its packaging strategies before 1917.

Film Packaging before the Feature Program, 1896–1914

The film distribution industry emerged as a sector recognizably separate from live-theatrical booking or cinema exhibition with the earliest film exchanges. Max Alvarez has admirably traced the history of these exchanges, noting that exchange entrepreneurs reconfigured the assumptions of manufacturers and exhibitors regarding the economic value of cinema. For most manufacturers in the earliest years, the most important salable attraction was not the films themselves, but the new technology of cameras, peep-show devices, and projectors. For the earliest exhibitors, films obviously had economic value, but always as part of a larger package of *exhibition* that included a projector and operator. Exchanges, which bought films outright from manufacturers but then rented them to anyone with a means to exhibit, or traded them with other exchanges, recognized the value of the film print itself as capital—as something that could return a dividend in the form of rental income. Venues, for their part, realized that renting film from an exchange, rather than buying it outright, could save a significant amount of money. For a small-time vaudeville house seeking to play several turns of film every day, investing in a projector, training the house electrician to be its operator, and renting films was cheaper in the long run than outsourcing those functions to an exhibition service.[5] As Musser notes, this was one factor in the transformation of many exhibition services into film exchanges and the separation of distribution and exhibition as sectors within the film industry.[6] The emergence of the earliest American film exchanges thus reflected not only a developing economic specialization within the industry, but also a recognition among both distributors and exhibitors that generating long-term economic value from the new medium required films to be released regularly and efficiently—in other words, programmatically.

Paul S. Moore has traced what is arguably the earliest form of the film exchange in North America to the classified section of the *New York Clipper*, which served as a primary communications channel for the market in secondhand films as early as 1896. As Moore notes, there was effectively no regime of copyright control over film exhibition before 1908, despite the Edison company's aggressive attempts to enforce its patents in film technology. Anyone in possession of a film print could rent, resell, copy, exchange, or exhibit it without having to pay manufacturers, creating the conditions for a robust secondhand market in films.[7] The supply side of this market was sustained by itinerant exhibitors' and exhibition services' constant need to refresh their programs with new films, and their very short length encouraged a voracious demand that could not be satiated with new productions alone. In its ad hoc informality, inefficient organization around individual transactions, and generally stochastic quality, the *Clipper* classified section could be likened to the Union Square "slave market" that had served as a primary site for live-theatrical booking in the mid- and late nineteenth century. While there were undoubtedly other networks for the market in secondhand films, film's mechanical reproducibility and status as an easily transportable physical good made print media classifieds well suited to marketing it to a wide swath of potential buyers, traders, or renters.

As Alvarez and Moore note, dedicated brick-and-mortar film exchanges tended to grow out of screen equipment suppliers who dealt in secondhand film as an adjunct to their main business of selling projectors, magic lanterns, song slides, and stereopticons.[8] The secondhand film rental business had become ubiquitous in New York and Chicago by late 1903, and by 1905 it had clearly surpassed the importance of equipment supply at exchanges. The nickelodeon boom of the subsequent years led to a concomitant growth in the exchange industry. By 1908, film exchanges could be found not only in the biggest cities but also in regional markets, such as Pittsburgh, St. Louis, and Kansas City. Chicago remained by far the most important center.[9]

Systematic circuiting of film by exchanges without an accompanying projector or operator was occurring by no later than the end of 1903, when the Miles brothers acquired a large supply of discounted films from Biograph and toured them between New York and San Francisco.[10] As recounted by Albert E. Smith, the Miles circuit was variously made up of theaters in "anywhere from ten to forty or fifty different towns," charging around ten dollars a week for films and films alone. Each theater—most of them probably small-time vaudeville houses—would have needed to supply its own projector and operator. At the conclusion of each booking, the theater sent the films on to the next house via an express service.[11] This circuiting model would eventually become known as the "lock system," whereby a particular package of films was "locked together" and distributed as a unit before returning to the exchange.[12]

Throughout this period, film manufacturers continued to sell films outright to anyone who would buy them. This is not to say that manufacturers never distributed films, but before around 1905 they almost always released exhibition packages that included the means to project the films. These packages were also typically outsourced to a separate business, as in the case of the Kinetoscope Company, a consortium of partnerships that handled the marketing and exhibition of the Edison peep-show device beginning in 1894.[13] Nevertheless, the model employed by manufacturers—via their surrogates—to distribute the service of cinema exhibition nationally would become the basis for idiosyncratic releasing in the film industry: the state rights system.

State rights distribution, whereby manufacturers sold the exclusive rights to market a product (film and its exhibition, in this case) to many independent state and regional companies, was another live-theatrical model that was adapted to the distribution of early feature films. As Ben Brewster notes, the exclusive contract in live theater, whereby an act agreed with the venue not to appear anywhere else in the local territory for some period of time, enabled theaters to both charge monopoly prices and market the attraction more effectively.[14] This economic model was the basis of state rights distribution for early features, where it fulfilled an important differentiating function for specially handled films. However, state rights was also a common approach to the national mass marketing of consumer goods—a context in which it is more commonly referred to as product franchising.

I cover the use of product franchising for multireel feature films in the early 1910s, including the state rights system, in more detail in chapter 4. For now, however, it is worth emphasizing that the state rights model was employed in the film industry from the very beginning, well before multireel features were a widespread phenomenon. In the earliest years of the film industry, state rights functioned less as a differentiation strategy for films than as an outgrowth of preexisting strategies for nationally marketing a variety of new technologies. The Edison company had used the system to regionally promote the phonograph and the Kinetoscope, for example. Beginning in 1896, two members of the old Kinetoscope Company, Norman Raff and Frank Gammon, organized a new venture in partnership with Edison to sell exclusive rights to that company's new projection machine, the Vitascope. As Musser details, dozens of entrepreneurs nationwide, most of them Edison franchisees for selling Kinetoscopes and phonographs, bought exclusive Vitascope rights at varying but quite large amounts, including $3,000 for Connecticut (William McConnell), $3,500 for California (J. R. Balsley and Richard Paine), and $5,000 for Ohio (Allen Rieser).[15] They then either exploited these rights themselves to exhibit the Vitascope or subdivided them to itinerant exhibitors and exhibition services for a further profit within their particular territory.

The state rights model was central to the early days of projected cinema, even in distribution situations where the primary marketable quality being sold was a singular filmed attraction as much as the novel technology of cinema exhibition. This was certainly true of the Veriscope Company's *Corbett-Fitzsimmons Fight* (Enoch Rector, 1897), which, as Dan Streible has shown, was the earliest instance of cinema distribution where "a commercial venture [took] its apparatus on the road with a single film subject." This single subject was not just another actuality to run through the Veriscope projector, but a draw in its own right. Technical considerations certainly played a large role in the film's exploitation— it had a one-hundred-minute runtime, a 63mm gauge, and a wide aspect ratio of 1.65:1—but the real attraction was its highly publicized subject matter: the bout between heavyweight champions James "Gentleman Jim" Corbett and Robert Fitzsimmons that had been organized specifically for the film. After the film's premiere at the New York Academy of Music in May 1897, Veriscope took it "on the road" along the model of a theatrical combination. The film's promoter, Dallas entrepreneur Dan Stuart, organized its distribution into eleven projection companies, a number that would eventually expand to at least twenty for the 1897–1898 theatrical season. Each company included the film itself, a Veriscope projector and operator, and a lecturer hired locally. Franchises to exploit these companies were then sold territorially.[16]

Streible has shown that the film's road distribution across the United States can be divided by exhibition context: first, in major venues, including grand opera houses, music academies, and legitimate houses in cities; second, in small-town opera houses; and third, at fairgrounds, amusement parks, and circuses.[17] While there was little in the way of a systematic national strategy governing the booking and circuiting of the *Corbett-Fitzsimmons Fight* beyond the sale of its state rights, the film's packaging as a theatrical attraction was designed such that local franchisees could bring it to nearly any venue in their territories and according to any circuiting strategy they thought appropriate. In enabling the idiosyncratic national distribution of a special attraction by outsourcing the local details of that distribution, the state rights system served an important function that itinerant exhibitors, exhibition services, and early exchanges typically did not: marketing individual films of unusual drawing potential.

Packaging strategies from live theater enabled distributors to emphasize—or *feature*—individual films alongside the technology of filmmaking. Of course, cinema was still so new in this period that for most audiences (and probably most exhibitors), there was little meaningful distinction between the appeal of individual films and that of cinema as a novel technology.[18] As evinced by the Shuberts' roadshow of *The Life of Our Saviour* nearly seventeen years after the *Corbett-Fitzsimmons Fight*, the combination-modeled packaging of individual titles with a projector and lecturer would continue to be used well into the 1910s. However, as the novelty of cinema wore off and structures of exhibition in the cinema industry became more regularized between 1906 and 1910, film distributors increasingly recognized that selling a package of films rather than a package of exhibition could be done much more cheaply and efficiently in many situations.

Film-exclusive distribution in the United States from 1906 to 1914—the one-reel period—took one of two forms: the state rights system and the variety program. These forms were largely incommensurate with each other in terms of packaging, pricing, run, and booking structure, as well as the kinds of films they were meant to deliver and the exhibition spaces they were meant to serve. The dominant model, and the one that would form the eventual systematic basis for multireel feature distribution after 1914, was the variety program, or "program system," which was structured around exchanges renting programs of short films to exhibitors.[19] By 1908, these programs were typically made up of three one-reel films, and local exchanges packaged them into groupings by age, with the knowledge that exhibitors would be changing their bills several times each week (and often every day). From a production standpoint, the program system encouraged the throughput of films above all else. Distributors purchased film from manufacturers at a flat rate of eight to twelve cents per foot of positive produced, then rented that film to exhibitors via standing contracts for very short runs. Film manufacturers were thus strongly motivated to standardize and control the costs of their films to turn a profit.

Frequent turnover in exhibition was the driving presumption of the program system. This was based on a combination of the economic reality of exhibition spaces and assumptions about film spectators. Most "picture theaters" (film-only venues) at the height of the one-reel period were small, seating less than three hundred patrons.[20] This meant that economies of scale in exhibition had to be accomplished temporally rather than spatially: if an exhibitor was to make any profit from rented films in a relatively small space, those films needed to be screened as frequently as possible. This encouraged distributors to rent—and manufacturers to produce—short films. Furthermore, exhibitors and distributors during the one-reel period catered to an imagined audience of "transient" spectators: passers-by or patrons seeking not a particular film, but general amusement at the picture show. The film industry of the late 1900s and early 1910s assumed the primacy of this audience and based its conduct around that assumption.[21] Exhibitors and distributors privileged not only the short length of films, but also the variety of the program and the frequency of its change, according to the logic that transient spectators would not have to wait long to see new and different films. This was the same logic B. F. Keith had used in programming his continuous vaudeville shows at the Bijou Theatre in Boston since the 1880s.

Indeed, the variety program's assumptions about what was valuable in exhibition—novelty, variety, well-appointed spaces, and programming that appealed to a broadly imagined (though assumed white) middle class—were essentially the same as those of vaudeville.[22] However, early variety program distribution differed somewhat from vaudeville booking in its packaging practices. First, early film programs distributed by exchanges were usually shorter than the average two-hour vaudeville program, with three or four reels giving a forty-five- to sixty-minute show. As a result, the work of assembling dramatic variation and flow across seven or nine turns that was so fundamental to vaudeville packaging was considerably less acute in film programs. Variety was still important, but the primary packaging questions film exchanges dealt with were the age of films and the status of the exhibitor renting them. The exhibitor willing to pay the most in rental fees would generally get a "first run" service contract, meaning the newest films an exchange had available. In these early days of programmatic film distribution, this notion had little to do with the structured runs of the later run/zone/clearance system; rather, it referred to the literal first run of a fresh print through a projector.[23] Less well-heeled houses could typically only afford a service contract with packages that mixed new films with older ones, or included only older ones. Exchanges often served theaters far outside their immediate vicinity— William H. Swanson's Chicago exchange shipped to houses as far as seven hundred miles away.[24] Such theaters were generally unable to pay for first-run service but were also more likely to lack competition, and so were often satisfied with all but the most worn-out prints if the price was right.

Film's mechanical reproducibility also altered the conditions structuring the work of circuiting at exchanges. In one respect, film circuiting was simpler: reels needed no food or accommodations, so their movement through exhibition networks was less spatially and temporally constrained. However, from the standpoint of making film economically attractive to exhibitors, circuiting was complicated by the destructive act of projection. The degradation of prints after every performance, even under the best of circumstances, lowered the exhibition value of each reel—although demand for film was so high in this period that the effect was somewhat moderated. Film's reproducibility presented another complication: a reel could conceivably compete with copies of itself within the same market by playing in neighboring theaters at the same time or shortly thereafter, decreasing its value to exhibitors and thus its rental price. This marketing problem applied not only to the vast quantities of duped product that circulated among exchanges, but also to release prints legitimately purchased from manufacturers. As with print quality, the sheer demand for films of any kind around 1906 and 1907 obviated these problems for exchanges. In the long term, however, they threatened the industry by restraining prices—especially those paid to manufacturers—and degrading the overall quality of film exhibition.

For these reasons, the primary role of local film exchanges within the larger economy of distribution as it developed in the 1900s and 1910s was to manage the *physical* condition and circulation of prints and advertising material. In that sense they were not analogous to vaudeville booking offices or agencies in legitimate theater, or any preexisting live-theatrical institution. Indeed, the stated goal of the United Film Services Protective Association, an organization of the larger exchanges and importers formed in November 1907 by Edison-aligned manufacturers, was to remove worn prints from circulation. Six months later, the same organization (renamed the Film Service Association) sought to establish a pricing schedule for reels by release date, centering the physical condition of prints as the main criterion of value in programmatic film distribution.[25]

The Motion Picture Patents Company (MPPC, or "Patents Company") created a more rationalized distribution apparatus, using a system of exchange licensing, following its founding in 1908. The system designated the 150 exchanges that signed on as licensed distributors of MPPC manufacturers' films and required them to implement several policies. These included purchasing film only from licensed manufacturers and importers; prohibiting duping, sub-renting, and secondhand selling of prints; and returning films to manufacturers for destruction after they had been played out. Licensed exchanges were also made agents of the Patents Company in collecting the two-dollar-a-week fee from exhibitors for using licensed projectors.[26] However, exchanges frequently ignored these policies, and the Edison licensing system was less a distribution system than a confederation of fiefdoms that followed the same rules only on paper. Although the MPPC licensed hundreds of exchanges throughout the United States in an attempt to shut out other manufacturers from distribution, exchanges continued to act in their own interests first.

Thus, there was no real film industry equivalent to the United Booking Office before 1910. Instead, booking, circuiting, and packaging were done at the level of individual exchanges, and those practices were far from uniform. Despite the rationalized packaging and pricing of films by age that the MPPC ostensibly enforced, exchanges continued renting the same films simultaneously to competing exhibitors, providing preferential service to theaters they owned, and engaging in other behaviors that depressed prices and made film distribution both unpredictable and disreputable. This changed in 1910, when the MPPC began buying out nearly all the licensed exchanges directly and established the General Film Company (GFC). As Robert Anderson has shown, the GFC rationalized film distribution on a national scale.[27] This was in part because it simply brought the exchanges under a single organization. Though it was not a completely centralized booking management office, the GFC did resemble vaudeville's United Booking Offices in its national scale and standardization of prices and practices at local exchanges (its equivalent to the UBO's geographically organized booking desks). By consolidating the multiple licensed exchanges that often coexisted within the same local market, the GFC created a national distribution monopoly on licensed film service.

However, the GFC also introduced new practices to film distribution, the most important of which was a variation on vaudeville practice: zoning. Just as the VMA granted theaters an effective local monopoly on artists they booked, the GFC granted certain exhibitors first-run status within a defined geographic area, giving them packages of all-new films released by the licensed MPPC manufacturers. Other exhibitors that were ranked lower in the GFC's hierarchy received packages in varying combinations, with some first-run, some second-run, and some subsequent-run films at successively lower rental prices. This zoning practice was not exclusive, meaning that exhibitors had no real clearance protection from rivals playing the same films at the same time. It was also common for the GFC to violate its own zoning hierarchies by offering some exhibitors a choice of service level independent of their location.[28] As a strategy of organizing film exhibition to optimize film circulation, the General Film Company's zoning practice was thus only partially successful. Despite this, the GFC's packaging of films according to a logical pricing scheme defined by release date constituted a vast improvement in distribution organization compared to the licensing system. Packaging individual films as part of full-service programs at predictable prices created various economies of scale within film distribution that strengthened that sector's relationship to exhibition. Exhibitors could now rent films in bulk contracts from a single exchange—the local GFC office—for all their programming needs.

The influence of the GFC's practices on film production was perhaps even more important; in effect, the organization combined the management of film production with that of programmatic film distribution through a standardized set of practices for the first time. This created a predictable set of conditions for the licensed manufacturers, enabling them to plan their productions for sale to what amounted to a single buyer rather than hundreds of different exchanges. That enabled producers to organize the pricing and planning of films more reliably. Film rental to exhibitors was now standardized per reel and based on the age of films, and the GFC exchanges purchased films from the MPPC manufacturers on standing orders at a fixed cost per foot of positive film, which varied between eight and twelve cents.[29] Thus, in 1914 prices, a print run of forty positives for a one-reel program film would predictably gross the manufacturer between $3,200 and $4,800 from the distributor. Uniform pricing stabilized budgets for manufacturers: prior to the formation of the GFC, when films were distributed through hundreds of independent exchanges, manufacturers had little incentive to raise the costs and quality of their films: pricing was unpredictable, and exchanges privileged newness and the availability of product above all else. Among exhibitors, the GFC's standardized pricing structure created an expectation of consistent quality within any given manufacturer's brand of film.

Because the GFC had the power to reject consistently poor brands of service from the program, manufacturers were also motivated to make films up to a particular standard. As Biograph's J. J. Kennedy argued in 1914, consistent pricing ensured consistent supply to exchanges, because an increase in the average quality of a particular manufacturer's films would, in theory, increase the average number of prints sold per subject.[30] This also meant that the popularity of manufacturers could be more accurately gauged. Prior to the formation of the GFC, a need for more prints might simply indicate inefficient distribution on the part of the exchanges. Now, prints made their way through the exchange system in a more rational way, according to zone, ensuring that any additional demand for prints corresponded (however roughly) to the greater popularity of a particular manufacturer. This overall pattern of *consistency*—of the quality of the industry's filmmaking, of manufacturers' and distributors' profits, and of trends in exhibition—was fundamental to the logic of program distribution.

Between 1910 and 1913, the program system evolved from an effective monopoly to a more competitive market. In 1910, concurrent with the formation of the GFC, a group of "independent" manufacturers, including Carl Laemmle's Independent Moving Pictures Company

(IMP) and Adam Kessel and Charles Baumann's New York Motion Picture Company, allied to create their own program service distributor, the Motion Picture Distributing and Sales Company (the "Sales Company"), out of exchanges that remained unlicensed by the Patents Company. They were eventually joined by other manufacturers, and by May 1910 the Sales Company was able to release twenty-one reels a week nationally, enough to satisfy the needs of most exhibitors. Two years later, in June 1912, when the Sales Company split into two separate and competing national distributors, Universal and Mutual, the GFC found itself in an even more competitive program market. With a circuit court ruling against the MPPC in August 1912, the independents were granted access to technology that had previously been exclusive to Edison-licensed manufacturers, allowing them to ramp up the quality and quantity of production significantly.[31]

General Film's emerging competitors copied its distribution model in most respects, attesting to the prevailing orthodoxy of the frequent-change program system before the mid-1910s.[32] The defining feature of that system was packaging: exchanges rented programs of films to exhibitors, whose service contracts specified a certain number of reels each week at a certain price per reel and rate of changeover (usually daily or every other day). As a result, the various manufacturing companies releasing through the program system between 1910 and 1914 centered their production on one- or two-reel films that were designed to be packaged together in a modular fashion.

However, the packaging strategy of the "independents" differed from that of the GFC in an important way. The GFC often restricted its licensed exhibitors from playing more than a specified number of reels at a time (generally three). The logic of this requirement was to discourage what was known as "bicycling" or "tagging" of reels, wherein two or more nearby exhibitors colluded to share films only one of them had paid for, by rushing them back and forth by bicycle or on foot.[33] The independent exchanges, by contrast, typically allowed exhibitors to rent as many reels at a time as they could pay for. Eileen Bowser argues that this packaging policy contributed to the growth of average program lengths among exhibitors starting in 1911, as the Sales Company used it to lure exhibitors away from the GFC.[34] Indeed, in the six years between the creation of the MPPC and the rise of feature programs in distribution, the average program length among exhibitors in urban markets essentially doubled. In 1914, *Motion Picture News* reported that the average

program in Los Angeles ran six reels, with some downtown houses showing as many as nine reels for a nickel and no exhibitor in the city showing fewer than four.[35] Similar lengths were the norm in San Francisco,
Albany, Baltimore, and New Haven, Connecticut, with markets such as
Milwaukee, Minneapolis, and Cincinnati averaging shorter programs of
four or five reels.[36] While program lengths certainly varied widely by the
dawn of feature programs at the end of 1914, three reels had become an
absolute minimum rather than an average.[37]

The increasing length of programs had important implications for
packaging at exchanges: it showed distributors—and especially the GFC's
competitors—that the program system *could* accommodate longer films.
This ultimately contributed to the decline of the variety program model
in distribution. Received histories of the General Film Company tend to
characterize its attitude toward films longer than three reels as indifferent at best. Robert Anderson, for example, counterposes the American
box-office success of eight-reel Italian epics, such as *Quo Vadis* (Enrico
Guazzoni, 1913) and *The Last Days of Pompeii* (Eleuterio Rodolfi, 1913),
with various memoranda in which GFC officials consider films longer
than three reels unsuitable for most motion picture theaters.[38] Michael
Quinn's work nuances Anderson's account by showing that the GFC did
attempt to integrate licensed features as long as three reels into its distribution system. However, that system failed to differentiate individual
films through special pricing, advertising, and systematically exclusive
access (i.e., clearance) for exhibitors—the idiosyncratic hallmarks of feature films handled by the state rights system in the early 1910s.[39]

The GFC's basic model, even as it was adopted by Mutual and Universal, had certain structural inadequacies when it came to the marketing
of features. Those inadequacies were exacerbated by the relatively short
length of licensed exhibitors' programs—three or four reels—which led
many GFC exchanges to release multireel films across multiple days. But
the GFC's distribution system was not, in principle, incompatible with
the packaging of longer films. The false conflation of "longer films" and
"features" is commonly pointed out in discussions of the one-reel period,
but the distinction was especially important to distributors as they developed packaging strategies for incorporating one or the other. "Features,"
in the early 1910s, were simply individual titles or acts that were differentiated on a particular program bill. While they could be longer than
other films on an exhibitor's program, they might also be differentiated
by subject matter, color, or some other idiosyncrasy.

The basic notion of the feature was therefore not incongruous with the variety program in the mid-1910s. In some exhibition contexts, such as small-time vaudeville theaters, it was in fact familiar, since feature films were an outgrowth of the vaudeville model of the featured act. In others—including the small picture-only exhibitors that formed the basis of the GFC's customers—there was resistance to longer features and programs. In early 1913, the Chicago Exhibitors' League (part of the Motion Picture Exhibitors League of America) resolved to limit its members' programs to three reels.[40] That September, the city's branch of the International Motion Picture Association (IMPA), representing some 150 exhibitors, adopted a policy of running three-reel programs for five cents, with five-reel programs requiring the higher admission price of ten cents.[41] The Detroit Exhibitors' League established the same standard.[42] This resistance was not confined to MPPC-licensed exhibitors but tended to come from houses in less competitive locations that lacked an incentive to offer more film for the same price. The anti-MPPC *Motion Picture News*, reporting on the IMPA policy, framed it as a sound one that would prevent the degradation of the industry's product: "The novelty of the motion picture must be sustained, and that by regulating the doses to be served to the public. To overeat is unhealthy, and to overfeed the public motion pictures is unhealthy for the business."[43] The GFC was thus hobbled in its feature strategies as much by its customer base and the conservatism of some exhibitors as by its own policies.

The daily change exhibition model and flat-fee pricing of the program system absolutely did limit the potential profitability of features, regardless of film length or type of theater, for reasons both structural and circumstantial. But the GFC's model had grown so fundamental to the motion picture industry by the mid-1910s that any firm venturing into programmatic feature distribution had to account for it. This is why none of the distributors that started releasing programs of features in 1914–1915 made them substantially longer than the typical program would have been at that time: four or five reels. Any industry-wide shift toward feature programs required a broad recognition that a film released as part of the daily change program could be nearly as long as the program itself, assuming that exhibitors were willing to either lengthen the program or accept less variety.

And many were. Mutual and Universal, serving exhibitors who were interested in longer programs, were able to fairly painlessly integrate two- and three-reel releases into their programs in 1912 and

1913. According to statistics aggregated by Ben Singer, the production of two-reel films increased almost tenfold between 1911 (12 films) and 1912 (116 films), and then fivefold again in 1913 (582 films). This compared to an 86 percent total increase in one-reel production over the same period (from 2,060 films to 3,841). By September 1913, Mutual's in-house magazine *Reel Life* was listing three or four two-reel releases every week and about one three-reeler every month on the company's program.[44] The tendency of both Mutual and Universal to package programs of multireel films more readily than the GFC was thus less a result of some greater business savvy about features than the fact that they were catering to a different set of customers who were more willing to embrace longer programs and films.

Nevertheless, as Quinn has emphasized, the GFC was conscious of the importance of multireel features, particularly by October 1913, when it experimented with an "exclusive service" strategy. Exclusive service was offered only to larger theaters, and at one hundred dollars a week was significantly more expensive than the GFC's typical program service. Exhibitors who purchased exclusive service received a four-reel program made up of two one-, two-, and occasionally three-reel films, changed three times a week. The service was differentiated in ways that had nothing to do with film or program length; exhibitors running it got color films from Kinemacolor, for example. Even more significantly, they got ninety days of clearance protection: a period during which no other exhibitor could book the films. This was a crucial differentiation strategy, as regular GFC service included no clearance at all.[45] Exclusive service also integrated some elements of idiosyncratic feature distribution—in particular, giving exhibitors the opportunity to advertise films in advance without the fear that they would be helping a competitor. However, exclusive service preserved the run structure of normal program service. Although it was not a daily change and it accommodated multireel films without splitting them across multiple days, there was no way to extend runs for individual films under the policy.

The exclusive service strategy exemplifies a central norm of the GFC model that would structure the conduct of the feature program distributors throughout the second half of the 1910s: short runs in exhibition. The short runs of the shorts-oriented program system continued into the feature-oriented program system even as the latter accommodated longer program lengths in exhibition. This practice had significant implications for distributors wishing to release higher-priced feature programs.

Because runs of early feature programs began on a specified release date and were generally short at any one theater—almost never more than a week, and for most exhibitors two or three days at the most—raising prices on programs in distribution to pay for features required strategies based on adding value to an exhibitor's service as a whole, rather than extending the runs of individual films to increase their value.[46] For distributors, this meant giving exhibitors exclusive access or long clearance, or even limiting feature programs to certain theaters. Because a consistent change in film programming continued to be common among exhibitors in the mid-1910s, it was an ingrained assumption for most distributors of program features.

The GFC's model of distribution practice remained dominant at the beginning of 1914. This dominance was a result of the structures of the exhibition market and the problems that the program system had helped to solve. As late as 1917, the basic distribution model of program service that the General Film Company had innovated continued to structure the releasing practice of the American film industry even as it was adapted in various ways for longer features after 1914.

The Paradox of the Feature Program, 1914–1917

Film historians have tended to contrast shorts programs and features as a way of emphasizing the marginalization of the former in favor of the latter over the course of the 1910s. But distributors could not simply repackage long features for the program overnight. They had to find middle-ground strategies for releasing films that they could integrate with pre-existing packages and that would also make enough money to justify the expense of differentiating them. The earliest feature programs were made up not of particularly long films but of films of four to six reels, with five becoming the standard by 1917.[47] The long features of eight to thirteen reels exemplified by the European spectaculars were never going to fit into even the longest programs at picture theaters—which is why they were distributed primarily to live-theatrical venues via the roadshow or the state rights system.

Just before the advent of feature programs, even those manufacturers that were deeply invested in the program short system began to make multireel features with increasing regularity, distributing them through effectively any system that would accommodate them. IMP's six-reel

Traffic in Souls (George Loane Tucker, 1913) was a prime example of this kind of idiosyncratically distributed production. After premiering on Broadway at Weber's Theater in November 1913, the film was released both on a roadshow tour, managed by Frank Miller of the Shubert Motion Picture Department, and via the United Booking Offices, for exhibition at both small- and big-time vaudeville houses.[48] Such strategies would continue even after the advent of Paramount's full-service two-features-a-week program in the fall of 1914. Elsewhere, I have examined Mutual's ambivalent approach in distributing a program of "Masterpictures" made by its manufacturers in 1915. Mutual offered these modestly priced four-reel features individually through its exchanges, framing them as an occasional substitute for or addition to its shorts service, rather than as a programmatic replacement for it. By advertising the Masterpictures in the *Saturday Evening Post* and emphasizing their theatrical sophistication, Mutual sought the ever-growing market of larger feature venues, many of them former legitimate or vaudeville houses. At the same time, by packaging the films separately from their shorts program, keeping them to four reels, and pricing them more reasonably than other features, Mutual hoped to make the films attractive enough for the smaller variety program exhibitors that remained their customer base.[49]

Given the possibility of releasing features idiosyncratically via state rights, the roadshow, or even exchanges, why did the American film distribution industry move away from a programmatic model that packaged mostly shorts to one that was centered on five-reel features? After all, live-theatrical distribution models such as state rights and roadshows could produce healthy profits when applied to cinema, and the program short system, though incompatible with the differentiation of individual films, produced consistent nationwide run practice, predictable pricing, and reliable profits for both distributors and producers. The answer ultimately boils down to the film manufacturers' interest in regularizing the much higher income that features could generate. The bifurcated film distribution market of early 1914, which maintained a programmatic system for shorts and an idiosyncratic one for multireel features, had to be integrated for this to happen. Program distribution, structured as it was around the short film and the daily change, encouraged manufacturers to strictly control their films' budgets and was difficult to reconcile with the growing length and expense of features. It also limited films' runs, blunting the profitability of individual titles. The fragmented state rights system had its own problems that made it unsuitable for releasing features in any kind of quantity (we will examine these in depth in chapter 4).

Solving the paradox of early feature distribution was not simply a matter of replacing short films of one or two reels with features of four or more reels on the weekly program. Film companies needed to rework their approaches to production *and* distribution to effectively compete in the emerging feature market. This meant not only altering their distribution policies to ensure the profitability of feature production, but also adopting strategies for producing features in enough quantity to fit the program system. Paramount succeeded because of its ability to negotiate both sides of this paradox. As Quinn has shown, the company's various innovations in feature distribution in 1914 ensured the profitability of feature production by borrowing policies from legitimate theater, such as dividing exhibitor rentals with its producers on a percentage basis (rather than a flat fee), structuring zone pricing around population, and enacting clearance policies to ensure that an exhibitor's advertising would not aid a competitor. At the same time, Paramount's producers were able to scale up production to the quantity the program system demanded by dividing their films into budget- and cast-based production classes, so that not every film on the program needed to be a "big" feature.[50]

Paramount's success as a feature distributor also stemmed from its beginnings as a state rights company—W. W. Hodkinson's Progressive Motion Picture Company in Utah—and the fact that its producers, Famous Players, Lasky, and Bosworth, had made prestige features from their inception. Paramount's production and distribution arms were both invested in features, so the company knew exactly how to make and distribute them profitably. The program system for features caught on like wildfire in the wider industry in 1915 as Triangle, Fox, Metro, and other distributors introduced their own feature programs. The success of the model lay in its programmatic nature; it allowed theaters to exhibit feature films, with all their attendant cultural cachet and economic advantages, but regularly and at a relatively affordable price compared to risky, expensive specials. Even more importantly, feature programs carried over expectations about film pricing and packaging from the older variety shorts system.

Between 1914 and 1917, the feature program system did much to regularize the exhibition of both features *and* shorts in many markets. Gregory Waller, in his study of Lexington, Kentucky, found that in 1917, film programming in that city was "quite systematic and regularized."

"Within the stable, efficient business of film exhibition in Lexington," he notes, "there was little, if any, place for the occasional oddball booking of the sort that had appeared at the city's moving picture shows even five years earlier."[51] In 1917, most cities in the United States with competitive exhibition markets probably resembled Lexington, where daily or triweekly changes remained the norm and many exhibitors played mixed bills of shorts and program features. In a February 1917 article advocating for the abolition of the daily change, *Motion Picture News* reported that smaller exhibitors were only just starting to move toward two-day runs in small markets such as Omaha and Iowa City, while in bigger cities, two- and three-day runs were typical for neighborhood theaters.[52] This assertion corroborates Richard Koszarski's findings that the average theater changed bills five times a week in 1916 but only three and a half times a week by 1922. Even by then, weeklong runs of a particular program were common only for the biggest first-run theaters.[53]

The increasing diversity in the length of films programmed in the second half of the 1910s, combined with the continued frequency of bill changes, explains why the full-service model of the shorts program system virtually had disappeared as the standard for feature distribution by 1918. Because distributors were now serving daily-change theaters *and* houses changing their bills twice weekly, they were encouraged to incorporate a degree of flexibility in their distribution methods that the program system could not sustain in its traditional form. Only the largest exhibitors could obtain a complete feature program service from any one distributor, because their longer runs meant they needed fewer films in a particular season. The transition to longer features and multiple-day runs as the primary format of film exhibition decisively shifted the work of packaging away from local exchanges and onto national distributors. Under the program shorts system, packaging had been a mostly *physical* and *logistical* question for exchanges: How many reels can this exhibitor use, and at what price and age? Under the feature program, it became a *marketing* question for sales representatives of national distributors attempting to profit from the idiosyncratic qualities of individual films.

Consider a hypothetical theater changing bills daily. In 1912, that theater would have only needed to sign up for standing service from one of the major shorts program distributors—General, Mutual, or Universal— to provide all its programming. In 1915, given the drawing power of features, the same theater might contract with two distributors, perhaps signing up for Paramount's program feature service for the weekend and the Mutual or General shorts program for weeknights. But by 1917, with feature distributors releasing two features every week, an exhibitor wanting a daily service of new features would have needed to sign contracts with at least four separate companies. All of Paramount's brands, including the Artcraft Pictures Corporation, formed in June 1916 to distribute Mary Pickford's films separately from their regular program service, could only supply half a service under those circumstances. The theater would need to round out its daily bills with additional service from Fox, World, Vitagraph, Metro, or Universal. Of course, an exhibitor changing its bill every day would be unlikely to play only features, but this hypothetical example attests to the fundamental film supply problem that theaters faced.

For frequent-change exhibitors, the continued dominance of short runs led them to prefer full-service programs—there were simply too many exhibition slots to fill. Thus, distributors that catered to such exhibitors, such as Universal and Fox, tended to cling closely to the program system into the twenties. For metropolitan theaters using weeklong runs, however, the program system was becoming too inflexible and inefficient. It forced them to take suboptimal product, monopolized screen time, prevented extended runs for hit films, and limited the variety of product they could put up on their screens. Some well-heeled exhibitors might even sign up for two or three different programs and only play the best films of each, leaving the weakest features "on the shelf."[54] Because such theaters provided the bulk of film rental income, the distributors that catered to them, including Paramount, Triangle, and Metro, were increasingly pressured to break their programs into smaller units throughout the 1910s.

The feature program system also presented problems when it came to the mechanics of booking. The foremost of these was the new system of contracting that was generally used for features. Under the variety shorts program, exhibitors' contracts with exchanges were for standing film service rather than any specific period. The contract generally specified only the details of the service: the number of reels to be furnished per week, the frequency of program changes, any specification of film ages (first-run, mixed, junk, etc.), and a price per week.[55] Exhibitors simply paid their local exchange in installments or took their films cash-on-delivery. With feature programs, however, individual films became a more central term of exhibition contracts, even if they were still packaged as a service. The sheer value of multireel feature films, even simply as a physical commodity, required some measure of collateral from exhibitors.

Because most exhibitors now had to deal with multiple distributors, specifics regarding playdates within exhibition contracts also became much more relevant. Consequently, most distributors of program features used a system of advance deposits to protect their prints and guarantee that exhibitors would carry out their contracts. Under this system, distributors required exhibitors to pay anywhere from two weeks' to a whole month's rental in advance in order to contract for a year's worth of a distributor's service.

Exhibitors fiercely resented advance deposits, mostly because they tied up exhibitors' limited cash assets. Four weeks' rental from Paramount, Metro, or another distributor could amount to several hundred dollars on top of an already expensive service. This was an onerous requirement for most exhibitors, purely from a standpoint of liquidity—but the deposits also paid no interest and were usually not insured against loss.[56] This was a departure from the standard practice of other industries that relied on deposit payments from retailers.[57] The problem of unsecured and uninsured deposits was not theoretical. Exhibitors in Brooklyn, New York, were threatened with the loss of hundreds of dollars' worth of deposits when Triangle's franchisee for distribution in that territory failed in early 1917.[58] *Moving Picture World* editor W. Stephen Bush claimed that even if a distributor waived the need for a deposit from a particular exhibitor, the distributor still held too much power to revoke an exhibitor's service in the event of a dispute. Stories abounded of "unsecured" exhibitors who found an unexpected deposit bill added on as a cash-on-delivery charge, owing to miscommunication or billing mistakes. This could lead to legal trouble, since exhibitors caught in such situations might well be forced to refuse delivery of the print.[59]

Distributors typically countered such claims, arguing that despite its inconvenience, the deposit system was necessary to avoid overbooking by exhibitors. As one exchange manager told *Variety* in April 1916, "I know one house in Brooklyn that has a $400 deposit with Paramount, $400 with Triangle, $100 with World, $100 with Bluebird, and $100 with Mutual, aggregating over $1,000, without a return, yet the exhibitors have nobody to blame but themselves. Before this system was put into effect, every day would find a number of shows on our shelves that were booked in good faith, but never called for."[60] The manager also complained of other exhibitor tactics, such as contracts being paid for with bad checks and films held well past their contract dates, ostensibly to be bicycled.

Opponents of open booking frequently used just such a line of attack—that of the unscrupulous, "fly-by-night" exhibitor who over-booked and then refused to play product, keeping it out of the hands of a competitor, or who simply did not pay rentals on time. Such exhibitors undoubtedly existed; their conduct was a common subject of discussion at the various Motion Picture Exhibitors League of America (MPELA) conventions of 1916. At the New York state league's meeting in Albany in March 1916, New York City exhibitor Louis Blumenthal granted that some exhibitors might not be "absolutely reliable and prompt in the payment of their film bills" but nevertheless decried the undue financial risks of the deposit system and urged all exhibitors to simply refuse to pay them.[61]

At the national MPELA meeting in Chicago that July, speakers articulated their own suspicions about the purpose of the deposit system, suggesting that distributors used deposit income to finance feature production.[62] The prominent Indiana exhibitor Frank Rembusch argued that in addition to financing production, advance deposits encouraged extravagant production spending, particularly for star salaries: "It is a case of 'come easy, go easy,' especially if you are spending another body's money."[63] As *Motography* pointed out, however, any official MPELA resolution to refuse advance deposits would expose the organization to charges of colluding to dictate distributors' business practices.[64] Thus, for exhibitors, advance deposits were more of a rhetorical term of the wider booking debate than an actionable issue. Indeed, deposits would continue to be a standard practice in film booking into the 1930s, albeit at much less onerous terms.[65]

Nevertheless, the Chicago MPELA meeting brought more fundamental weaknesses of the program system to a bigger industry stage. No one articulated them more self-aggrandizingly than Lewis Selznick, who had been positioning himself as the industry's most vigorous critic of the feature program system for several months—despite having been an early adopter of it as vice president and general manager of the World Film Corporation.[66] Selznick's boosterism for more open booking was no accident. In April 1916, a few months after being ousted by World's board of directors, he partnered with former World star Clara Kimball Young to distribute her films as a unit, independent of any program, a move that likely gave Mary Pickford leverage to do the same thing with Adolph Zukor the subsequent June. Upon the announcement of his partnership with Young, Selznick described the program system as an absurd version of wholesaling: "As the contract system works today, the exhibitor must buy gold, silver, brass and tin at the same price. The producer lumps all these metals together, and to get the gold the exhibitor must buy the tin as well. In other words, under the present system the exhibitor, in order to get features like the Clara Kimball Young pictures, must also book a lot of pictorial junk that does not draw a dollar to his box office."[67]

Selznick's argument drove at a fundamental assumption about pricing in the program system: that exhibitors were willing to pay for an entire yearlong feature service just to get a handful of individual films. This inflexibility was becoming a real problem by 1916, as many exhibitors now used a feature service at least part of the week. Selznick's plan, by contrast, emphasized the star as an independent, flexible package of distribution; exhibitors could get Young's pictures—and only her pictures—without having to book any other Selznick-distributed films. Selznick also planned to distribute the films of other stars in the same way. By the end of 1916, this releasing format would increasingly become known as the "star series," but early ads for the Young Corporation simply described Selznick's model as "open booking" and claimed that it sounded "the death knell of the program system."[68] Stars and other idiosyncratic qualities of individual films would end up killing the program system. But they did not end programmatic releasing—in fact, they proved vital to its transformation into a more flexible system of packaging and pricing.

3 THE PACKAGE, PART II

Reprogramming the Studio System

The Rise of Open Booking, 1916–1922

The years 1916 and 1917 saw a fundamental transformation in the way feature films were distributed programmatically in the United States. At the beginning of 1916, the feature program system reigned supreme; exhibitors who wanted regular multireel features from any one of the major distributors were generally obliged to contract for all the releases of a particular distributor for the entire release season. By the end of 1917, however, all but one of these same distributors had abandoned exclusive use of the program system in favor of what was referred to in the trade press as "open booking." Open booking was less a coherent alternative to program booking than an umbrella term encompassing a variety of different releasing models, including the star series, tiered sub-programs, and even selective booking of individual films. The only commonality of these models was that they were more flexible—more "open"—than the program system and did not require exhibitors to take a distributor's complete service.

This chapter examines this shift in the industry's dominant model of distribution and proposes several causes for it, including the inflexibility of program distribution, the increased importance of stars to the valuation of both programs and individual films in distribution, tensions between exhibitors and distributors, competition from new distributors using more open booking methods, and wartime taxes and inflation. Chief among these causes, however, was the ever-diversifying character of exhibition in the United States. Between 1917 and 1921, the disparity in run lengths and rental income between urban first-run theaters and small-town exhibitors grew quickly. While increased rental income from premium exhibitors created competition for ever higher-priced films and stars, the continued prevalence of short runs in exhibition created a large and constantly churning market for more affordable feature films. At the same time, however, shorts did not disappear from the distribution landscape; they continued to be popular in theaters of all sizes and types, particularly before 1920, even as they were increasingly defined as adjuncts to multireel features. All of these factors created space for distributors to venture into new markets for their primary product, which would increasingly be defined not as the feature program, but as the individual feature film.

Programmatic Feature Distribution and the Rise of Open Booking, 1916–1917

Service programs had done much to stabilize the distribution market during the one-reel period, making costs much more predictable for producers and providing for the regularized production of feature films. Why, then, was the program system increasingly marginalized after 1916? Previous scholars have suggested multiple causes of the program's demise, but the generally accepted view is the one offered by Michael Quinn: the flat distribution rental fees and restricted run structure of the program system could not accommodate the rising costs of film production, and particularly star salaries, in the latter half of the 1910s. The Artcraft Pictures Corporation, the Paramount entity formed to distribute Mary Pickford's films, is often cited as an important example of this trend. Pickford's Artcraft contract, in addition to stipulating that her films could not be packaged with other Paramount product, mandated percentage-based pricing of her films to exhibitors—making every screening of a Pickford film a benefit performance for Artcraft. Pickford's contract showed that the increasing scale and expense of productions centered on popular stars required more open booking formats, such as the star series or selective (individual) booking, as well as percentage-based rentals to exhibitors that could bring in greater profits for individual hits.[1]

The Pickford-Artcraft case certainly explains the incentive for changes in distribution from the perspective of the most lucrative segment of the distribution market—the segment interested in high-budget production and well-known stars. However, we should not neglect tensions and debates in the wider industry that were arguably more important factors in the move away from the program system after 1916. It is important to remember that most of the industry—exhibitors in particular—remained program oriented in the mid-1910s, and certain industry players were hesitant to abandon the program as the standard distribution structure for features. Program booking may have been increasingly untenable for Pickford, Famous Players–Lasky (FPL), and other high-profile producers and distributors, but for the wider industry the yearly program was an established and mostly successful norm. Furthermore, the percentage-based rentals that exhibitors had to pay for Pickford's Artcraft films were exceptional during this period—only the largest stars could garner them, and the vast majority of booking contracts continued to rely on flat fees. Explaining the abandonment of the program system and the rise of open booking requires us to go beyond the familiar narrative of Pickford and Paramount. What other incentives did industry entities—and particularly distributors and exhibitors—have for accepting changes in the established system of film booking?

One was a simple desire for more flexibility in film packaging. The idea of exhibitor choice in the matter of individual film bookings was not a new one in the mid-1910s. "Open booking" had, in fact, been a common term among exchange managers since at least the early years of the one-reel period, when it was used to designate one of the common systems for booking shorts services to exhibitors. Under open booking (also referred to as "pick-up" booking), exhibitors signed up for standing service from their local exchange, but the exact combination of ages and makes of films to be booked each day was negotiable. This practice contrasted with what was known as "schedule booking," where exhibitors were required to stipulate the age and brand makeup of their daily programs in advance and received their films according to the manufacturers' predetermined release schedules. Exchanges generally operated under one system or the other according to the crowdedness of the market in question: in general, localities with multiple neighboring theaters using the same service were booked by schedule as a way of avoiding conflicting service, while smaller markets, or those dominated by a handful of exhibitors (or even a single theater), could leverage more open booking.[2]

Open booking during the one-reel period—as during the early feature period—was something of a misnomer. Although it provided exhibitors with a certain level of control over their own programming, in practice, under the open booking system, theater managers in competitive markets had a say over only around half the reels on their programs—the rest were dictated by the exchanges. Exchanges using pick-up booking also prioritized exhibitors' requests for films of a particular age over requests for certain brands of films. Theaters wishing to substitute for a particular brand could do so but generally had to take the first available reel of that make—which would almost certainly be an older (and thus less valuable) title. Thus, open booking was only "open" relative to its alternative. As a matter of practice, however, most exhibitors during the one-reel period prioritized the newness of the films on their daily bills anyway. The flexibility of being able to choose those reels was less important. Because changes in bills were so frequent, open booking offered exhibitors a defensive strategy against the losses incurred by persistently underperforming brands of films, unexpected flops booked for a longer-than-usual run, or holes in the normal booking schedule. Furthermore, as outlined in the previous chapter, the whole point of the program from the perspective of film distributors was to provide a consistently high-quality product at regular, reliable intervals—pick-up booking was ideally supposed to be an aberration, not the norm.

Nevertheless, open booking would become a central topic of debate in the industry as the shortcomings of the feature program system became apparent in 1916. By far the most popular form of packaging for open booking was the star series. Howard T. Lewis describes this series model as a "short-lived" phenomenon that lasted for only about two years, 1917–1919.[3] These dates may be correct for up-market distributors, such as Paramount; more program-oriented companies, such as Fox and Universal, however, adopted the star-series model slightly later than that, around 1919–1920, and used it as late as 1923. Although historians tend to footnote the star series, describing it as a failed practice or a mere step on the road to block booking, it was a very common distribution strategy in the late 1910s and early 1920s.[4] Star series distribution was a drastic change from program booking in terms of the amount of information it gave exhibitors. Rather than booking a generic program of films on a service basis, exhibitors using star series distribution now at least knew the names of the stars they were paying for, and how many films they could expect from them, even if the promised output did not live up to expectations.[5]

The most common size of the star series was seven or eight films—the number of features a single star might reasonably produce in a single season—although they might have been as small as two films or as large as twelve.[6] Generally, the bigger the star, the fewer films they had to make for their series. Fox's booking sheets for the 1921–1922 season, for example, promised only three pictures from William Farnum, but seven from Buck Jones.[7] While distributors promised a certain number of films at the time of booking, in practice this number could change as a result of production problems or simply miscalculation. The changes could be quite drastic: Fox originally planned for seven Dustin Farnum features for 1921–1922 but eventually had to cut that output to four. By the same token, a star series might produce more than the promised quantity, as happened with William Russell the same season.[8]

The star series was the first open-booking alternative to gain serious traction against the feature program system and was covered widely in the trade press. In the lead-up to the 1916 Chicago MPELA convention, where Lewis Selznick would pitch the star series as a welcome alternative to the program system's packaging of "gold, silver, brass and tin at the same price," *Variety* anticipated a rhetorical showdown between Selznick and his rivals—especially Adolph Zukor, who warned that the new open booking system Selznick was proposing would disrupt the entire industry.[9] There was a certain irony to Zukor's objections, given that he and Lasky had wrested control of Paramount from W. W. Hodkinson just two weeks earlier in their formation of FPL and would soon begin releasing Pickford's Artcraft films.[10] As Selznick pointed out, "Why, the very people who are making the biggest outcry against me are copying my proposition for Mary Pickford. All the big stars see the advantage of being presented as a separate proposition, like Miss Young, and want to emulate us. . . . The intelligent exhibitor would be only too glad to pay four or five times what he now pays for a big feature if he could eliminate the rest of the trash on the program and double his receipts."[11]

Selznick's argument for open booking acknowledged its increased cost but emphasized that a series model would give the ordinary exhibitor greater access to stars, increasing box-office receipts and growing the whole industry. In theory, this was an attractive proposition for exhibitors, but even Selznick's own hypothetical rental prices for his system betrayed that it was viable only for well-heeled theaters: "Let us presume that the seven biggest stars in the business were being presented along lines similar to our plans for Miss Young's pictures. Suppose an exhibitor could play Mary Pickford, Clara Kimball Young, Marguerite Clark, Francis Bushman, Douglas Fairbanks, Fanny Ward and Anita Stewart on alternate days throughout the week. Don't you think he could afford to pay $100 a day for each of those pictures and make twice the money he does now?"[12]

For most exhibitors in 1916, paying $700 a week for the industry's biggest stars was simply not an option. Just two years previously, even the largest metropolitan first-run theaters paid only $500 a week for full Paramount service at two features a week, and most daily-change exhibitors in the mid-1910s paid a quarter of that amount in weekly rentals.[13] Selznick's critics seized on open booking's pricing problem as its most obvious weakness; the system priced in a level of choice that most exhibitors simply did not need. Furthermore, Selznick shrewdly appropriated the most attractive aspects of the program in making his case for the star series by implying that all his stars would be priced evenly at $100 per day—glossing over the likelihood that market pressure would differentiate the pricing of gold (Mary Pickford's films) fairly drastically from tin (Fanny Ward's or Anita Stewart's films). But there is little doubt that Selznick's open-booking model was attractive for exhibitors who could afford it, and the fact that Selznick promised to release *fifty-two* pictures for the 1916–1917 season was an unmistakable signal to exhibitors that they could still book his films as a weekly program if they wanted to. Open booking, he argued, would force producers to raise the standard of their filmmaking and exhibitors to improve their houses, "materially increasing motion picture patronage."[14]

In a widely publicized speech at the 1916 MPELA convention, Zukor responded by defending the program system, arguing that it enabled exhibitors to fill their playing time efficiently while also keeping rental prices and distribution costs down. He argued that Selznick's system would almost surely disrupt the pricing model that program distribution had rationalized: "It is an accepted fact that in order to change twice a week [the exhibitor] must have one hundred and four pictures a year, and as most theatres change three, four, and six times weekly, if they give their support to individual producers and individual stars they are going to demoralize the program at the expense of their own investments, because I do not believe that the exhibitor can exist if he has to pay a different price for every production he presents."[15]

Zukor argued that open booking would cause untenable and haphazard inflation in the price of features, as well as introducing inefficiency and anarchic competition to the distribution sector. Overbooking and exploding prices would therefore stifle the growth of the industry. Specifically, Zukor predicted, exhibitors would be encouraged to use booking as a purely competitive strategy, denying neighboring theaters particular stars or films without intending to actually play them.[16] Here he followed the general argument of other critics of open booking, who said it was an inefficient and costly system of distribution that encouraged unscrupulous practices among exhibitors. Of course, Zukor had an obvious interest in defending the program. FPL's two-features-a-week program was the dominant feature service, and it was soon to become even more dominant, with Triangle's overpriced and underdrawing program quickly losing its appeal as 1916 went on. As we will see in chapter 5, some of Zukor's predictions about open booking's effect on the distribution market would come to pass just a few years later.

Despite his defense of the program system, Zukor clearly understood that its days as the dominant form of feature distribution in the United States were numbered. From the production side, the industry's biggest stars—Pickford, Young, Douglas Fairbanks, and Charlie Chaplin among them—were gaining enough market power in 1915 and 1916 to leverage not only higher salaries but also favorable distribution on an individual basis.[17] *Photoplay* mordantly called this phenomenon "stellaritis" and suggested that it would undermine the industry's rationalized system of distribution in favor of a "wildcatting of personalities."[18] Whether the distributors liked it or not, stellaritis reduced the extent to which individual players could be used to sell an entire year's program. This trend was not necessarily bad for distributors; the fact that many exhibitors in key markets were now willing and able to pay advanced prices for the films of such stars mitigated the consequent decline in income from yearlong program contracts. Exhibitors were also changing their bills less frequently in general, which decreased the total number of films they needed to book.[19] These combined factors made the smaller programming batches exemplified by star series and other forms of open booking a more viable option in the second half of the 1910s.

This is not to suggest that all exhibitors welcomed open booking.

Smaller exhibitors echoed Zukor's sentiments that it would upset film pricing, often framing their objections in terms of the removal of stars from regular programs. Because they changed bills so frequently, small exhibitors got very little out of star series other than a price increase for the top-drawing stars that had previously been part of the program. In October 1916, the Alameda County Motion Picture Exhibitors' League in California "adopted strong resolutions against the 'star system' and express[ed] confidence in 'a daily consistent program.'" Their resolution argued that "encouraging the individual star system . . . will weaken the daily program exchanges by drawing from their company the best drawing cards."[20]

That same month, *Motion Picture News* published the opinions of several Michigan exhibitors. One argued that "the open booking policy is feasible, logical, and practical only with a few week-stand theatres and on possibly two or three nights a week of theatres that are playing a policy of daily change. . . . The individual star program is simply a case of getting all the exhibitors in one town together to see who is willing to pay the most for it."[21] Another theater manager, while not opposed in principle to open booking, was annoyed by the uncertainty it caused: "If we knew positively that certain stars would remain on certain programs, then we would go out and select our program and feel assured that we would get those stars by signing up with certain producers. . . . [K]eep the stars on the regular programs and exhibitors will forget open booking."[22] Even in the major urban market of Detroit, theater managers doubted that open booking could work as an everyday policy in their houses, although all advocated keeping at least one night of the week "open."

This general reticence about open booking may be why, at the beginning of 1917, only two major distributors offered any of their films through a true star series booking model: Paramount (via Artcraft) and Selznick. For much of 1916, it seemed that the program might survive the challenge of open booking. In addition to Zukor, other highly respected figures in the distribution sector defended the program system, including W. W. Hodkinson and William A. Brady of World Pictures.[23] Nevertheless, developments by prominent industry players in late 1916 and early 1917 accelerated the industry's switch to open booking. In December 1916, Samuel "Roxy" Rothafel, the prominent manager of the two-thousand-seat Rialto in New York, announced that the theater would switch from the Triangle program to open booking.[24] In March 1917, both Paramount and Triangle said they would begin allowing exhibitors to book some of their product openly.[25] As *Variety* reported, "both companies, in instances where the bookings are of pictures with stars who have won a big following with the public, have raised the ante, and are asking more rental than on regular contract for the entire output."[26] In other words, each distributor was now willing to negotiate with exhibitors who wanted only particular stars or films on their program—as long as they were willing to pay advanced prices for them. According to *Variety*, one "well known" New York exhibitor predicted that the distribution market would be "split wide open" within six months. Only two weeks later, Triangle went even further by abolishing the deposit system for its contracts, instead having exhibitors place much smaller deposits with an independent bonding company.[27] This was another surprising reversal from Triangle Distributing's president, W. W. Hodkinson, who as head of Paramount had been a pioneer of both the feature program and the deposit system.[28]

Perhaps the most important tipping point in pushing the industry toward open booking was the incorporation of the First National Exhibitors' Circuit on April 24, 1917.[29] A combine of more than 200 of the largest exhibitors in the United States and Canada, First National was effectively a nationally organized circuit of state rights distributors cooperating to purchase and distribute independent productions. Each First National franchisee paid a particular percentage for each production based on its expected rental income in that territory, in exchange receiving the exclusive right to sublease it to local theaters independently. That First National played a key role in spurring FPL to vertically integrate into exhibition is part of the canonical narrative in previous histories of this period. As Quinn and others have pointed out, First National combined the exhibition and production sectors of the American film industry on a new kind of scale—and with an unprecedented degree of market power—that threatened Paramount's dominant position as a producer-distributor.[30]

Less emphasized, however, is the extent to which First National's distribution system encouraged its affiliated exhibitors, most of them chains or large theaters with significant clout in their local markets, to abandon full-service programs. *Moving Picture World* took special note of the fact that First National was not a "closed [exclusive] corporation." Franchisees could not only purchase any films they wished for their own territory, independently of the national organization, but also distribute First National features to sub-franchisees in any way they saw fit.[31] Much has been made of First National's scale in exhibition, but the organization was also a threat to Paramount in the same way the Shuberts had been a threat to the Syndicate: through the prospect of completely open booking policies. Strictly speaking, First National—like the Shuberts—did not practice what it preached, because it actually used a form of program booking. Franchisees did have to take all of First National's films and pay their proportion of the production advance for each. However, the details for sub-franchising and contracting were left up to the twenty-nine initial franchise members, and production contracts were entered into only after two-thirds of all the members approved.[32] For its first few years, First National gave a kind of latitude for open booking that no other major distributor, save perhaps Selznick, offered.[33]

In the months following First National's incorporation, most of the other major distributors announced either the option to acquire some of their films separately from the program or an explicit reorganization of their releasing model around star series or other smaller packages. Studios that lacked enough well-known stars to believably offer their films in star series typically split their programs up into smaller branded packages of sub-programs. Fox, for example, split its features for the 1918–1919 season into four sub-programs, each sold at a different pricing tier: specials (four films), "Standard Pictures" (twenty-six films), the "Victory" brand (twenty-six films), and the "Excel" brand (twenty-six films).[34] Though branded sub-programs tended to be larger than star series, they functioned as a useful compromise between full-service programs and star series for distributors with a more program-oriented customer base.

On May 5, 1917, Paramount announced it would switch to open booking as a default, eventually settling on star series distribution by the time the new season began in August.[35] The same month, *Variety* reported that William Fox was contemplating open booking for his own exchanges.[36] At the end of July, Metro announced it would use star series booking for the 1917–1918 season.[37] *Variety*, looking ahead to distribution conditions in 1918, mused, "The probability is that some such method as the open market, with modifications, will prevail in time to come. The exhibitor is growing in importance and quality every day. It is improbable that he will for long be satisfied to remain tied to any program which limits his discretionary powers. Meantime, the program is advantageous perhaps for the less experienced showman in the remoter districts. But even he is being educated constantly and will soon outgrow his swaddling clothes."[38]

Certainly, *Variety*'s optimism about open booking in the key markets was not unfounded, but its condescension for the program system and subsequent-run exhibitors obscures how important the program still was outside of key markets at the end of 1917. Just because most distributors booked "openly" did not mean they stopped making full programs available to exhibitors who wanted them. Nor did they stop pushing their full programs on theaters through pricing incentives. Fox, Universal, and World continued to market their regular weekly feature programs as such for the 1917–1918 season, and for good reason: most exhibitors continued to use programs for at least some portion of their weekly bills. *Motography* pointed out that the program system and open booking were hardly mutually exclusive, and that the choice between them was really about who took on the labor of packaging: "The best of showmen running miscellaneous features will pick a lemon once in a while, just as the best of producers will make one occasionally. It is just a question of whether the exhibitor is safer to rely on his own judgment or the judgment of the program producer."[39] The paper might have added that for theaters changing their bills three, five, or six times a week, no single program could possibly supply enough features at a reasonable price; such exhibitors *had* to mix open booking with programs, if they used open booking at all.

What really changed in exhibition over the course of 1916 and 1917 was the extent to which theaters in the most lucrative markets stopped using program service. This happened not only because such theaters were changing their bills less frequently and had access to openly booked product from distributors such as Selznick, Artcraft, and (eventually) First National, but also because many were not exclusively film oriented. As *Variety* reported in March, "One of the developments of the Selznick and Artcraft [open booking] systems is the fact that vaudeville theatres showing a feature picture and making a change twice weekly, are gradually eliminating the weekly program picture, preferring the other system of booking. . . . This situation has caused a scurry among the exchanges to take up contracts among smaller exhibitors."[40] In other words, by differentiating star series releases through open booking, distributors were effectively pushing programs down-market, to film-only theaters in metropolitan neighborhoods as well as smaller cities and towns. As much as they needed the greater rental income of the key cities, distributors also needed the *reliable* (if modest) income of regular program contracts in *Variety*'s "remoter districts."

The Great Open-Market Bunk: Selective Distribution, 1918–1922

By the early 1920s, it was no longer sufficient for studios simply to bifurcate their distribution slates, offering lavish specials to one market while centering most of their feature production around a regular program made cheaply and sold in bulk to another. Rather, program films needed to be made and distributed more flexibly, such that new stars could be quickly advanced to more lucrative markets, and budgets set to accurately reflect a film's potential in distribution. Fundamentally, the major distributors sought to increase the rental grosses of *all* the films they released. Beginning with the 1918–1919 season and lasting through the end of the 1921–1922 season, up-market distributors concentrated on a "selective booking" strategy in their quest for higher rentals. This strategy would help to create a period of heightened competition among distributors. Alongside developments brought about by World War I, this resulted in inflation of various kinds, from the number of features distributors released, to the number of separate sales contracts they sold, to the prices exhibitors were willing to pay for them.

Films sold via selective booking, also called "open-market" or "wide-open" booking, were made available on individual contracts, ostensibly without being tied to other product. Because selective booking packaged individual titles, it was the most extreme form of open booking. Although it was used occasionally during the earliest years of feature programs, in the mid-1910s, the distributors that used the strategy this early on, including VLSE and Goldwyn, tended not to do so for very long, since selling the model required much higher expenditures than program booking did. As Quinn points out, selective booking "worked best when it did not work at all"—that is, when exhibitors selected as much of a distributor's output as possible on their contracts.[41]

Why did the industry adopt an expensive and ostensibly unworkable strategy for selling individual features? In answering this question, it is important to emphasize that distributors, no matter their size, almost always tried to sell exhibitors more product than the exhibitors originally intended to buy, using pricing incentives and tied arrangements to achieve that objective. Exhibitors who selected only a single film from a distributor's offerings could expect to pay a hefty price for it. Those who picked out a group of three, six, or ten could expect a more reasonable per-film price, and those who "selected" the entire program paid even less.

"Selective booking" was therefore mostly a marketing term specifically crafted to articulate a sense of exhibitor choice in the realm of film sales. Paramount's marketing department likely coined the term, using it to refer to their own booking practices in the 1919–1920 season. Other distributors had their own designations: Goldwyn called it "merit booking," for instance. Whatever the precise terminology different distributors used, selective booking was essentially little more than a promise to exhibitors that they could technically rent films on an individual basis. Exhibitors continued to book films mostly programmatically during the selective booking period, and distributors encouraged them to, through volume pricing. Thus, selective booking operated *within* the program, not outside of it. Nevertheless, it was a lure for both exhibitors and producers, and it became an important tool for distributors, who used it not only to boost rental grosses, but also to determine accurate pricing for their product in distribution.

While selective booking succeeded in driving up rental prices, its most important effect was to show distributors the value of *pricing* films on an individual basis while *booking* them programmatically. Though selective booking had the potential for much higher rentals, it was also a more idiosyncratic—and thus riskier—form of distribution than the program system. The program system had provided a reliable estimate for a program's per-film rental gross from exhibitors, allowing production budgets to be carefully adjusted according to that amount and applied to many films at once. Selective booking made it more difficult for distributors to predict how much any film would yield in distribution. Because it made each film's performance in the marketplace a direct function of its own individual value to exhibitors, determining the budget for a selectively booked film required an assessment of its value in advance—what distributors called its "exhibition value." By pricing films individually to exhibitors under selective booking—even if they pushed them to buy several "selectively booked" films programmatically on a single contract—distributors were able to acquire much more granular data about the exhibition value of features. All these strategies would form the basis of the industry's distribution practice after 1922, but to understand it, we must first account for the exhibition context that framed it.

A key characteristic of selective booking was that it was much more expensive on a per-feature basis than even the star series. This meant it most clearly benefited the first-run exhibitors who could regularly afford it. The richest exhibitors could book most or all their films selectively if they chose, but most theaters could use selective booking only sparingly. More programmatic distribution strategies remained a viable option for companies that catered to smaller houses, such as Fox and Universal. However, small exhibitors were caught in a bind created by the growing market for ever bigger feature films and expensive stars. The increasing prices of features, and the new differentiation of stars from the rest of the distribution program via the star series, increasingly meant that the program system did not earn enough to justify being the sole booking method. At the same time, runs for small exhibitors were still so short that some programmatic booking remained essential to keeping rental expenses down. As a result, exhibitors outside urban first runs could no longer rely on a single model—they needed to use a mix of the program system, the star series, and selectively booked films.

Selective booking was not a completely unprecedented phenomenon in 1918; as we have seen, the state rights system was essentially individualized film booking conducted under special terms, and nearly every distributor released a handful of "specials" every season that theaters contracted for independently from their regular program. In the early years of feature distribution, features themselves were distinguished by the fact that they were rented on individual terms rather than as part of a film service. Even as feature distribution became regularized in the mid-1910s, with feature programs, the biggest films were still distributed individually through the state rights system, via roadshows, or sometimes directly from the distributor or an affiliated company.

However, two major differences distinguished selective booking from these earlier forms of distribution. The first was that it operated systematically and on a national scale. Exhibitors negotiated with the distributor directly over the rental of selectively booked films, which meant that the latter could rationally organize selective booking according to the normal system of runs, zones, and clearance. The state rights system, by contrast, was a largely ad hoc arrangement between a film's producer and regional companies. Roadshows, while slightly more systematic, were still typically subcontracted out to specialist companies that handled distribution separately from the regular release system. Selective booking made the individual booking of films a centralized process that distributors directly controlled, just as the GFC had systematized and nationalized the shorts exchanges of the Edison licensing system.

The other major feature of selective booking that separated it from state rights was the extent to which it operated in conjunction with more programmatic forms of booking. Just because exhibitors could book films selectively did not mean that they signed single-film contracts with distributors. Rather, most exhibitors who took advantage of a distributor's offer of selective booking would book several films at once, a practice that benefited both them (because of the reduced price of the volume purchase) and the distributor (because of the reduced relative selling cost of each additional film). Selectively booked films were thus often bought in quantities and packages not dissimilar to star series. In 1921, Illinois exhibitor Thomas Watson booked twenty-one films on a selective basis from the W. W. Hodkinson corporation, for example, paying anywhere from $15 to $150 for each individual title (for a total rental of about $1,300).[42] This one contract would have accounted for almost fifty days' worth of Watson's playing time. Selective booking was thus a modification of more programmatic forms of booking rather than a full-scale replacement of them.

Despite its differences from the state rights system, selective booking's rise was influenced by an increase in the amount of product available from independent producers on the state rights market in the spring of 1917.[43] State rights distributor Benjamin Friedman attributed the bullish market to a new recognition of the returns on investment possible through the system.[44] While the boom created a larger market for the special productions that had always been associated with state rights, such as Maurice Tourneur's eight-reel horse melodrama *The Whip* (Paragon Films, 1917), more modest features were increasingly booked this way as well. These included films such as *In the Hands of the Law* (Ben Goetz, 1917), a Balboa five-reeler distributed by B. S. Moss, and surprise hits, including *A Mormon Maid* (Robert Leonard, 1917), a Lasky anti-Mormon film originally intended for program release from Paramount but cut from the company's release slate.[45] Even if state rights continued to be associated with prestige production through the mid-1910s, by the end of 1917 it was a market in which significant numbers of features were available from a broad cross-section of producers.

The increasing availability of individually booked product from the "open market" (as opposed to the major distributors) was evident in the trade press. *Exhibitors Herald*, for instance, listed the features available in any given week in 1917 and 1918 according to two broad categories: "program films" and "the open market," with the latter divided into "state rights issues," consisting of smaller films from independent

distributors, and "special productions" from the major distributors.[46]
Moving Picture World began a section dedicated to covering state rights
releases in May 1917, and it was listing such pictures systematically
by the end of July.[47] One commentator for *Variety* noted that the box-
office performance of many independent open-market productions did
not justify the publicity surrounding them, resulting in "a loss to everyone concerned except the actors and the Eastman Company."[48] The
practice of booking films individually was still confined primarily to independent state rights features in the 1917–1918 and 1918–1919 seasons,
and the bulk of the major distributors' releases—apart from specials—
remained packaged in programs or star series. Individually available films
continued to be associated primarily with state rights and independent
production well into 1918. When Metro began accepting independent
productions for selective release on its Screen Classics brand of specials
in May of that year, it hastened to assure exhibitors that the films were
of high enough quality for them and would be required to "pass the tests
in the matter of bigness of theme, beauty of photography and power of
story and action."[49]

Even if the major distributors were still cautious about releasing
individually booked productions themselves, the increasing competition
from independent distributors demonstrated that exhibitors both inside
and outside the major first-run markets were increasingly willing to book
substantial portions of their output selectively. Large theaters had more
direct reasons than small ones for accepting selective booking, and their
growing power relative to small exhibitors shaped the distribution market. They had much more power to negotiate booking terms with distributors; even those distributors with their own localized first-run holdings
in exhibition, such as Fox, were forced to cater their booking and releasing models to the demands of first-run exhibitors to some degree if they
wanted national distribution for their films. Because of the various economies of scale afforded to first-run houses in terms of run length, size,
and location, they could more easily afford their pick of the most promising films released by all the distributors, not simply a prestigious program
from one company or a set of star series from three or four companies.

The longer runs used by urban first-run theaters—one or even two
weeks—also reduced the number of playdates they needed to book, making star series or selective booking feasible from the standpoint of the
labor of programming. Theaters in urban markets tended to be relatively

close to an exchange, which meant not only that films could be more easily previewed before booking, but also that distributors' expenses on a per-contract basis when renting to such theaters were much reduced. Unlike towns or rural markets that required a costly long-distance visit from sales personnel (at least relative to the eventual rental amount), urban theaters could be serviced repeatedly at a low cost if the distributor had an exchange in the city. Finally, urban first runs tended to have much larger seating capacities, which meant they could afford to pay much higher rental prices for individual features while still keeping ticket prices relatively low.

Selective booking became normalized in distribution practice thanks in part to the lengthening of runs in exhibition. In the mid-1910s, runs of more than a week or two were specifically associated with specials and not programmers. By the late 1910s, however, it became increasingly common for diverse types of multireel features to become popular enough to enjoy an extended run. This was made possible by an active strategy that distributors used in urban theaters: run exhibition (also referred to as "exploitation exhibition"). William Paul defines run exhibition as the practice of playing a particular film for an extended run of many weeks—specifically in New York at first—to promote its drawing power prior to entering the normal release system of first, second, and subsequent runs.[50]

As Paul indicates, run exhibition had developed into a quite intricate system by the late 1920s, when regular prereleases, roadshows, and regular releases premiered in defined types of cinemas according to how distributors positioned them in the marketplace. However, early run exhibition in the mid- and late 1910s was not nearly as rationalized, owing to the sharp distinction between specials and programmers. As we have seen, specials and other high-budget, high-prestige films tended to be strictly separated from the regular program in the mid-1910s, but as the 1910s ended, fewer first-run theaters were willing to sign up for an entire program (or even a star series) to obtain such films. Apart from the previously mentioned reasons for this shift, first-run exhibitors increasingly chafed against the problem posed by restricted runs in distribution. The program made it very difficult to extend the run of any individual film past one or two weeks. In the mid-1910s, films that were expected to garner significant run time in distribution were typically handled as part of a separate distribution system that could accommodate long runs, often in venues that were not dedicated to motion pictures (such as opera houses or legitimate theaters). By the late 1910s, however, with the increasing market power of first-run dedicated picture houses, distributors shifted away from this bifurcated system and toward run exhibition, which was specifically designed to accommodate extended runs and holdovers.

The earliest examples of run exhibition from the period 1915–1917 were previously roadshowed specials introduced into the regular distribution system, where they played in regular first-run picture theaters for a significantly longer time than the standard week—typically three weeks or more. This practice was made possible by a form of selective booking that industry parlance commonly referred to as the film's flat "rental-basis" run, in contradistinction to the percentage basis contract that usually governed runs as specials.[51] Unlike the later "prerelease" forms of run exhibition in the 1920s, the rental-basis release of a special was still the "first run" of the film. It marked the first time a film was made available in the normal distribution system at normal admission prices rather than the one- to two-dollar scale normally charged for special engagements. However, rental-basis runs were also given relatively long clearance to accommodate any exhibitor requests for "holdovers"—extensions of their run of the film.[52] Under the full-service program model, even first-run theaters typically lacked the ability to hold a film an extra week past its original playdate—runs and clearance were simply too short and too concentrated, and prints had to be sent on to the next run. By contrast, rental-basis runs allowed films to be booked for an initial run of as long as four or five weeks, and holdovers might extend that run even further. As a result, the theaters that played rental-basis runs of specials were typically purpose-built picture theaters—the earliest of the large "presentation houses" modeled on the Strand in New York—and they often advertised an "indefinite run" policy.[53]

Rental-basis first-run exhibition of films for a month or more became commonplace in 1917 and 1918, and the distinction in run lengths between specials and program features became increasingly blurred. This convergence seems to have happened relatively quickly. In early 1917, a standard program run in a city could be defined as anything from three days to a week, depending on the exhibitor.[54] A year later, in May 1918, *Motion Picture News* suggested that a week's run was the perfect length for most first-run theaters, and urged big-city houses not to be too exuberant by running any program film longer than two weeks.[55] A mere three months after that, press coverage of the rental-basis release of Fox's special *Cleopatra* suggests that runs of two weeks for such contracts were standard, with exceptional rental-basis runs for the film lasting three weeks in Boston, Chicago, and Cleveland. By comparison, when the film had originally been roadshowed in the winter and spring of 1917–1918, it played for five weeks at the Washington Theatre in Detroit and the Colonial in Chicago (on percentage, and for premium admission prices of one dollar).[56]

Thus, successful rental-basis runs for specials in first-run theaters could now last almost as long as they had in their previous roadshow engagement. *Moving Picture World*—by way of what was likely Fox-provided copy—noted as exceptional that many of the *same* theaters that had played the film as a special were rebooking it on rental.[57] The Rose Theatre in Chicago, having witnessed the film's success as a special at the nearby Colonial, booked the film for a two-week rental-basis run but eventually asked Fox for an extension to three weeks. Fox itself had held over *Cleopatra* for a third week at its own special engagement of the film in San Francisco the previous March.[58] These examples suggest that while repeat bookings and holdovers were still relatively risky and exceptional practices as of mid-1918—even for films that had done strong business as prereleased specials—two- and three-week rental-basis runs were becoming normal for big films.

The extension of run lengths in urban first-run theaters, in combination with the normalization of run exhibition and holdovers after 1918, allowed program films to be convincingly marketed as "specials" in first-run distribution, especially if they were offered on a selective booking policy. With the end of the program system for first-run theaters and the rise of star-centered strategies of distribution, a new space opened up for any distributor looking to market a slate composed of "all specials." Extended run lengths allowed individual films to gross much higher amounts in distribution, which ultimately resulted in a distributor push in 1918 and 1919 to make "fewer and better" pictures.[59] Even Carl Laemmle—who just two years earlier had signed his name to a Universal ad that likened multireel features to "cheese cake" unsuitable for regular consumption—encouraged exhibitors in the summer of 1918 to book films individually and preview them whenever possible.[60] Indeed, 1919 would prove a crucial year in the shift toward selective booking.

Compared to urban first-run theaters, small-town theaters had fewer reasons to adopt selective booking as a widespread practice, and for the most part such houses remained program oriented. However, small theaters did occasionally use selective booking, even for program films. They, too, were pressured by the nationwide shift toward longer runs, and small theaters were an important part of distributors' strategic push toward selective booking. Even before the transition to program features, distributors had had an incentive to increase run lengths in theaters of all types. From their perspective, frequent changes put unnecessary strain and expense on the circulation of prints while also limiting the potential rental grosses of films. This sentiment is obvious in the scores of polemics against the daily change in the trade press throughout the first half of the 1910s.[61] The transition to program features put the antiquated status of the daily change into even sharper relief, as ever more expensive features were being churned through a distribution system that structurally limited their grosses. William A. Johnston railed against the daily change in his *Motion Picture News* column seemingly every week in 1917, arguing that it encouraged overproduction and depressed rentals by "overfeeding" movie fans while at the same time failing to properly market films for more casual moviegoers.[62]

Distributors recognized that daily changes overvalued the newness of films—and encouraged the overproduction of cheap negatives—at the expense of distribution's ability to widen and deepen the audience for any particular film. Hostility to the daily change was a question not only of marketing, but also of physical distribution. Increasing the standard run of small theaters to two days instead of one would not only allow distributors to charge increased rentals, but also reduce the amount of time that prints spent being physically distributed—that is, sitting in train cars or trucks rather than being projected. As the *News* would later point out, "[A] print which would in the event of a one-day stand spend the following day in transportation can in many cases be obtained at a smaller proportionate price for . . . two days."[63]

However, most small theaters did not lengthen their standard runs to two days until the 1920s.[64] The year 1919 seems to have been pivotal in this shift. According to a survey of exhibitors released by First National in early 1920, "one hundred and fifty more theaters are playing productions for week-stands this year [1919] than in 1918; this year five hundred and thirty more theaters are changing programs twice a week than the number last year and nearly seventy per cent of the daily-change theaters have adopted the two-day engagement plan within the last twelve months."[65] Thus, longer runs alone cannot explain small exhibitors' increasing use of selective booking after 1917. A more direct explanation has to do with the increasing variety of product on the market and the ever more diverse ways that distributors packaged that product.

Consider a series of parodic articles that *Motion Picture News* published in April 1918. Titled "Letters from a Self-Made Exhibitor to His Son"—a send-up of George Horace Lorimer's "Letters from a Self-Made Merchant to His Son"—the parody presented the correspondence of a fictional exhibitor, "Bill Grimm," to his recent college graduate son, Cuthbert. Recently bitten by the movie bug, Cuthbert has invested $10,000 from his trust fund in a movie theater—against the advice of his father. Through his witty grumbling about the various problems facing contemporary small theater owners, "Grimm" lays out the common methods of feature booking used by exhibitors around early 1918. Though somewhat tongue-in-cheek, the series gives us an insight into the small exhibitor's perspective on various booking practices:

> Let us assume you were being canvassed by frank, honest [distributor] salesmen representing each plan of booking. (I know what you are thinking, but this is only supposition.)
>
> Here's the program man: "We are turning out fifty-two pictures a year, one a week, and you must use them in order, selecting none and skipping none. Some are great; some are fair and some are just plain rotten. We make you a price which is very moderate and offer you a program which averages up well. If you bought our GREAT stuff in the open market it would cost you much coin. At the same time, I'll admit that you could buy our poorer stuff at a lower price than we are asking. But it's a good 'average' proposition."
>
> Now the star series man: "We sell our pictures by the series, each series featuring a star. We have great stars, fair stars, and poor stars. If you take all our stuff we'll let you have ALL the great stars, but if you are only going to take a portion of our output we will have to split the big stars between you and your competitor. The big stars are going to cost you many yen; the fair stars will set you back a little more than the average program price, and the poor stars will run at about program prices. Yes, we are making our big stars carry our fair and poor ones, naturally. But it's a good average proposition."
>
> Finally you have the independent man: "I have 'steen pictures and about half of them are worldbeaters and cost me a

wad of dough. The rest are pure mouse bait. Take all I've got and I'll make you an interesting price, but if you are going to pick out my winners and leave me holding the bag with the lemons I'll have to soak you good and plenty so as to cover what I DON'T get on the flivvers. It's just an average proposition."[66]

The fact that Johnston equated the program system, the star series, and selective booking in terms of each method's tendency to exploit the small exhibitor suggests that even if most small houses still booked most of their features via programs, the other two options were fairly common by early 1918. Grimm's conclusion as to the best booking method was that there wasn't one: "As the polite murderer said: 'How would you prefer to die: shooting, knifing, or strangling?'"[67] For small exhibitors—even those using a daily change—the primary motivation to adopt wide-open or selective booking was to differentiate themselves from their competitors. The same was true for many larger exhibitors, but because they tended to be in much more competitive zones and could play films for much longer runs, selective booking became a more frequent part of their booking practice.

Grimm's account of the "flivvers" and "mouse bait" available on the open market also highlights the fact that individual booking strategies were increasingly being used not only for specials that could garner extended runs, but also for films that were effectively programmers but for their distribution. Smaller companies provided many such films. In 1921, Thomas Watson signed a $300 selective booking contract with the independent distributor Robertson-Cole for three films in his three-hundred-seat Superba: $125 for *One Man in a Million* (Sol Lesser / George Beban, six reels), $100 for *Seven Years Bad Luck* (Max Linder, five reels), and $75 for *The First Born* (Colin Campbell / Sessue Hayakawa, six reels).[68] Each of the films on Watson's contract was produced semi-independently by a star with widespread name recognition—none were "mouse bait." However, their five- and six-reel lengths meant that they were nowhere close to specials; they were clearly intended for the program. As a result, while the $100 per picture Watson paid for these films was much higher than the $50–$75 he paid for the programmers he booked in bulk around the same time, it was still lower than the $250 (plus a percentage of the gross) he paid for the Fox special *Blind Wives* (Charles Brabin, nine reels, 1920) a few months later.[69] Markets like

Watson's were increasingly opening up to somewhat pricier product that filled a gap between programmers and specials.

Exhibitors in the cities, for their part, had internalized the logic of rental-basis run exhibition by 1920, when both extended runs and holdovers of films were common not only for specials but for a wider cross-section of films. In September of that year, *Motion Picture News* began publishing a section titled "What the Big Houses Say," which featured reports from first-run theaters on how recent releases, all of which ran for at least one or two weeks, were performing with their spectators. In four months' worth of issues, nearly every installment reported at least one run of three or more weeks in downtown houses. Some runs were much longer, including Frank Borzage's *Humoresque* (Paramount-Artcraft, six reels), which ran for as long as seven weeks in its first run.[70] Holdovers were also relatively frequent by this time: every week, between two and five out of the sixty or so published reports explicitly mentioned that a film had been held over for another week.[71] This applied not only to the productions of the major distributors, but also to independent products such as Clara Kimball Young's *Mid-Channel* (Equity, Harry Garson, six reels)[72] and B. A. Rolfe's *Madonnas and Men* (Jans Pictures, seven reels).[73] By the 1920s, selective booking had opened up a space within the distribution norms of the program—in both urban first-runs and smaller theaters—for films that were neither specials nor programmers, many of which were made by independent producers. These changes happened in the aftermath of a drive for longer runs and higher rentals that had begun in earnest in the 1918–1919 season.

"Fewer and Better": Distributors' Drive for Selective Booking, 1918–1919

The interstitial status of selective booking promised distributors a new way to differentiate individual films and increase their rental grosses, escalating the pattern that had begun with the star series. In 1916, star series distribution through Artcraft had been enough to differentiate Mary Pickford from her peers, but by 1918–1919, Charlie Chaplin's "million-dollar contract" films for First National were booked individually (as Hodkinson vice president F. B. Warren noted, "Mr. Chaplin knows his values too well to see them delivered in one package").[74] Because selective booking automatically lent features a certain aura of prestige, simply advertising films as being available on the "open market" was a useful strategy for distributors who sought to encourage upward pressure on rental prices. Selective booking was also at least partially driven by increases in star salaries. Because distributors needed higher rental fees from exhibitors to pay those salaries, they instituted ever more flexible models of distribution that in turn increased stars' value. This practice combined with wartime price inflation to drive up production costs considerably in 1917 and 1918.[75]

Though World War I might seem far removed from the American film industry's distribution practices, there is ample evidence to suggest that it increased pressure on exhibitors to raise prices, lengthen runs, and book films more frequently on an individual basis—all of which primed the postwar distribution market for more selective policies. Apart from the wider inflation in the American economy brought about by the war, one of its most important and widely discussed effects was the new tax regime imposed as part of the War Revenue Act, which took effect November 1, 1917.[76] The act included a 10 percent federal war tax on all admission tickets sold by places of amusement (later reduced to 5 percent), as well as a footage tax of one-quarter of a cent per foot of raw film stock and one-half a cent per foot on positive prints.[77] Exhibitors were responsible for the admissions tax, and as lawmakers had intended, most passed the extra one- to three-cent ticket surcharge on to their patrons. The bill had likewise intended for distributors to bear the footage tax. However, it did not specifically provide for that fact, and as Kia Afra has detailed, distributors passed the tax on to exhibitors in the form of a fifteen-cent-per-reel daily charge on all rentals—a charge that the distributors not only broke even on, but actually profited from.[78] A second revenue bill that went into effect in May 1919 replaced the footage tax with a 5 percent tax on the total rental amount—this time, explicitly payable by distributors (though again, it was usually passed on to exhibitors).[79] The taxes on both rentals and admissions lasted well beyond the conclusion of the war and were not repealed until 1922.

Though they certainly caused no small amount of tension with distributors, one practical effect of these taxes on exhibitors was to encourage them to book bigger films for higher prices and longer runs. The admissions tax did hurt theaters in some markets, but it did very little to dent movie attendance nationally. Arguably, the one- to three-cent increase in ticket prices that the tax imposed brought admission prices up to a more economically optimal level. Some exhibitors even took advantage of it to round prices up to the nearest five cents—ostensibly to avoid having to make change in pennies. In any event, moviegoers were generally willing and able to pay the increased prices, and some felt it was their patriotic duty.[80] The distributors' fifteen-cent reel tax, however, was widely resented—particularly by small exhibitors. The admissions tax at least hit theaters in direct proportion to the number of tickets they sold; the reel tax was seen as regressive, especially because small exhibitors had less seating capacity over which to spread the flat daily charge.[81] In practice, the reel tax encouraged exhibitors to book more "specials" to justify significantly higher ticket prices, and distributors positioned themselves to serve the demand. One state rights distributor, Hiller & Wilk, encouraged exhibitors in New York to selectively book a big production for a week's run every three or four weeks, such that they might "raise their admission price to a figure that will allow them to assume the tax."[82]

The especially harsh winter of 1917–1918 also encouraged exhibitors to change their pricing and booking policies, thanks to the rationing policies instituted by Harry A. Garfield of the Federal Fuel Administration. In an effort to conserve the nation's coal supply, Garfield ordered that nonessential places of business east of the Mississippi, including all places of amusement, go without heat on Mondays over the course of a ten-week period from late January through March 1918. Many businesses simply closed on "heatless Mondays" as a result. Film theaters successfully lobbied to turn off the heat on Tuesdays instead, since that was traditionally the weakest box-office day and it allowed exhibitors to take advantage of the crowd of now-idle Monday workers. Like the admissions tax, this policy had little negative effect on box office and was in fact beneficial for some exhibitors, since it effectively extended the weekend.[83] Theaters that may have run features only on Sundays now had a reason to extend the run of those films for an extra day, and those theaters that already ran features but used a daily change had a tempting opportunity to extend their runs to three days or more. Because the Fuel Administration also instituted a "lightless Sundays and Mondays" policy—from which theaters were exempted—many large and midsize exhibitors saw significant boosts in box-office receipts during those days.[84] At the same time, the fuel holiday put the weaknesses of the program system into sharp relief for those exhibitors who still used it. Paramount, for example, refused to refund payment for the affected playdates on program contracts signed before Garfield's edict.[85]

Given the blurring of the distinction between specials and program features, as well as the longer runs brought about by the war and by run exhibition, the American film industry was primed to accept open-market booking by 1919. The tipping point came in January of that year, when Mary Pickford, Douglas Fairbanks, D. W. Griffith, and Charlie Chaplin announced that they would incorporate United Artists.[86] UA's distribution model was fundamentally idiosyncratic: each of the star's films would effectively be a special, booked and released individually to exhibitors under percentage rental arrangements.[87] In their formal announcement of the combination to the press, as well as their various individual statements, the four stars articulated their company's exclusive use of selective booking as arising from a desire to "protect the exhibitor and the industry itself" from program-minded distributors forcing unwanted product onto the market.[88]

Despite its lofty goals, UA's entry onto the industry stage ended up benefiting the long-standing efforts of distributors to make film distribution more profitable. By normalizing the idea of an all-special, all-selective slate offered at advanced prices, the UA model framed higher prices for all features as a progressive idea that would benefit the entire industry, when it mostly benefited the distributors who offered big specials, and the large exhibitors who could afford to pay for them.[89] UA did not release enough product early on to be more than a boutique distributor, but it helped to create a demand among exhibitors for selectively booked big films from big stars that the other distributors were happy to supply. And unlike UA, those distributors had plenty of product that they could offer programmatically on the side, using their specials as leverage.

The first distributor to follow UA's lead in terms of adopting selective booking was W. W. Hodkinson, the former head of Paramount, who had pioneered the feature program system in 1914.[90] Hodkinson's company announced the change in distribution policy in April 1919 through a series of emphatic ads.[91] The hype over the so-called open market was such that some distributors—First National in particular—scrambled to claim that they had offered selectively booked films for *years* before Hodkinson.[92] UA and Hodkinson's plunge into the open market set off an industry-wide shift; over the course of the following spring and summer, Paramount, Metro, Goldwyn, and Vitagraph all declared that they would offer the bulk of their slates on the open market beginning in the fall.[93] World and Fox remained doggedly programmatic ("Fox provides for all theatres; not merely for one class"), although both were effectively forced to introduce star series plans.[94] As for Universal, while the company's marketing cagily implied that it had always offered its product selectively—it had not—it followed Fox and World in moving toward the star series and putting more emphasis on specials.[95]

Many exhibitors recognized that the distributors' ostensible commitment to exhibitor choice was, as *Variety* put it, "plain bunk" and a "shell game." Fundamentally, selective booking encouraged speculative and competitive bidding among exhibitors, raising the price of rental contracts across the entire slate.[96] The key to the scheme was that it did away with the formalized, structured units of distribution—the program and the star series—that had been built into previous contracts, and instead made booking a more flexible pricing negotiation between distributor and exhibitor. Those programmatic distribution units had always provided exhibitors with important information (the star they were paying for, or the assurance of a bulk-priced program) that helped them make judgments about fair pricing. However, now that films were sold "on their own merits," distributors suddenly had the flexibility to find exceptional merit in any production the exhibitor might want. Simply by inviting the exhibitor to actively select individual films, distributors gained the upper hand in negotiating contract prices. This meant that much of a distributor's slate could be sold on the merit of a handful of films. As *Variety* pointed out, "Where in former times the producer was content to give the exhibitor one good crushing with a contract hooking the exhibitor up to, say eight pictures a year, now in the new plan he can give the theatre boob eight good macerations by making him come across to the limit every time the producer throws a new Pickford, Fairbanks, Chaplin, or other self-seller on the market."[97]

Although most exhibitors agreed with the basic principle of open-market booking, this process of up-bidding explains why they tended to prefer the star series as a matter of practice. The series at least gave exhibitors enough information about a film to obviate previewing it, while still offering a programmatic and (relatively) reasonably priced contract.[98] This was especially important for exhibitors outside of urban markets, who were particularly put off by selective booking:

> The exhibitor so placed that he must buy his pictures without seeing them is saying unreservedly to the producers that all their literature about the abolition of the star system [i.e., star series] so that cheaper and better pictures can be made is

just sheer bunk. [The star series] is the only plan that gives him any sort of guarantee of the quality of a picture, for, it stands to reason, he declares, that no star of any account will hook up to any but a production that has a chance, but that where the star is missing, the assurance of quality must be missing also.[99]

While selective booking increased certain stars' value significantly in production, it also reduced the overall importance of stars in organizing most of the studios' distribution slates. Big films were increasingly sold based on distributors' own valuation of them through marketing, rather than on the presence of any star. Distributor valuation of selectively booked product was referred to as "scale," or "exhibition value," and it became a common tool of film distribution. When Paramount began selling contracts for George Loane Tucker's *The Miracle Man* in the summer of 1919, it estimated the film's value in domestic rentals at $1 million. *Variety* saw this as sheer delusion for a film with no stars based on an undistinguished George M. Cohan play: "With a million asked from the whole country for 'The Miracle Man,' New York's percentage quota scales at 14. At the rating, the local exhibitor can't see where he gets off, unless he takes it off the low jumping-off place of the Brooklyn Bridge. There isn't an exhibitor between Montauk Point and the Sawmill River tip of the Bronx that can see where $140,000 is coming out of New York for rental for any picture save a sensation."[100] As it turned out, Paramount had underestimated *The Miracle Man*; the film performed spectacularly, earning about $3 million worldwide.[101] Benjamin Hampton wrote that the film "seriously shook the faith of producers in the star system."[102]

However, Paramount executives recognized the imperfections of the star series as early as the fall of 1918, and it is clear that distributors had already begun to deemphasize stars in their distribution strategies.[103] This did not mean making every film a "special production without stars," as William Fox had once described it; program films continued to be produced.[104] The entire point was to focus attention around the specials so that they could carry the rest of the program. Rather, *The Miracle Man*'s status as an independently produced film from the Mayflower Photoplay Company was even more important than its lack of stars. This was because the film's success seemed to validate the United Artists model of distributing boutique productions, and its $126,000 cost showed that those productions need not be half-a-million-dollar super-specials.[105]

Mayflower's president, Benjamin Prager, positioned the success of his company's film as the result of a corporate philosophy he called the "Mayflower idea," a privileging of the director's "centralized authority" according to "the firm belief that photoplays should be created and not 'made'": "In the large corporations, the scenario department selects the story; the financial department sets a maximum figure on the cost; the costuming department makes the wardrobe, according to its own ideas of the requirements, and so on down the line. Hence, five or six factors that contribute to the production place five or six interpretations on the story and its spirit. . . . During the making of [*The Miracle Man*], Tucker, under his Mayflower contract, had perfect freedom to create an artistic photoplay as he alone thought it should be."[106] Prager's rhetoric should not be taken at face value, but the relationship between production and distribution he describes aligns with what Matthew Bernstein has described as "semi-independent production," which he defined as "the procedure by which major Hollywood talents from the 1910s onward form[ed] their own companies, hire[d] their own artists and technicians, and deliver[ed] a completed, high-budget negative to a national distributor."[107]

Prager's rosy characterization of Mayflower as a semi-independent production company was of a piece with a broader industry rhetoric that distinguished the quality of semi-independent films from the programmers churned out by the distributors' own production departments. For Prager, *The Miracle Man* was a high-quality production because of the company's supposed centralization of authority around the director as a creative artist. Paramount marketed many of its other independent releases in a similar way. In the lead-up to the 1919–1920 season, Jesse Lasky highlighted the use of independent releases from Mayflower, Sydney Chaplin, Cosmopolitan, and the New Art Film Company at Famous Players–Lasky, boasting that each of FPL's pictures was a "unit by itself" and that "for the first time in the history of the motion picture, genius will be given absolute and unlimited opportunity to assert itself."[108]

Another way distributors attempted to differentiate their programmers beginning in 1919 was by linking independent production with a certain discourse of literary prestige. Goldwyn touted the "literary quality" independent production made possible when it reorganized roughly a quarter of its program releases into a brand known as Eminent Authors (figures 3.1.1 and 3.1.2). Although Goldwyn attempted to convince exhibitors that Eminent Authors was a semi-independent producer, it was simply a brand for Goldwyn films adapted from works by well-known

ANNOUNCING EMINENT

EMINENT Authors' Pictures, Inc., organized by Rex Beach and Samuel Goldwyn, unites in one producing organization the greatest American novelists of today. It insures the exclusive presentation of their stories on the screen and each author's cooperation in production. These authors are:—

Rex Beach	Gertrude Atherton	Mary Roberts Rinehart
Rupert Hughes	Gouverneur Morris	Basil King
	Leroy Scott	

The creation of Eminent Authors' Pictures, Inc., is the natural outgrowth of the association of Mr. Beach and Mr. Goldwyn in the making of such successes as "The Crimson Gardenia," "The Brand," "The Auction Block."

It is safe to say that the authors in Eminent Authors' Pictures, Inc., are known to every reading individual.

Their popularity in the motion picture theatres can be no less than their popularity in the newspapers, magazines, and books. If anything, it must be greater.

Figures **3.1.1** *and* **3.1.2**. *Goldwyn ad for Eminent Authors*, Moving Picture World, *July 12, 1919, 175.*

SAMUEL GOLDWYN

AUTHORS' PICTURES

Editors and magazines vie with one another to secure the manuscripts of these writers. They pay large sums for the exclusive rights to their works. Every word of these men and women is contracted for, both for serial and book publication, months in advance.

Every picture will be as popular an achievement for the motion picture world as the story has been in literature. It will not be offered for release until the author has given his personal approval to it. The picture must first pass the severest critic that it will ever meet—the author of the story.

During the year each author of the corporation will be represented by at least two stories. These splendid productions will be sold *only in the projection rooms* of the Goldwyn exchanges one at a time—on merit.

The stories are right. That is settled by the approval of the millions. The casts will be models of excellence. Every part of the production will have the quality that is always the hallmark of Goldwyn.

The formation of Eminent Authors' Pictures is a great step forward in the betterment of the industry.

writers, such as Rex Beach, Gertrude Atherton, and Mary Roberts Rinehart, who ostensibly "supervise[d] the adaptation of their own stories in motion picture form."[109] This marketing-driven approach was less successful than Paramount's strategy of signing actual distribution contracts with independent production companies. *Variety* noted that the Eminent Authors brand, while successful for a short time, was "scarcely a ripple beyond the normal program quality," and Goldwyn's in-house scenario writers often stonewalled the creative input of the authors, "whose brilliance [the company] placarded as far as the nether limits of the moon."[110]

Eminent Authors and Mayflower instantiated a common pattern among distributors, however, in that they both marketed what were essentially program films as special releases by downplaying any sense that they were produced according to programmatic methods. The usefulness of giving independent production this kind of marketing was twofold: it enabled the distributors to farm out significant portions of their programs to specialized producers while allowing their production departments to pay greater attention to their own films. As a result, the use of semi-independent production grew rapidly in the two years following 1919. First National, for its part, doubled its output from 25 films in 1919 to 50 in 1920, with all 50 provided by contracted semi-independent producers. Of the 117 features distributed by Paramount and Artcraft in 1919, slightly over a third were made by semi-independent companies.[111] The growing market for films made by independent producers resulted in an increase in the total number of releases. After a significant decrease in production brought about by the solidification of open booking from 1918 (841 releases) to 1919 (646), the number of releases grew 23 percent in 1920 (796) and another 7 percent in 1921 (854).[112] This was despite the growing length of the average run, which in theory should have encouraged distributors to release *fewer* films.

While selective booking affected the total number of films the industry made, it had even more crucial implications for studio production strategies. As early as 1918, distributors realized that integrating selective booking policies into the sale of their programs would require new attention to production control and planning across the yearly slate. In an October 1919 letter to general manager Charles Eyton, FPL's production manager, Whitman Bennett, laid out the challenges of a new production planning system the studio had instituted to guide the process of scenario selection. He explained that under the program system, Paramount's production divisions had not needed to consult the distribution department in any meaningful way about the kinds of scenarios that were to be produced. This changed in 1918, however, in anticipation of the move to selective booking:

> So long as Paramount and Artcraft distributed the films on the program basis, selling almost entirely on the reputation of various stars, the system [of scenario planning] did not radically differ from previous procedure, except that *we consulted the distribution department about the selection of stars.* The new order of things, as it is now developing, began only about a year ago [the fall of 1918]—when it became apparent that the program system was antiquated and that each film must be considered as an individual venture and as an *individual sales problem.* [Emphasis added.][113]

Because individual features that had formerly been sold on the basis of the program or the star were now "individual sales problems," selecting scenarios for non-special productions was no longer primarily the purview of producers who saw it as a function of cost control or program-wide quality. Instead, it became a direct point of interest for distribution as well: "When the distribution department considers the sale of each film separately, it is not to be wondered at that it wants some say as to the character of the productions," as Bennett put it. In other words, by 1919, integrated producer-distributors, including FPL, were selecting scenarios across their yearly slates with an attention to their individual marketability. This had previously applied only to special productions meant for idiosyncratic release.

Bennett's chronology suggests that FPL's implementation of its new distribution-centered scenario-selection practice occurred in anticipation of Paramount's announcement of selective booking as a slate-wide policy for the 1919–1920 season. It was therefore a highly calculated strategy, and as Bennett's letter reveals, it was based on a preliminary set of data about the performance of individual films in the distribution market:

> Although the distribution department is just as important as it ever was, it has assumed a totally new character. It is no longer a piece of mechanism. It is simply the artery through which

we get into direct contact with the public through the theatres. Now, that we have also begun to acquire theatres, the distribution department must eventually become to a large degree an exploitation and exhibition department; and we shall have the same *direct contact with the public* that is enjoyed by a Frohman production on the legitimate stage playing in a Frohman theatre. In fact, we already have that exact contact in some few instances, where we have played pictures for sharing engagements in theatres of which we ourselves control the leases.

By the same token that the distribution department has come into closer contact with theatres and audiences on the one hand, it has come into closer contact with the producing department on the other hand. And, because the distribution department has, more than formerly, exact information as to the kind of material the public wants (by reason of its closer contact) we of the producing department have depended upon it more and more for advice. [Emphasis added.][114]

By "direct contact with the public," Bennett did not simply mean better advertising or determination of the public's tastes—he meant hard data about how much money films made in ticket sales. "Sharing engagements"—another term for percentage rentals—explicitly revealed this data, which was one reason that exhibitors had always been reluctant to accept them.[115] By the early twenties, a sophisticated statistical division in Paramount's distribution department allowed for a much clearer picture of the value of individual productions than had been possible under the program system or the star series, which made selective booking much more workable as a strategy.[116]

Even when it did not include a percentage arrangement, selective booking, at the very least, gave distributors better data on exhibitor demand for individual films in distribution. This was information that both the program system and the star series had obscured, because exhibitors bought those packages at a uniform price per film. Selective booking enabled distributors to continue to rent films programmatically in groups while pricing them individually within the package of sale. This practice helped immensely in predicting an accurate exhibition value for subsequent films—which, in turn, dictated their pricing and budgeting. As film distribution practice continued to evolve in the 1920s, synchronizing the operations of production with those of distribution—and vice versa—would become even more important.

In the late 1910s, the major distributors' valuation of films shifted away from strong distinctions between individually handled specials and bulk-priced programs and toward the idea of each film on the program as an "individual sales proposition." This change motivated distributors to take more direct control over all aspects of production to more specifically tailor individual films for distribution. Nevertheless, distributors were obliged to use independent producers to release entire programs of films that they could position highly enough to boost those grosses. By incorporating individual pricing into a sales package that remained fundamentally programmatic, selective booking enabled distributors to gather more granular data about the popularity of individual stars and films in particular theaters. Selective booking was not especially cost effective due to its increased sales and distribution costs, but it did help to centralize distributors' control over production (through financing) and film pricing (through setting exhibition values). Selective booking was a lure not only for exhibitors, who were subject to price manipulation thanks to the practice, but also for producers, who saw in it an opportunity for higher speculative returns on their filmmaking investments.

As a packaging practice, selective booking was not without its risks for distributors. In chapter 5, we will see how it encouraged exhibitors to cancel contracts, withhold playdates, and otherwise complicate distributors' desire for controlled, rationalized, and programmatic circulation of film product at standardized prices. In their responses to this exhibitor conduct, distributors adopted three strategies of temporal management in both distribution and production: block booking, uniform contract terms, and run exhibition. The integration of these strategies into distribution practice after 1921 expanded on the advantages of selective booking as a packaging practice—its combination of programmatic distribution and idiosyncratic, granular pricing—by strengthening distributors' control of exhibitors' playdates. This would set the stage for the transformation of the studio system in the 1920s. Before we can understand the industry's strategies for controlling exhibitors temporally, however, we must examine how and why Hollywood developed a centralized model for controlling the national distribution market spatially.

4 SPACE

From Franchising to Merchandising
Marketing Films Locally and Nationally, 1914–1923

So far in this book I have attended to the development of film distribution's packaging strategies in the 1910s, with occasional forays into pricing and production, intentionally deferring discussion of distribution as a practice of circulation. This is not because I wish to downplay the latter; the organization and control of space was obviously important for the film distribution industry. The reliable physical transportation of prints to exhibitors, usually by express companies, was by no means automatic or assured even in 1920, and questions about where and when films played get at the heart of cinema's cultural importance. However, to understand the industry's drive for spatial control as it pertains to practices of industrial capitalism, we must understand space not as a literal or geographic quality, but in capitalism's terms: as a *market*. In this chapter I therefore concentrate on how film distributors variously understood the national cinema market in the 1910s and early 1920s, and how they spatially organized their strategies for selling to—and creating demand in—that market.

The traditional narrative about the spatial transformation of silent-era film distribution in the United States goes something like this: over the course of roughly twenty years, what had been an intensely local enterprise came under the sway of a centralized regime of control in New

York City. This story originates with the itinerant exhibitors of the first decade or so of cinema, who purchased films directly from manufacturers and showcased them to local markets one venue at a time across an extended span of time. It then moves on to the local independent film exchanges of the early one-reel period—with their endless demand for daily product—and then to the coalescing national shorts distribution systems of the General Film Company, Mutual, and Universal. The narrative's logic asserts that as early as 1910, film distribution in the United States had become a largely rationalized and centrally controlled system releasing one- and two-reel films at a national scale.

Within this same narrative, the handling of longer features of four or more reels after 1910 essentially mirrors the pattern of film distribution before the General Film Company. Distribution of features begins with the state rights system, whereby manufacturers directly sold "special" films to many independent state and regional distributors for large sums. It advances to the centralized national distribution systems of the first program feature distributors in 1914, and concludes with the vertically integrated producer-distributor oligopoly of the 1920s. Michael Quinn's work on Paramount—the first company to successfully distribute features programmatically when it inaugurated a twice-a-week five-reel feature service—carefully details a canonical example of this phenomenon of centralization, concluding that Paramount adapted the General Film Company's model to multireel features.[1] And Ben Singer writes that "beginning around mid-1914, the feature distribution business underwent a major transformation from a haphazard regional enterprise fragmented among hundreds of state rights firms to a national enterprise dominated by about ten big companies."[2]

As a diachronic pattern of change, this narrative is correct in its essential outline. There is little doubt that the various systems of film distribution in the United States in 1920 were more centralized than those of 1914, which were in turn more centralized than those of 1905. However, because of the linearity of this historiography, the extent to which local concerns and interests continued to determine distribution patterns and practice, particularly for features in the period 1914–1919, has been significantly underestimated. This is partially a function of the discourse of business efficiency so widely promulgated by the industry itself. The trade press made constant reference to the systematizing of film exchanges in an effort to, as Gregory Waller puts it, "conjure up a thriving industry that [was] open to both quick-thinking entrepreneurs and also to ambitious corporations with national business strategies."[3] Scholars in recent years have begun to trace the importance of regional distribution in the early 1910s. Maureen Rogers has emphasized the importance of the regional distribution practices of the state rights system to the rise of the star system and the centralized program feature distributors of the mid-1910s.[4] But to what extent did the influence of state rights and other regional entities continue into the mid-teens and beyond? And what implications did these regional considerations have once more centralized, nationally organized practices of feature film distribution became the norm in the 1920s?

Answering these questions once again requires us to look at management practices in both cinema and the industries adjacent to it. While live show business offered Hollywood useful models for booking, packaging, and physically circulating its product, the fundamental difference between the product being distributed—human performers versus the positive film print—meant that the nascent film industry had to look elsewhere when it came to questions of marketing films to retailers at a national scale. Live performance, by definition, constitutes a different product in every booking, and even the largest plays touring in duplicate companies in the 1880s and 1890s could mount only about twenty simultaneous performances nationwide. Cinema, in contrast, by virtue of its mechanical reproducibility, is a mass-market good in a more fundamental sense. The physical extent of film distribution in the 1910s and 1920s was limited only by the number of positive prints that could be produced from a single negative before it wore out: at least 250 in the 1910s. Even when one- and two-reel films were expected to completely run their course in two or three months, a print run constituted at least twenty-five positives (one for each exchange territory), with particularly popular films justifying the manufacture of additional prints.[5]

In the mid-1910s, the need for strategies to market the emerging program feature presented new challenges to established models of film distribution. As features, these films constituted a new "special" form of cinema and called for individuated attention; at the same time, the impetus to release them as a programmatic, standardized product necessitated models of distribution that accounted simultaneously for the twin questions of national scale and local tailoring. Shorts cinema had required less attention to local marketing, because the run of any one film through the national market was so brief; local preferences were reflected less in the popularity of individual films than in the success of the larger brands of which they were a part. Features, by contrast, depended on longer runs and advertising to generate the larger grosses that justified their additional expense. A different approach was needed to market such films, and early in the history of features, manufacturers adopted models from live show business. However, as the teens went on, it became clear that selling program features—which constituted the bulk of the industry's production—called for a marketing approach rooted less in live show business than in mass-market merchandising.

This chapter covers the development of centralized feature marketing as a distribution practice from the mid-1910s to the early 1920s. While the practices that governed the circulation of feature films were, in general, as centralized as those used for shorts, the practices distributors used to bring them to market—selling and booking, in particular—continued to be outsourced to independent local firms at many distributors until late in the 1910s. Through an examination of this hybrid form of national feature distribution, which I term the "franchise system," we will see why distributors continued to use decentralized, theatrically influenced forms of marketing up until the 1920s. The weaknesses of the franchise system also point to the advantages of more centralized marketing practices, helping to clarify why techniques from mass-market merchandising, rather than decentralized franchising, became ubiquitous in film distribution by the early 1920s.

Franchising before 1915, outside and within the Film Industry

According to business historian Thomas Dicke, franchising is a system of industrial organization in which "one firm is granted the exclusive right to market the goods or services of another company in a given area." A key aspect of this right is that "producer and distributor are legally independent of one another, and the relationship between them is closely defined and controlled by contract." Dicke distinguishes between two types of franchising: system franchising and product franchising. System franchising, also known as business format franchising, is exemplified by the fast food industry and is the most familiar form of the practice. In system franchising, the fundamental product being sold by the national firm (McDonald's, for example) to its franchisee is not the retailed output itself (hamburgers), but the right to operate a particular branded outlet (a McDonald's location) along with that brand's reputation and a set of standardized production, marketing, and training procedures. From the perspective of the producer in system franchising, the real customer is less the retail consumer than the franchisee, who pays for the use of the producer's standardized methods of marketing and manufacturing.[6]

Product franchising, by contrast, is fundamentally a form of distribution rather than one of selling a manufacturing or marketing format. In product franchising (also known as product-distribution franchising), manufacturers use franchise contracts with local entities to build and maintain a national distribution network. The most familiar example of this type of franchising in the United States is the car dealership. Nearly all car manufacturers sell franchise agreements to local dealers or regional dealer chains, who assume the overhead costs of owning and operating the outlet in exchange for the right to retail the cars and to offer maintenance and financing services associated with the manufacturer's brand. As a consequence, the manufacturer is able to minimize distribution and retail costs, outsource sales and marketing strategy to local entities who are presumed to be more attuned to their markets, and roll out new products quickly and efficiently on a national basis.

Franchising is often thought of as a post–World War II phenomenon closely associated with chain restaurants and hotels. However, this is true only for system franchising, which, according to Dicke, was not possible in the United States until the 1920s. Product franchising, by contrast, had been a common strategy for creating national sales networks since well before the 1920s, having been used as early as the mid-nineteenth century to sell farm implements and sewing machines. By the first years of the twentieth century, the system was commonly employed to sell a variety of high-cost durable goods that were difficult to market locally through the traditional system of manufacturer-controlled agencies. This older agency system, which involved manufacturers contracting with established wholesalers of similar products acting as the manufacturer's legal agents, made the manufacturer and the agent-distributor indistinguishable from a legal standpoint. Auto manufacturers, who early on sold their products through the agency system, increasingly moved toward franchise dealerships in the 1900s and 1910s. This approach obviated the need to account for frequently changing local laws regarding automobile sales while simultaneously allowing the companies to build national sales networks quickly. It also provided a stable cash flow to the manufacturers, as cars were now sold directly to dealers rather than consigned—at no small amount of risk—to agents.[7]

Given product franchising's advantages for selling durable goods, its utility for film distribution from around the turn of the twentieth century through the 1910s might not seem obvious. Positive film prints could hardly be described as a durable product; indeed, during the one-reel period they were rarely conceived of as having value in distribution for more than a few weeks. The widely imitated success of the General Film Company's model was a result of its conception of film as a low-cost generic good, one that could be efficiently moved through the national exhibition market—via exchanges it centrally owned and operated—for modest but predictable profits. Franchising made little sense under this conception since the short film's profitability was determined by quick throughput rather than long-term durability. For film manufacturers making less generic, "special" negatives in smaller quantities and at considerable cost, product franchising offered a compelling model of distribution for the exact reason that it outsourced distribution and marketing to local entities. In offering something like the filmic equivalent of a durable good, manufacturers could charge their local franchisee-distributors higher prices for that good without having to devote additional resources to the marketing details needed to ensure its profitability at the local level. As Dicke argues, "Distributors of non-generic goods were unable to exploit fully the potentials of the economies of speed [that enabled mass marketing in the twentieth century], since the specialized nature of their products forced them to concentrate on a limited product line that did not allow for a large flow of goods through retail outlets. As a result, there was less need to internalize the transactions between the producer and the final distributor and fewer reasons to turn to newer, more elaborate methods of organization."[8]

Product franchising was an attractive option for feature producers in the 1910s because the GFC's dominant model of film distribution during the period was tailored around a conception of cinema as a high-turnover generic good rather than a specialized and individuated product. Though the GFC was more open to longer, specialized features in the 1910s than is generally acknowledged, it was ill equipped at the local level of distribution to sell such product profitably. The fundamental purpose of local exchanges, both when they acted as independent entities and after they were consolidated under the control of the GFC in 1910, was to efficiently manage the physical circulation of films rather than marketing differentiated product to exhibitors.[9] Such marketing was essential to feature makers, but it was also complicated and represented a significant financial risk. Outsourcing marketing to specialized local firms via product franchising was fundamentally a strategy for managing that risk; meanwhile, the physical circulation of films could, for the most part, continue to employ preexisting models established for shorts cinema.

In its early years, national feature film distribution in the American context is thus better understood as a hodgepodge of external and highly local transactions between manufacturers and independent distribution entities than as an inevitable march toward centralization and vertical integration. Even though centralization had obvious advantages from the strict standpoint of circulation, marketing features nationally required different, or at least hybrid, distribution strategies. The earliest form of idiosyncratic film distribution that was clearly influenced by product franchising in other industries was the state rights system. Under state rights, manufacturers sold exclusive distribution rights for an individual film to many buyers throughout the country on a territorial basis, typically for extended periods (usually five years, according to Quinn). Those buyers could then rent the film to exhibitors, subdivide the distribution rights to other companies, exhibit the film directly, or employ some combination thereof—they effectively had complete control over the distribution of their print(s) of the film.[10] State rights had its origins in the practice of the theatrical exclusive contract, which allowed theaters to charge much higher prices for acts over which they essentially had a monopoly.[11] The system thus allowed extended runs for individual films. It also encouraged the state rights firms and exhibitors to advertise films extensively in their local markets to build up audience interest in a particular production. This approach differed significantly from the variety program model of the General Film Company, where advertising focused on particular brands of program service rather than individual films. As a result, the state rights system could generate significant profits for the manufacturer on individual films—much greater than was possible in the program system.

Furthermore, state rights distributors tended to contract for exhibition in larger and more prestigious venues than were generally used in the variety program model, such as opera houses and legitimate theaters, which could charge higher ticket prices and seat larger audiences.[12] This is one reason why the state rights system was the most common method of feature distribution before 1914; it was more effective at generating the kinds of grosses in exhibition that might allow distributors and producers to recoup the higher costs of specialized feature production. Under the variety program model, the General Film Company or Mutual circa 1914 might pay a manufacturer $4,000 for forty positives of a one-reel film. The state rights to distribute a single feature could be sold for ten times that amount across the country, or even more. *Tillie's Punctured Romance* (Mack Sennett, 1914) was produced at Keystone for $9,000, but the manufacturer sold the film to the state rights distributor Alco for $70,000.[13] At Majestic that same year, D. W. Griffith's *The Avenging Conscience* was offered on the state rights market for $6,000 in Illinois and $2,400 in Wisconsin; the rights for just those two states earned back two-thirds of the film's $12,800 negative cost.[14]

In its delegation of distribution authority to local companies independent from the manufacturer, the state rights system was a clear example of product franchising. Indeed, from the teens and throughout the studio period, trade press ads for the state rights of a particular feature frequently described manufacturers' contracts with territorial distributors as franchises.[15] State rights was the dominant method of feature distribution in the early 1910s, but after 1914, the system began to manifest problems that the modified franchise system sought to remedy. Despite its profit potential, state rights distribution was simply too haphazard to be practical at a national or programmatic scale. While it worked reasonably well for specialty producers (or for the special productions of a manufacturer that otherwise made shorts), any feature producer hoping to nationally distribute more than a few films through the system faced problems. The most obvious of these was the issue of logistical coordination. Because the rights for each film were sold to territories on an individual basis, manufacturers that used state rights had to deal with many separate local distributors at once. A manufacturer wishing to release a film nationally through the system circa 1913 would have needed to maintain relationships with around 150 separate companies. This meant 150 separate negotiations over pricing, release dates, payment schedules, quality control of prints, and so forth. The duplicated costs to the manufacturer of selling individual films to so many distributors blunted the cost advantages of outsourcing distribution in the first place.[16]

Perhaps more importantly, the haphazard structure of the state rights system tended to give pricing advantages to the regional franchisees in the long term. As Quinn shows, operating a state rights distributor required very little startup capital when compared to the amounts needed to actually produce features. This meant that state rights companies were often fly-by-night operations organized to distribute one or two films, and they could generally afford to hold out for lower prices when negotiating with producers for local distribution rights. Feature producers, by contrast, tended to need capital quickly to amortize debts incurred on previous productions, and so had less leverage to bargain over pricing. Furthermore, because producers typically sold their territorial distribution rights for a flat fee, they tended not to share in the profits of unusually successful films.[17]

For these reasons, previous histories have tended to characterize state rights as either a marginalized distribution practice or one that was subsumed into more centralized releasing after 1914, when major distributors, including Warner's Features and Paramount, began offering nationally coordinated feature programs of a certain number of releases every week. However, the state rights system was central to the creation of these centralized national distribution networks. Rogers has emphasized that the May 1914 combination of Famous Players' exchanges and the exchange holdings of W. W. Hodkinson to form Paramount was only one major step in a more continuous process of coalescence: "Paramount Pictures' national distribution network grew out of the state rights market; in effect, Hodkinson recruited existing state rights franchisees to operate as their exclusive exchanges."[18] Even after this combination, Paramount was not, technically speaking, a national distributor; as Quinn points out, the company was obliged to sell additional sub-franchises to cover the entire territory of the United States.[19]

The product franchising model of the state rights system continued to be an important norm of feature distribution into the mid-teens. Paramount consolidated its long-term relationships with local state rights franchisees ever further to become a centralized producer-distributor, effectively completing that process with Zukor's hostile takeover of Hodkinson's holdings to form Famous Players–Lasky in July 1916. However, newer firms continued to rely on the vestiges of state rights to create national distribution networks through modified systems of franchising.[20] As the teens went on, approaches to product franchising in the film industry increasingly coalesced around locally influential exhibition entities as well as state rights companies. These magnates, whose theaters and chains in key cities and territories gave them power in their local market, were extremely useful to producers as part of a national product-franchising strategy. They tended to represent long-standing businesses rather than fly-by-nights, had an understanding of the idiosyncrasies of their local markets, and, perhaps most crucially, could leverage the reputations of their houses in marketing the new phenomenon of the feature program. The Triangle Film Corporation, to which we now turn as our first case study of such an exhibition-centered product-franchising system, instantiated both its strengths and its weaknesses.

The Franchise System at Triangle, 1915–1917

In mid-1915, many of the major manufacturers who had made films for the Mutual Film Corporation, including D. W. Griffith's Majestic, Thomas Ince's New York Motion Picture Company, and Mack Sennett's Keystone Studios, departed from the shorts-oriented national distributor and aligned themselves with a new feature concern, the Triangle Film Corporation, organized by former Mutual heads Harry and Roy Aitken. From the outset, Triangle modeled its feature production strategies on those of Paramount. These included its structuring of contracts with producers to encourage higher-cost filmmaking, its programmatic output of two features and two shorts a week, and its premium price. However, whereas Paramount refined these strategies over the course of the mid-1910s, while consolidating its producers and distributor-franchisees, Triangle's distribution model continued to rely on the much more decentralized releasing strategies of the state rights system. This was in part out of necessity. After their ouster from Mutual, the Aitkens had to build Triangle's national distribution system quickly. The most straightforward way to do that was to leverage preexisting relationships with the state rights companies that had handled Aitken-produced features, such as *The Birth of a Nation*. State rights had also proven a lucrative approach in the past, and, as we have seen, its cash-flow benefits were considerable.

Triangle's system was not a simple reversion to state rights. It combined the advantages of a nationally coordinated feature program with the income potential of state rights in a hybrid franchise system. Unlike in state rights, Triangle's entire *program* was franchised, rather than individual films being franchised. This innovation enabled the company to coordinate national release dates and advertising—a crucial aspect of the feature program. Triangle's luxurious "model theaters" are often cited as an early example of the vertical integration of the industry into exhibition, but most of Triangle's model theaters were the centerpieces of independent distribution franchises operated by local exhibition magnates.[21] By contracting with franchisees for the distribution of its films while at the same time putting certain contractual limitations on their distribution, Triangle maximized profitability in distribution at the expense of flexibility and a certain measure of control over their releasing. Additionally, Triangle operated its own exchanges in most major cities, sometimes alongside independent franchisees, completing its national network while reducing the costs of managing that network. According to Kalton Lahue, this company-owned exchange system cost around $500,000 to initially set up. However, it theoretically ensured that recurring distribution costs to Triangle were limited to those of physically circulating prints, with sales and marketing expenses mostly taken up by franchisees. In its emphasis on efficient circulation and throughput of product, Triangle's own exchange system was conceptualized according to the General Film Company model. The Aitkens even hired former GFC distribution head J. R. Naulty to manage it.[22]

In theory, at least, this strategy of separating the circulation and marketing aspects of film distribution eliminated many of the problems of the state rights system while preserving its advantages. The rights to Triangle franchises were a source of significant potential income, which is why well-heeled exhibitors, many of them with experience as state rights distributors, were willing to pay handsomely for them. Franchises with well-known exhibitors also served as useful advertising copy for Triangle in the fall of 1915 as the company sought to expand its fledgling distribution and exhibition networks. Trade press ads touted the company's franchises with William H. Kemble in Brooklyn, S. M. Hexter in Cleveland, the Archer Brothers in Chicago, E. H. Hulsey in Texas, and others.[23] This advertising benefited franchisees as well, by positioning their own theaters as bellwether exhibition sites in their local markets—a clear instance of the "show window" function of first-run theaters in the emerging studio system.

Triangle's November 1915 contract with Harry Garson and Pliny Craft, owners of the Broadway Strand and Miles theaters in Detroit, outlines the details of their franchise with the company. The deal would have been a familiar one for Craft, who was a pioneer in the use of state rights for feature distribution, having been instrumental in the state rights release of *The Birth of a Nation*.[24] Garson and Craft agreed to pay Triangle $2,000 a week for a year of Triangle service—an incredible sum, given that Paramount service for a theater in a city the size of Detroit would have cost only around $600 or $700 a week during this period.[25] What this hefty price bought, however, was an effective exhibition *and* distribution monopoly on Triangle service in the city. Triangle made Garson and Craft's two theaters their model exhibition spaces for the zone encompassing the entire city for all of 1916. In addition, the company gave them authority over all bookings of the Triangle program to subsequent-run theaters in Detroit.[26] All of these sub-rentals were subject to Triangle's approval, and prints were shipped directly from Triangle's own exchanges, but the contract made no provision for additional payments to Triangle from rentals to these subsequent-run theaters. Garson and Craft were free to charge the theaters whatever they wished for subsequent-run bookings and could keep all of the rental income.

This subsequent-run booking privilege was the key to Triangle's franchise strategy. It justified the high cost of the franchise and provided Triangle weekly cash flow from its releases in franchised territories without the accompanying expenses entailed by selling and contracting for subsequent-run distribution. In its basic form, this franchise system was effectively the state rights model, but applied to programmatic booking. Triangle's franchise contracts make clear that it anticipated that some territories it franchised would bring in almost as much on a weekly basis as the state rights system might have earned in a single flat payment. Garson and Craft got their Triangle service in Detroit for a relative bargain compared to state rights distributor William H. Kemble of Brooklyn, whose Big "T" Film Corporation paid $4,000 a week for the Triangle franchise covering all of Long Island, with first runs at the Crescent Theatre in Flatbush.[27] The owners of the Southwestern Triangle Film Corporation were so confident in their three-year franchise for all of Missouri and Texas that in their contract with Triangle, they accepted an increase in the price of their service from $3,800 a week for the first year to almost $5,000 a week for the second year, and $6,000 for the third.[28] Compared to the $6,000 flat fee paid to Majestic for the state rights in Illinois for *The Avenging Conscience* in 1914, this was serious money.

The exact terms of each franchise could differ significantly from contract to contract. Although Garson and Craft's contract lasted only for a year, others had two- or three-year terms. Some franchise contracts had percentage-based pricing systems rather than weekly flat fees; others resembled state rights in paying a lump sum. Ernest Fenton's two-year contract for distribution in Canada, for instance, specified no weekly charge but required Fenton to pay Triangle 50 percent of all weekly net rental profits plus six cents per foot of positive for each film.[29] In New York, Chicago, and Philadelphia, where Triangle leased its flagship model

theaters and directly profited from ticket sales, the company distributed
to subsequent-run theaters in some zones directly but sold franchises to
cover other zones in the same market. In New York in late 1915, Triangle was distributing directly to Broadway and downtown theaters after
showings at the leased Knickerbocker, while selling franchises to the 81st
Street Theater for the west side of Manhattan (at $750 a week), the Clas-
sic Theater in Washington Heights (at $500 a week), and David Picker's
Berlin Casino in the Bronx (at $700 a week).[30] In Philadelphia, Trian-
gle's own exchange, which centered on first-run showings at the Chestnut
Street opera house, was less than successful in selling the company's program directly. As a result, in December 1915, the company sold a one-
year exclusive franchise for the entire city to Harry Schwalbe's Electric
Theatre Supply Company for $250,000, payable monthly (equivalent to
about $4,800 a week).[31] Triangle's own exchange continued to handle
subsequent-run theaters outside the bounds of the city itself.[32]

Despite being modeled on the state rights system, Triangle implemented several centralizing strategies in its distribution. Given the varying terms of the franchise contracts (one to three years rather than the
five years common in state rights), Triangle's franchise system may not
have been intended as a long-term arrangement—the company may have
been planning to take a more active role in its own distribution after
1916. Indeed, Garson and Craft's Detroit franchise was canceled after
only four months because of a dispute with the company, and Triangle
opened its own exchange in the city.[33] Yet by June 1917 this exchange
had been replaced by another franchise centered on the Orpheum Theater on Lafayette Avenue.[34] Thus, the franchise system proved useful to
the company both in building a national distribution network quickly
and in mitigating the failures of its own distribution management that
would become increasingly apparent in 1916.

Nevertheless, Triangle's franchise contracts imposed certain booking and screening limitations on its franchisees and any subsequent-run
exhibitors to whom they sub-rented. These limitations forced a more programmatic, coordinated, and nationally focused structure on the company's releases than would have been possible under state rights. Like
Paramount, Triangle offered a full-service program and gave franchisees
no option to book films individually. Although none of the contracts in
the Aitken collection explicitly required that its franchisees play Triangle
films exclusively, the program's cost, as well as its booking provisions,
effectively made anything but exclusivity impractical. Crucially, Triangle

prevented its franchisees from extending the runs of its films past a one-week maximum. Garson and Craft's Detroit contract obliged them to play Triangle releases at either the Broadway Strand or the Miles Theater "and not elsewhere, during the first week of each release, and at no other time." Each week's releases—two features and two Keystone shorts—had to be screened either as a full fourteen-reel program or evenly split by showing a particular Griffith / Fine Arts or Ince / New York Motion Picture Company release along with its corresponding Keystone for the first half of the week, and the other feature and short for the second half (the latter was by far the more common arrangement).[35]

Other stipulations guided franchisees' sub-rentals, the contracts for which had to be expressly approved by Triangle at least a week in advance. Prints for subleases came directly from Triangle's own exchanges and were to be returned directly to the same. Interestingly, subleases were generally limited to short runs as well, and always in theaters of at least four hundred seats that charged ten cents admission or more for evening performances. Garson and Craft's contract allowed them thirty-five *one-day* bookings for each Triangle five-reeler—always paired with a corresponding Keystone—and required that all sub-rentals be booked within a four-month window beginning after a thirty-day clearance period from the first run.[36] Thus, though a particular Triangle bill might be in distribution in Detroit for as long as five months, it would stay in any one subsequent-run theater for only a single day. This was not the case in all franchisee contracts; Kemble did not have such a restriction in Long Island, for example. However, Triangle's practice of splitting the weekly program in half suggests that for most subsequent-run theaters around the country, Triangle bills lasted three days at an absolute maximum.

The product-franchising distribution model used by Triangle differed in important respects from the strategies used at Paramount. First, it was much more decentralized in terms of its pricing, particularly for showings beyond the first run. Since 1914, Paramount had structured its pricing based on exhibitors' local markets and the length of the desired run (which could be up to two weeks). As Quinn points out, this pricing model was adapted from contemporary theatrical practice, and it applied to all contracts for Paramount service, whether a franchisee was involved or not.[37] Triangle, by contrast, charged its franchisees a lump sum for their contracts that was based on a calculation of the value of distributing within their larger territory—the same practice used in state rights. Apart from the physical circulation of prints and the ultimate approval or disapproval of sub-run contracts, Triangle's contract did not stipulate the rental fees that franchisees charged for its service.

Second, Triangle conceived of the value of its product fundamentally at the level of the program as a whole rather than at the level of individual films. This attitude manifested itself in the company's restrictions of both the length of its films' runs and the theaters with which it did business. While Paramount was also program oriented, it clearly saw the potential of longer runs early on, as evidenced by the fact that its exhibition contracts had a pricing tier for two-week runs. By the end of 1916, the company was already institutionalizing longer and more flexible runs in its Artcraft service. Triangle runs, by contrast, could not be extended even by Triangle's own franchisees, who had paid hefty prices for the company's program. Triangle's continued emphasis on the weekly release—if at a more expensive scale—was effectively a direct extension of the variety cinema model of the GFC and Mutual. Furthermore, because Triangle effectively forbade theaters with less than four hundred seats from renting its program regardless of run, it intentionally limited the distribution of its program. This practice was in keeping with what Rob King has shown about the company's strategy of appealing to upper-class audiences and tastes.[38] Combined with the minimum ten-cent ticket price, the size requirement effectively restricted the Triangle program to newer and more well-appointed houses. However, Triangle's model also employed some of the contemporary strategies of the national shorts distributors as the company attempted to adapt to the arrival of features. The General Film Company had offered a premium "exclusive service" program of two- and three-reel films in 1913, available only to larger theaters charging a minimum price, that enabled exhibitors to advertise films in advance while preserving the run structure of normal program service.[39] Triangle's program-oriented distribution similarly attempted to concentrate the value of short runs in its franchise contracts.

Finally, Triangle's distribution strategy encouraged a different kind of relationship with its producers than obtained at Paramount. Triangle's payments to its three producers in 1915–1916 were based on flat fees for each production and incorporated a percentage payment of rentals past a certain amount. Triangle's three-year contract with D. W. Griffith, signed in July 1915, stipulated flat payments to Majestic of $40,000 for the negative and twenty-five positive prints of each film, along with 25 percent of the film's gross rentals "after such gross receipts shall have equalled 175 percent of the cost of such photoplay to [Triangle]."[40] Paramount, by contrast, paid its producers through a percentage arrangement—65 percent of the gross after recouping their production advance—giving producers a much greater stake in the success of individual films. On top of that, Triangle's contract with Majestic provided that Triangle could, "from time to time," assign its own high-priced theater actors (such as DeWolf Hopper and Sir Herbert Beerbohm Tree) to the films at a cost to the producer of $1,000 a week. As with its franchising strategy, Triangle imposed specific contractual restrictions on its producers, with the goal of differentiating its films from those of other feature programs.

By attempting to concentrate the value of short runs through the terms of its franchise contracts rather than managing its booking more directly, Triangle was left unable to adapt to the strategy's increasingly apparent problems in 1916–1917. Based on the collected evidence of trade press accounts throughout 1916, which make far more frequent reference to franchises than to Triangle's own exchanges, the latter seem to have been ill equipped to sell and market the company's product locally. Although Triangle was successful in centralizing the physical *circulation* of its films—all domestic franchise contracts routed prints through the company's own exchanges—it was unable to structure its *booking* practices for optimal efficiency and profitability on both local and national scales. In October 1916, Triangle announced in the trade press that it would offer all twenty-one of the key city exchanges it directly owned for sale to "independent exchange men" on the open market.[41] While franchisees had been handling most of the company's booking since the beginning, ostensibly reducing costs, Triangle's own exchange system had been unable to "pay its own keep," according to Kalton Lahue.[42] Triangle's films simply did not bring in enough in rentals to defray the overall costs of distributing them. It is telling that as the company began to flounder, Harry and Roy Aitken thought of their own exchange system not as a crucial part of a strategy to save the company, but as an asset to be liquidated.

Much of the problem stemmed from the relationship between production and distribution at Triangle. The usual explanation of Triangle's failure is production based, emphasizing the company's use of highly paid theatrical stars who lacked appeal for cinemagoers. However, the structural inadequacy of Triangle's franchise distribution system was also an important factor in the studio's downfall. Because Triangle's system encouraged upward pressure on the price of its program as a whole in distribution, its producers were pressured to spend more than was needed to keep the perceived quality of the program high. According to Lahue, "[Triangle's] New York office begged Sennett to spend more money on his comedies and studio manager George W. Stout obliged Kessel and Baumann by raising the salaries of the minor actors."[43] This logic came straight from the received wisdom of the one-reel program: the higher the costs enabled by the distribution program, the higher the average quality of that program. This was a common belief among the program shorts producers in the mid-1910s. Biograph's J. J. Kennedy expressed it in his 1914 claim that under the GFC's system, an increase in the "average quality" of the program tended to lead to more copies (positives) being sold of each film.[44] Triangle's franchise strategy melded this programmatic logic with the state rights system's assumed suitability for marketing premium films at a local level. Harry Aitken, justifying the sale of Triangle's exchanges, claimed in *Moving Picture World* that the company's new system was a "semi-cooperative plan of distribution which permits the return to active participation in film circulation of the independent exchange man": "A man in business for himself will invariably give better service to his customers than the same man as a representative of a distant corporation. Not only the producer and the exchange man, but each individual benefits greatly from extra promotion effort on each film. Moreover, the more prints of a film that are bought by exchanges, the better it is possible to make the pictures."[45]

Aitken's discourse here came directly from the logic of the variety program in its emphasis on the local exchange and on the purchase of additional prints (rather than extended runs) as an index of success, as well as in its overall characterization of film as a mass-market generic good. Even though Triangle's program was made up of expensive features with highly paid stars, the methods used to distribute it were in keeping with this increasingly outdated programmatic logic. Because Triangle service was so expensive for franchisees, the program as a whole— virtually every film—had to be a solid performer in exhibition to justify that cost. Furthermore, Triangle's pricing system, both from franchisees and to producers, was still based largely on contractually locked-in flat-rate payments. As a result, the system encouraged consistently high costs in production, rather than a separation of productions into distinct cost tiers, as had long been the practice at Famous Players.[46] Thus, when Triangle's product proved less of a draw than its franchisees had hoped, many began renegotiating or canceling their contracts in 1916, causing a downward spiral in the average cost of Triangle features. At Triangle's

Fine Arts studio at 4500 Sunset Boulevard, supervised by D. W. Griffith, average negative costs dropped measurably in the second half of 1916, settling at around $20,000 rather than $35,000. This was despite Fine Arts' percentage share of rentals; the production company could theoretically make more money by keeping a portion of Triangle's $40,000 production reimbursement than it could hope to make in new rentals for the program.[47]

These weaknesses in Triangle's franchise model were obvious by the fall of 1916, when the company was forced to change its production and rental policies. That October, in conjunction with the sale of its exchanges, the company allowed its program to be rented on the open market, including exchanges independent from Triangle. This strategy had decidedly mixed results: while it made Triangle's program more widely available to theaters without the intermediary of a franchisee, its high price continued to keep it out of most theaters as a practical matter. Lahue estimates that no more than 15 percent of all the cinema houses in the United States ever played a Triangle film, even in rerelease.[48] Franchisees also reacted negatively to the revelation that the "exclusive service" they had paid for no longer applied. As King shows, they were particularly annoyed when Triangle replaced the two-reel Keystones with one-reelers on the program so that they could be sold separately; this decision further soured their relationships with exhibitors and devalued their franchises.[49] In November, the Aitkens finally sold the company-owned exchanges to W. W. Hodkinson for $600,000, and Hodkinson combined them with his own Superpictures, Inc., to form the Triangle Distributing Corporation. The sale cleared some of the Aitkens' debts and helped keep the producing end of Triangle afloat, but its status as a more centralized distribution company independent from the Aitkens signaled the beginning of the end for Triangle's franchise system.

Franchisees continued to handle Triangle's distribution in some domestic territories at least through the summer of 1917 and in Canada through the end of that year. Well before then, it was clear to producers that Triangle's original distribution concept—the high-cost feature program sold to franchisees for select exhibition venues at advanced prices—was no longer feasible. Triangle's payment system to producers was changed to a pure percentage basis in February 1917, suggesting that the company's cash flow was no longer sufficient to pay Ince and Griffith $40,000 a week. A month later, Griffith ended his association with Triangle, and by the end of June both Ince and Sennett had sold back their stakes in the company. Around the same time, the Aitkens hired Universal's H. O. Davis to economize production.[50] By 1919, the producing side of the company was effectively defunct, though the Aitkens and others would gradually liquidate the remaining elements of the production side of Triangle throughout the early twenties.[51]

Triangle Distributing continued to limp along until early 1920 with the help of William S. Hart and Douglas Fairbanks reissues and other low-cost fare. A vestige of the original franchise system continued to operate there, though less as a coherent strategy of distribution than as a vehicle for personal enrichment. In May 1917, Stephen A. Lynch, who controlled a chain of dozens of theaters in the Southeast, bought out his partner Hodkinson's shares in Triangle Distributing and took control of the company.[52] Lynch's notorious "dynamite gang" tactics had earned him a bad reputation as a Paramount franchisee in 1914 and 1915, and his leadership of Triangle took on a similarly disreputable character.[53] According to Lahue, in the second half of 1917, he not only made his own Southern Enterprises Triangle's franchisee for the Southeast, but replaced the Triangle title cards on the prints he distributed, promoting the films as his own. Lynch also instituted a suspiciously flexible booking system that allowed exhibitors to set aside a brand new Triangle release in favor of a cheaper Triangle reissue, or even a film from another company—Famous Players–Lasky, for instance, which Lynch was heavily invested in, and whose franchise for distribution in the Southeast he continued to hold. Indeed, three years after the dissolution of Triangle Distributing in the spring of 1920, Lynch would sell that FPL franchise, as well as his holdings of around two hundred theaters, back to Zukor.[54]

As Eric Hoyt has argued, any discussion of Triangle's mismanagement at any level of the industry, be it production, distribution, or exhibition, must be couched in the knowledge that the studio's leadership ran it on an essentially fraudulent basis. Its principals frequently transferred Triangle's assets to their own private company, Western Import, enriching both themselves and their associates.[55] Triangle's distribution franchise to Australia, New Zealand, and Tasmania was sold to Hyman Winik, Western Import's manager.[56] We should therefore be careful not to uncritically characterize Triangle's use of the franchise system as merely a well-intentioned strategy to finance high-cost program production. It may have simply been the easiest way for the Aitkens to perpetrate their schemes, and Lynch certainly used it to his own advantage. Nevertheless, the fact that so many franchisees and exhibitors—not to mention three of the industry's leading production companies—bought into Triangle's franchise system in 1915 demonstrates the extent to which it was taken as a possible way forward for programmatic feature production. Despite the system's failure, Triangle's distribution and production policies for features were structured according to the fundamental assumptions of the variety shorts program and the state rights system.

These assumptions were not limited to Triangle—they were intrinsic to the industry's evolving conception of feature marketing through the mid-1910s. At the beginning of the decade, when most films were considered a generic high-turnover good, franchise distribution via the state rights system offered a specialized outlet for marketing individuated feature films of higher value. Even as the new feature companies were obliged to coordinate their releases in various ways according to the demands of programmatic distribution, Triangle's founders clearly believed that distribution franchises were a fast and profitable way to build their national release network. This attitude continued to hold significant sway over the industry well into the teens—at least through 1917, based on the structure of First National at its founding (discussed in the previous chapter). Product franchising did not disappear as a method of film distribution. In the 1920s and 1930s, the state rights system continued to be a key strategy of independent producers and Poverty Row studios. Because these producers worked with low budgets and were typically unable to release their product through the major distributors' networks, they used state rights as a way of bypassing the studio oligopoly and distributing their films nationally. According to Robert Read, the state rights market remained robust through much of the 1920s, bolstering Poverty Row production. Several of the Poverty Row companies of the mid-1920s likely had distribution models not unlike Triangle's, combining their own exchanges in key markets and circulation hubs with franchise arrangements to enable national releasing.[57]

However, for the major distributors, more centralized, mass-market models of distribution would obtain beginning in the late teens. By then, shifts in distribution practice had marginalized the franchise as a viable release strategy for the major distributors. As we saw in chapter 3, the most important was the rise of so-called open booking models that decentered the yearlong release program and emphasized more flexible units of distribution, including the star series and selective booking. By freeing the major distributors from the restricted run and release schedule of the program system, these new forms of block booking encouraged even more attention among the studios to the nationwide marketing of individual films. Because this made showcasing releases in first-run theaters even more important, studios were encouraged to centralize their distribution so that they could exert greater control over rental pricing and release patterns.

Distributor-controlled exchanges and sales offices, combined with these new flexible forms of booking, enabled companies to profitably extend the runs of very successful films and to bury failures quickly in a way that the franchise system simply could not accommodate. Circulation and marketing—equally important but undeniably different as practices of distribution—were increasingly integrated within the local exchange. By the 1920s, the office that sold exhibitors their rental contracts was likely to be the same one that booked their dates and shipped their prints. It was also likely to answer to a controlling central office in New York.

Film Distribution as Mass-Market Merchandising: Centralizing Marketing Control in the Late 1910s

In her book on the development of mass-marketing practices in the late nineteenth and early twentieth centuries, Susan Strasser has argued that the dominant model of retail distribution in the United States around 1918 continued to emphasize wholesalers with substantial power in their local markets: "On a systemic level, the enormous output made possible by the new processes of mass production was being introduced into an unwieldy and old-fashioned distribution system, dominated by still-powerful regional wholesalers who supplied credit and goods to a multitude of small shopkeepers, many with unstable businesses. Merchants did not develop into dealers as fast as manufacturers wanted them to; distribution continued to rest on the personal relationships that they formed with wholesalers' salesmen and with customers in the communities they served."[58] Strasser's description of retail distribution might just as well apply to the film industry as it entered the second half of the 1910s. While producer-distributors increasingly recognized that more centralized control over marketing was a prerequisite for selling program features nationally, feature distribution at many companies continued to rely on regional firms and magnates.

Here, the distinction between the circulatory and marketing functions of distribution should be reemphasized. The circulation of feature programs had been centrally organized to a large extent since their emergence, to ensure the coordination of release dates and runs. Marketing, however—the selling of contracts, enforcement of playdates, and expansion of a distributor's business—was by definition market specific: that is, local. National distributors had to send some local representative to sell their wares to exhibitors, whether that representative was the distributor's employee or a contracted franchisee. National feature distributors increasingly centralized their marketing after 1917, even as the circulation of feature films had been centrally coordinated at some companies since 1914.

Understanding the process by which the centralization of feature marketing occurred requires us to contextualize it within the wider history of mass marketing in the United States. Business historians have characterized the period between 1870 and 1920 as a crucial one for changes in retail product distribution. With the emergence of reliable nationwide rail transport in the 1870s, distribution began to be dominated by regional wholesalers—"jobbers"—who bought goods from manufacturers and brought them to retailers, either through their offices or direct from the manufacturer. Jobbers tended to specialize in a particular category of good, such as dry goods (Marshall Field, Chicago), hardware (Simmons and Company, St. Louis), or drugs (McKesson and Robbins, New York). Alfred Chandler notes that they were some of the earliest "modern multiunit enterprise[s]," with managed sales forces, credit and collections, and purchasing departments.[59]

Beginning in the 1880s, regional jobbers were increasingly replaced by new retail structures that integrated distribution with other economic functions. The department store combined distribution with retail in urban markets, and mail-order houses (Montgomery Ward or Sears, Roebuck, for example) performed a similar function for rural customers. At the other end of the product chain, many manufacturers built their own in-house distribution and marketing networks.[60] What linked these new and more nationally scaled forms of retail was the same administrative structure that had characterized the jobbers: the combination of the physical circulation of goods with the centralized coordination of sales. Strasser points to the Scott Paper Company, which ceased dealing with jobbers in 1909 and began distributing its various product lines directly through an internal sales force. Though costly, this force enabled "promotion by a salesman devoted to Scottissue or Sanitissue, 'not, like the jobber's salesmen, spreading his interest thin over a multitude of things.'"[61] Thus, although regional wholesalers continued to be important entities in retail distribution through the 1910s, there was also recognition, particularly among manufacturers, that the in-house integration of national circulation and marketing was ideal for highly standardized products.

How did these changes in retail distribution influence the film industry? While historians have noted the influence of chain retailers on film exhibition in this period, the majors also modeled many of their distribution practices after those of mass marketers.[62] As we established in chapter 2, manufacturers used brands to package films in distribution through the earliest years of the industry. Janet Staiger has written about studios' use of brand names to foster consumer identification of film through advertising in the 1910s.[63] However, by far the most important of the retail practices imported into the film industry was the hierarchically managed sales force.

As Strasser emphasizes, salaried sales forces were expensive, particularly for firms intending to sell their products nationally. But they were necessary for the young American film industry in the 1910s, as national distribution demanded new forms of marketing and circulation. Throughout that decade, the structure of distributors' sales forces tended to be closely linked to the packages that films were booked in. In the program shorts system, the emphasis on release dates and film throughput—with exhibitors placing standing orders for so many reels of a particular manufacturer's brand every week, irrespective of individual titles—tended to make film sales a relatively straightforward matter of expanding the spread of the distributor's program. In the early years of the full-service feature program, as we have seen, sales costs tended to be outsourced to local franchisees with a high degree of autonomy, with the distributor's centralized costs limited to those of film circulation and national advertising.

Another factor that shaped the role of distributors' sales forces in the 1910s was the corporate relationship between the distributor and its film manufacturers. At the shorts distributors (General Film, Mutual, Universal) and in the early years of feature distribution (Paramount before 1916, Triangle), production companies tended to be independent firms attached to a distributor through a contractual relationship rather than by direct ownership. As a result, distributors' sales forces were faced with the typical marketing problem of defining the product being sold: Was it the individual production company brands (Kay-Bee, Reliance, American), or the distributor's program (Mutual)? Most, unsurprisingly, chose the latter, because what sales forces sold in the field was the program as a totality, even if individual film brands were an important aspect of that sale for exhibitors. However, as was the case when the Aitkens left Mutual, this arrangement could create tension between distributors and production companies—as the latter might have a very different conception than the former about how to position their products in the marketplace. Additionally, production firms might have their own limited sales staff separate from the distributor's, particularly for the purpose of selling features on the state rights market.

As a result of these factors, distributor sales forces modeled on those of true mass marketers that both produced their products and distributed them, such as the Scott Paper Company, were rare in the film industry before 1916. As open-booking models such as the star series began to replace the full-service program and producers began to integrate with distributors, the work of distribution expanded beyond the efficient circulation of films to encompass the marketing of individual stars and films to exhibitors with an increasing array of choices in the film marketplace. The franchise system had allowed distributors to concentrate their in-house staffs on the former, and most of the expense of feature distribution would continue to be circulatory.[64] After 1916, however, sales forces in the film industry became larger, more marketing-oriented, and more specialized.

July 1916 saw Adolph Zukor's takeover of his distributor Paramount from founder W. W. Hodkinson, and the resulting Famous Players–Lasky Corporation was the preeminent example in the late 1910s of a centralized, "rationalized" national distributor with a permanent sales force. The company made much of its sales force in *The Story of the Famous Players–Lasky Corporation*, a 1919 promotional document that reveals several qualities the company foregrounded as attractive to potential investors. One such quality was the sheer scale of FPL's marketing and film circulation capacity: "The Department of Distribution includes a field force of 1241 persons apportioned to twenty-six branch exchanges throughout the United States so located that few motion-picture theaters are distant more than twenty-four hours by express shipment from an exchange. Each exchange has film storage vaults as required by the underwriters, personnel and all equipment necessary to take care of exhibitors in its territory. This field force is supported by a staff of 300 at the home office in New York."[65]

The potential exaggeration of this passage aside, FPL clearly had one of the largest sales forces in the film industry, as well as a national reach. What distinguished Paramount's sales force was not simply brute scale, however, but the degree to which sales personnel collected and used granular data about the markets they worked. These included data about "population and resources, type and seating capacity of every motion picture theater, train service and all else likely to be of service in fixing an equitable rental for films and for serving exhibitors."[66] Since 1914, Paramount had directly tied the price of renting its program to the size of the town a theater was located in, a practice adopted from legitimate theater.[67] This more granular system, however, was sensitive to the prices that exhibitors could pay for films. Sales personnel offered individual theaters tailored prices for star series, blocks, and individual films based on the collected data, which would become a common practice in the marketing of features in the years after the decline of the full-service program.

Pricing to exhibitors under FPL's system was also centrally coordinated in New York to a much greater degree than at the General Film Company, where exhibitors paid fixed prices per reel based on their placement in the run hierarchy. It was also more centralized than in franchising, where prices were generally negotiated at the level of the local franchisee. According to FPL in the 1919 document, "This data is on file at the branch exchange concerned, and also at the home office. From the former source it is passed on to the salesmen together with a thorough understanding of the pictures they have to offer, so that these gentlemen may approach a potential customer with a full knowledge of all conditions likely to affect a bargain." Through a musical metaphor, the company pointedly characterized local theaters and exchanges as literal instruments of New York: "Like an organist at his console, the general manager . . . plays upon the motion-picture theaters of the nation, for every operation of every exchange is absolutely controlled by the home office."[68]

Indeed, for distributors, administrative structures for governing the sales force were at least as important as data about exhibitors. FPL had a preferred word for any kind of administrative control within the company, one that the company's managers repeated ad nauseam in *The Story of the Famous Players–Lasky Corporation* and other publications, as well as in the trade press: "supervision." Supervision often went hand in hand with "system" and "scientific management" as buzzwords of rationalization in early twentieth-century business discourse, but for the specific purposes of FPL's distribution division the term tended to center various strategies of disciplining—in multiple senses of the word—the sales force.

As a matter of positioning the company for capital investment, FPL emphasized the organizational connotation of "discipline," in the sense that the distributor's supervision over sales had a kind of military-grade precision: "Salesmen who handle Paramount-Artcraft pictures are never told, as has been known to happen in more primitive days, to 'go out an' get some business'; on the contrary, they are as carefully rehearsed for each onslaught, and as rigidly restricted to limited objectives as were the gentlemen who accompanied Marshal Foch on his personally conducted tour to the Rhine." This was in part a conscious effort to differentiate Paramount from the wider distribution market, which was quite unsettled in the late teens and early twenties. As a matter of actual practice, however, FPL disciplined its sales force in the Foucauldian sense, through long-standing sales management strategies. These strategies included setting quotas for new and settled exhibition contracts, awarding bonuses for sales past a certain threshold, and instituting standardized systems for reporting results to a central authority. Continuing the musical metaphor, FPL asserted, in *The Story of the Famous Players–Lasky Corporation*, that "one of the methods devised for keeping salesmen keyed up to concert pitch is a system of duplicate daily reports to general headquarters in New York, as well as to the branch exchange. Thus, even while in uttermost Dismalburg, the salesman is made to feel that the sleepless eye of the home office is always upon him."[69]

This surveillance-based approach to marketing control exposed the true goal of supervision in FPL's distribution division after 1916: sell as many contracts for as many films to as many theaters as possible. Though such an approach may seem unsurprising, it was a shift from the general philosophy behind feature distribution at other companies in the early and mid-teens. While state rights and the franchise system had emphasized the differentiated qualities of the feature through high rentals, select exhibition spaces, and exclusivity, Paramount sold its features as merchandise for the mass market. Wide releases and exhibitor-centered pricing maximized the returns of each individual film by booking it as widely as possible, even in venues of marginal profitability. The company thus recognized that an integrated sales force could sell features on a truly national scale, not just to the upscale trade of legitimate theaters and opera houses.

The Internal House Organ as a Sales Supervision Practice

Another sales management practice that centralized producer-distributors imported from mass marketing in the 1910s was the internal house publication. Company publications, published both internally for a company's workers and externally to the wider trade, were a major part of merchandising and retail in the early twentieth century. Effectively all national retail firms published internal house organs for their sales forces and distributed them regularly to their field offices by the late teens, with a particular burgeoning of the form in the years after World War I. A 1921 survey of five hundred US companies using internal publications found that 71 percent of them began publishing their house organs between 1917 and 1920.[70] The decreasing cost of duplicating machines made them a popular management strategy even for smaller firms, and how-to guides for writing and publishing internal publications proliferated in this period.[71]

Externally oriented house publications, including Mutual's *Reel Life* and *The Universal Weekly*, had been published in the film industry since the one-reel period. Even feature producers releasing via state rights occasionally published them; Frank J. Seng's national distribution campaign for *Parentage* (Hobart Henley, 1917) involved the publication of a six-month run of a house organ titled *The Parentage Messenger*, which was directly mailed to state rights firms.[72] External house publications were thus in part an extension of the practices of mail-order retailers into film marketing. Although such publications have long been familiar to film historians, little has been written about the industry's use of internal magazines intended for consumption only by studio employees. By 1920, most of the major producer-distributors were releasing internal publications in addition to their trade journals, including Famous Players–Lasky (*Paramount Pep*), Fox (*Fox Folks*), and Selznick (*The Brain Exchange*). Internal house publications could be aimed at any category of employee; Goldwyn's *Studio Skeleton*, for example, was produced primarily for production workers at its Culver City plant ("Get it at the Main Gate; contributions expected from everyone").[73] The internal magazines that were intended for workers in distribution were among the most important for studio management, as they served as a regular, public, and top-down channel of communication between the home office and the sales force working at local company exchanges.

Business history scholar JoAnne Yates has outlined the primary functions of internal house organs during this period: humanizing an otherwise impersonal workplace, educating employees, building morale, and communicating management's position.[74] Film distributors' internal publications performed these functions in addition to the more specific work of sales management. By both praising and shaming individual exchanges—and sometimes individual employees—according to various company-designed measures of sales effectiveness, distributors disciplined the behavior of their sales forces in an internal forum. For contemporary managers, this was a core function of these types of publications: "The Internal House Organ increases sales by stimulating employes [*sic*] to greater effort in the firm's behalf, no matter what line of work the employe is engaged in. He may be in the unproductive class, as the manufacturer divides his working forces, but by encouraging team-work and loyalty, greater business is bound to result."[75]

An in-depth look at *The Brain Exchange*, the internal publication of the Selznick Organization's distribution division, shows these functions at work at a centralized producer-distributor. The *Exchange* was published weekly at Selznick from 1919 until at least October 1922. In the spring of 1919, Lewis Selznick wrested control of his company back from Adolph Zukor, who had owned a half stake in it since 1917. Selznick went on to operate Selznick Pictures until it went bankrupt in 1923. The company's distribution arm was technically divided into separate exchange networks, known as Republic and Select, through the 1919–1920 season, after which they were consolidated into a single entity, Select. For all practical purposes they were part of the same company, and the *Exchange* made little distinction between the two. The publication was housed in Selznick's publicity department with a succession of editors at the helm, including John Cutting, Randolph Bartlett, Watt Parker, and Tamar Lane.

Like many film industry publications of the period, much of *The Brain Exchange* is an esoteric read. Its pages abound with sales advice to exchanges about star series (the dominant form of distribution at Selznick during this period), pieces about exhibitors' conventions and executive promotions, and weekly aphorisms dubiously credited to Lewis Selznick himself. However, the magazine was more consistent than most in its attempts to humanize the Selznick Organization as a workplace. Even the dourest of "shop papers" included some lighthearted material, whether articles about employees' personal lives and interests, news about marriages and babies, cartoons and caricatures, jokes, or bits of comic verse.

This kind of content was considered especially important for house organs oriented toward sales forces, because sales personnel were often on the road: "Alone in his territory, the salesman ordinarily knows little as to what is going on at 'home' and among the other 'boys,' and it should be part of the mission of the house organ to keep him informed. . . . If that little dream of a stenographer, Lilly Jones, has plunged the office into gloom by suddenly leaving to get married, the salesmen want to 'gloom' with the office force, too."[76] House organs almost always imagined a male employee-reader, and the *Exchange* was no different—despite the fact that Select employed hundreds of women, who worked as sales representatives, bookers, film inspectors, and clerks. Women made up half of the office staff at many exchanges. Profiles of "girl employees" and their interests were a common feature of the magazine ("Girls! Send in Your Pictures to the Editor").[77] Sexism aside, this kind of material was the primary appeal of *The Brain Exchange* for ordinary distribution workers, to the extent that poor handling of it by the publication's editor was likely to result in swift removal. In May 1921, newly minted editor Randolph Bartlett threatened to make the *Exchange* a "straight business sheet," complaining that not enough exchanges were sending in news. He warned that "if you would rather know that Goldie Gezink, the blonde stenographer, had her toenails trimmed last week, than keep in touch with policies and facts concerning the organization, drop a line to L. J. and possibly he can fix it for you."[78] Bartlett was replaced by the end of the month.

Though he perhaps lacked the finesse to succeed as editor, Bartlett had a point. Although lighter material was never lacking in its pages, the *Exchange*'s primary purpose as a tool of sales management was to discipline the practices of Selznick exchanges and distribution workers, including exchange managers, bookers, and sales personnel. The most frequent and visible manifestation of this was the "Honor List" published at the end of each week's issue, which ranked Selznick's local exchanges, and eventually individual managers and salesmen, from best to worst in order of various quantitative measures of effectiveness. From late 1919 to May 1921, the Honor List ranked exchange offices according to three categories: Rental Efficiency, Collection Efficiency, and Operating Cost Efficiency. The publication explained the various categories as functions of the branch's rentals and costs in relation to its sales quota, giving them the appearance of objective "scientific measurements."[79] However, they were almost certainly manipulated by the Selznick home office to encourage exchanges to improve their overall performance, by either increasing rentals or decreasing costs. The quotas upon which rental and operating cost efficiency were based were completely arbitrary and could be set by the home office at any desired level of reasonableness.

Furthermore, the Honor Lists never published actual dollar amounts, instead rewarding exchanges with abstract percentage scores based on a 1,000-point scale. This method of calculating the scores obscured the actual rental income being brought in, enabling Selznick to encourage even the most profitable exchanges to increase their performance, by giving them a lower standing on a given week's Honor List. The home office had good reason not to publish rental and collections numbers that were too accurate, as such data might be used by competitors. As one contemporary how-to guide advised, "Copies of your house organ will fall into hands other than those of your salesmen, so for this reason the information given cannot be too confidential."[80]

In addition to being a general signal of week-to-week performance, the Honor Lists provided a convenient forum for Selznick to encourage participation in sales contests, another strategy that came from retail merchandising. Sales contests took many forms, and their ultimate goal was not to reward the best salesperson, but to increase the performance of all sales personnel working for the company. A common strategy was for firms to divide their sales force into separate levels of ability, ostensibly encouraging higher performance from even the weakest salespeople. Another model was to split the sales force into teams and pit them against one another to increase sales for the company as a whole; the basic structure of distributors' exchange networks was well suited to this approach.[81] In March 1921, as the recession of 1920–1921 began to hit the wider industry with force, Selznick was faced with a significant decline in the number of fulfilled rental contracts. In response, the company organized an eight-week collections contest among all Select exchanges, with the *Exchange* serving as the contest's primary arbiter and cheerleader. The top ten exchanges would share a total of $5,000 in prize money, with the leader getting $1,500. As usual, the ranking was determined by a home office quota, and the *Exchange* promised that President Selznick would keep in "personal touch" with each branch: "Each night he will check up the returns as they come in and the laggards may expect to receive gentle reminders that they are running below form."[82]

The *Exchange*'s coverage of this contest instantiates the variety of disciplinary tones and approaches taken by the magazine in assessing sales performance. In general, examples of praise for good performance tended to outnumber instances of shaming, but many issues did take exchanges and individual salespeople to task. When it thought such an approach necessary, the magazine's default position tended to be one of playful chiding: "The week of August 5, Old Man New Haven batted out some contracts, while Charlotte was packing up her duds for a bush league berth. . . . Charlotte is still peacefully asleep!"[83] This chummy voice was typical; George Frederick Wilson's how-to book on internal house publications advised that "courtesy, promptness, service, etc., should be preached in the house organ, but these are best effective when sugar coated."[84] However, the *Exchange* could also be brutal, particularly in cases of perceived incompetence. One dressing-down of a Kansas City salesman had a particularly nasty and antisemitic quality: "H. S. Stultz—our Irish salesman (from Jerusalem)—has had honorary membership conferred upon him in the Local Order of Dumb Bells, for his scrupulous attention in getting exhibitors' signatures on the wrong line of contracts."[85]

While this disciplinary strategy was primarily aimed at underperformers, it could also be deployed against over-promisers and "big talkers." After the manager of Select's St. Louis exchange, a Mr. Fox, confidently wired Selznick's vice president, Sam E. Morris, to suggest that he "watch our speed" in selling the special *The Greatest Love*, the *Exchange* offered this reply: "Take a look at the special chart on page 7 of last week's issue, Mr. Fox. What has happened to your speed?"[86] Even otherwise effective sellers who had a poor week could fall victim to public embarrassment on the magazine's pages. "What has happened to the Boston twins, Shafer and Gruber, who, after keeping among the elect for five weeks, are now discovered opposite numbers 73 and 74? And the altitude achieved by Harter of Pittsburgh last week, when he edged in as 10, seems to have caused some sort of dizziness, for he has tumbled to the bottom."[87] Exchanges could also be called out for reasons besides sales performance, such as insufficient communication with the home office or with *The Exchange* itself ("Los Angeles!! San Francisco!! Denver!! Salt Lake!! *PLEASE WRITE*").[88]

Not all the communication in *The Brain Exchange* was top-down—much of the paper's exchange news and social content was provided by the exchanges themselves, and letters to the editor from employees were published in a weekly section when it suited management's purposes. Although sales personnel or clerks were occasionally published, most of the letters approved for the *Exchange* were from exchange managers or other more senior workers looking to advance their careers. The paper printed a signed letter from the aforementioned Mr. Fox and his staff at the St. Louis exchange, addressed to Lewis Selznick himself, vowing that they would win the spring 1921 collections contest.[89] The letter certainly worked toward the typical house organ goal of building company morale, but it also offered a particular articulation of the role of the exchange in the modern production-distribution firm: as a dedicated, loyal dealer of its company's films rather than a coequal partner in circulation. At the same time, the letter served the home office's interest in paying lip service to the idea that the magazine was a forum for the whole company, employees included, instead of the management tool that it was.

Demanding regular communication from branches served another important management function: asserting the centralized control of the New York home office over the local branches. This function was typically performed in the context of standardizing actual distribution practice, as this November 1920 request from the home office printed in the *Exchange* indicates:

> President Lewis J. Selznick, General Manager Sam E. Morris and the Home Office executives are extremely gratified to learn that the men in the field have been busy with their thinking apparatus lately to such an extent that innumerable sales promotion and operating cost ideas have been circulated throughout the organization. They do not, however, believe that the policy of sending these from one branch to another without first forwarding them to the executive offices to be advisable.
>
> It is believed that all such ideas should be forwarded to the home office and then if they have sufficient merit they will be relayed to every branch.[90]

Communication between branches was one of the central goals of the *Exchange*, but not when such communication might hamper the goals of the New York office. Controlled lines of communication and authority were essential aspects of modern mass merchandising, and the fact that an appeal for upward rather than lateral communication was published in the *Exchange* suggests that certain vestiges of an older distribution environment—when local exchanges had greater freedom to tailor their practices to the local market and shared ideas and resources with their peers—remained at Selznick in the early 1920s.

Another recurring space in the paper, the "Barter Column," offers insight into the role *The Brain Exchange* played as a contested channel of communication *between* exchanges rather than simply from the home office on down. The Barter Column was effectively a want ad section; branches needing a particular film could request it there, while those with unneeded or unrented prints could place them on offer. In addition to film, branches could exchange advertising matter ("paper") or office fixtures.[91] Because Selznick had an interest in keeping prints in constant circulation for as long as they would rent ("Prints Earn Only When They Work"), the Barter Column served a valuable income-generating function.[92] Before mid-1922, Select exchanges essentially used the space to initiate communication with each other, shipping any needed prints directly among themselves. However, by August of that year, the *Exchange* had stopped printing ads from exchanges in the Barter Column and instead published simple lists of wanted and needed films. Exchanges now shipped needed films to a central point of distribution in New York, and the home office sent them back to where they were needed.

Selznick's changes to the Barter Column were indicative of rapidly centralizing distribution structures among the major studios. For the most part, exchanges were no longer film jobbers or independent franchisees; they were local marketing representatives of the New York office. This required a fundamental shift in distributors' conceptions of the primary product they sold, feature films, away from the prestigious connotations of the mid-teens and toward the assumption that all features—from specials to programmers—were mass-market merchandise. Merchandise might be advertised and branded in various ways to differentiate it, but the profitability of film distribution lay in its mass salability through a centralized marketing structure. Selznick vice president Sam E. Morris explicitly made this case in an article printed in the *Exchange* in August 1921, extolling the virtues of the star series:

> Pictures have developed a more general appeal in the fifteen or twenty years which they have been a commercial proposition than any other form of similar entertainment. . . . To me this is convincing that the motion picture exhibitor cannot look to the "showman" for all his guidance. He comes pretty nearly

[to] being a merchant and must use at least an approach to merchandising methods if he hopes to make any lasting success of his business. . . . [T]he growing popularity of the star series plan of motion picture distribution illustrates my point. It is a merchandising—not a showmanship—idea that lasting success depends upon a vender identifying himself in the public mind as a man who is selling a line of goods which can always be depended upon to satisfy a certain proportion of the people in the community.[93]

Morris's argument was that the now feature-centered film industry had grown beyond an idiosyncratic reliance on novelty, spectacle, and "big attractions" sold by "specialized effort"; these were, for Morris, strategies based in live-theatrical show business rather than retail. Cinemagoers—and the exhibitors who catered to them—now thought of feature films as consistently-turned-over programmatic merchandise and would buy certain brands of it dependably, just as they would clothing, soap, or toilet tissue. Put in Strasser's terms, cinemagoers were now consumers. For distributors, this did not mean giving up the "big attraction" or "showmanship," nor did it mean a return to the program short. But it did mean strategic marketing of branded packages of film—star series, at Selznick—across a national market. Certain stars might sell better than others in certain territories, but the centralized merchandising of the entire product line across the country by disciplined local exchanges evened out these differences, ensuring the profitability of the distribution slate as a whole. *The Brain Exchange* and other house organs served as active instruments of that merchandising strategy, shaming employees and setting semi-public sales expectations while encouraging the centralization of corporate policy in the New York home office.

As it turned out, the star series that Morris touted, and that Select tended to use in packaging its films, was in its waning days. Problems in the relationship between distributors and exhibitors that had been growing since the decline of the program system were coming to a head. While the model of mass merchandising had created an organized market for feature distribution in a spatial sense, significant temporal problems had yet to be solved. In the next chapter, we will see how distributors solved those problems and, in the process, took control of the screen time they had always assumed belonged to them.

5 TIME

The Battle for Playdates

*Temporally Controlling the Distribution Business,
1921–1925*

The trend among distributors of renting ever more diverse packages of
programming—star series, sub-programs, individual films—to exhibitors
for a greater variety of run durations meant that by the early 1920s, the
national film distribution market was increasingly defined by a hodgepodge of booking arrangements. Long-standing practices were causing
problems in both distribution and production, including unsustainable
rental prices and an oversupply of films. By far the most widespread of
these problems was overbooking and underplaying on the part of exhibitors. It was very common for theaters to book much more product than
they played during this period, not only to deny competing houses promising titles, but also as insurance against unexpected scheduling changes,
delivery failures, or underperformance by a particular feature or star.
These problems in booking practice were exacerbated by a wider recession in the American economy that began to hit the film industry in early
1921. As a result, distributors began to adopt new strategies. Over the
course of 1921–1922 and the release seasons that followed, the industry
adopted three new strategies for systematizing feature distribution.

The first strategy, distribution blocks, organized a distributor's entire slate into temporally defined subsections of a distributor's program for the year. This system was the mature form of what scholars have traditionally referred to simply as "block booking," and it refined the booking packages distributors used in ways that helped to mitigate the disadvantages of the program and star series. Blocks varied in size but were offered successively to exhibitors over the course of the release season. In basic form, this was the version of block booking that would structure distribution in American cinema for the next twenty-five years. While Paramount used block booking as early as 1920–1921, the wider industry did not settle on it as a distribution strategy until 1923–1924. Distribution blocks worked in concert with the second strategy, uniform contract terms to exhibitors, to give distributors an extensive measure of control over theaters' playdates. These terms were negotiated by the industry's new trade association, the Motion Picture Producers and Distributors of America (MPPDA), in a successful campaign to implement a Uniform Exhibition Contract in 1923.

Finally, distributors began to temporally manage their releases more systematically through run exhibition—the playing of films for extended runs before they entered the normal release system.[1] By the 1920s, run exhibition included the direct "prerelease" of films to Broadway theaters, often forgoing an extensive nationwide roadshow. By prereleasing certain films in legitimate theaters or dedicated picture houses, distributors could maximize their value before they entered the regular distribution system.

These methods maximized distributors' control over film pricing and circulation through the temporal management of feature distribution. Temporal management practices gave distributors even more flexibility to determine and act on a film's actual value in exhibition. Unlike earlier models of distribution, which had determined this value based on the newness of films, or on a declared amount estimated from past experience (exhibition value), strategies of temporal management were designed according to the understanding that for certain films, exhibition value could actually grow during a film's run. Because a film's popularity could not necessarily be predicted, temporal control over playing time became an important way for distributors to extract value from the films they released while managing the risks of that release.

In the first part of this chapter I situate these strategies of temporal management as responses to a specific problem in distribution: overbooking. My account of this problem draws on two bodies of evidence that articulated different industry perspectives on overbooking.

The first of these sources, the trade press, tended to frame the unsettled distribution market as a threat to the interests of the major producer-distributors, although exhibitor views were also included to an extent. This trade press evidence illuminates the logic of distributors' conduct during the early 1920s. The second body of evidence is the correspondence of Freeport, Illinois, exhibitor Thomas Watson, who operated the three-hundred-seat Superba Theatre in the early 1920s.[2] Watson's pugnacious and often overtly anti-Semitic back-and-forth with companies such as Fox, Metro, Paramount, and Pathé suggests that distributors' frequent complaints that exhibitors were overbooking and not playing contracted films were not unfounded. Watson's correspondence also provides insight into the logic of exhibitor overbuying, which was itself partially driven by distributor conduct.

In the second part of the chapter I examine the particular distribution and production strategies of a single company, Paramount, as a specific instance of how distributors navigated the changes occurring in the early 1920s. Based on a combination of trade press coverage, testimony given by various witnesses at the company's trial before the Federal Trade Commission, and internal company correspondence, I offer Paramount as a case study of temporal distribution and production management as it stood among the major producer-distributors in the first half of the 1920s. Received historiography on the company tends to make much of the company's control of first-run theaters, but Paramount's domination of exhibitors' playdates through block booking, uniform contracting, and prereleases was a co-requisite to that control. Famous Players–Lasky instituted changes in production that dovetailed with these distribution strategies, including a temporally focused system of production control based on coordinated scheduling and a "supervisor" system of unit production.

These production and distribution strategies went beyond the logic of the program system. They did not simply prioritize keeping feature and distribution costs down; rather, they more effectively synchronized production and distribution through strategies of temporal management. Block booking, like the program system, reserved playdates for a particular distributor's films—but unlike the program, it did not lock features into a specific run pattern far in advance of their release. Instead, it gave distributors much greater control over when to release individual features to certain theaters, allowing those films to live up to their earning potential in distribution. Temporally defined distribution blocks, aided by the provisions of the Uniform Exhibition Contract, enabled distributors to more easily extend the runs of successful films in prerelease and first-run theaters.

This flexibility in distribution helped to produce flexibility in production. Doing away with the explicitly tiered format of the star series and other branded packages reduced the long-standing emphasis among distributors on releasing a reliable program of consistent quality. Instead, block booking gave distributors greater flexibility to produce films of mixed quality, and to distribute those films more profitably in tied packages. Because the block system retained selective booking's ability to negotiate the pricing of individual features within a block, production could be planned according to granular and flexible *pricing* tiers rather than broad and inflexible *distribution* tiers, mitigating the risks of all levels of production. Production could now be more easily tailored to the shifting tastes of audiences across a particular release season, which reduced the dependence on consistently strong output from any one star or director in distribution slates. For distributors, block booking essentially solved the wholesale pricing problems of the program system—its selling of "gold, silver, brass and tin at the same price," as Selznick had put it in 1916—by combining the best features of programmatic distribution with the profit potential and pricing advantages of selective booking.[3]

Overbuying and Its Effects: The Unsettled Distribution Market of the Early 1920s

Understanding overbuying requires a brief overview of the process of film booking, which in practice occurred in two separate stages during this period. The first was the booking itself, which in the years of the program, series, and selective booking generally took place in the late spring, three or four months before the beginning of the subsequent release season in September. Depending on the distributor and exhibitor, another round of booking might occur in the fall, for spring and summer releases. After negotiating the exact programs, series, blocks, or films to be rented, along with the price of the rentals and the payment of any advance deposits, exhibitors signed a contract with a distributor, either after a visit from a sales representative or by going to a local exchange directly. It was at this stage that the exhibitor effectively promised the distributor a certain portion of playing time.

The second stage, playdate determination ("dating"), was an ongoing process that involved the provision of the exact playdates for the individual films on a rental contract. Exhibition contracts generally reserved the distributor's right to dictate an exhibitor's playdates at any point after the signing of the contract; in practice, however, dating was a somewhat flexible process in the early 1920s. This was because there was remarkably little certainty about the temporal availability of a particular film or playdate at the initial stage of booking.[4] A variety of contingencies could arise: an exhibitor might pick up a spot booking for a particular playdate, or the distributor might face an unexpected delay in the release of a film. The initial contract might end up being canceled by either party. As a result, distributors often allowed exhibitors to put off the confirmation of playdates until just a few weeks before a film's release date. As a film's release date approached, distributors sent exhibitors program bills or other reminders to set their playdates. In the October 1921 example of a dating form Fox sent to Thomas Watson, the pictures Watson had played are crossed out, those with agreed-upon playdates are dated accordingly, and those for which Fox has requested dates are checked (figure 5.1). In the dating stage, the distributor essentially collected on the exhibitor's promise of playing time. Ideally, that collection went smoothly, with the exhibitor supplying a playdate, paying the rental a week in advance, and accepting the film shipment.

In practice, however, exhibitors often refused to do some or all of these things because they had contracted for more films than they could actually play. The most common strategy that overbooked exhibitors employed was to delay the playdate on a particular film ("setting it out," or "holding it back," in booking argot) until a later point in time when an alternate playdate might open up. This was a less-than-ideal situation, especially if a first-run exhibitor held back a film, because it upset the booking schedules of all subsequent runs. Nevertheless, distributors often accepted the practice. The same amount of rental money was (in principle) due to them regardless of when the film played, and in markets dominated by a single powerful exhibitor, accepting such delays was often necessary for distributors wishing to maintain access to the market.[5]

The problem arose when delayed playdates began to pile up past the point where they could be reasonably carried out within the term of the contract, or when exhibitors simply refused to give distributors playdates in the first place. Both conditions meant that exhibitors were not paying the balance of their unplayed rentals, depriving distributors of expected

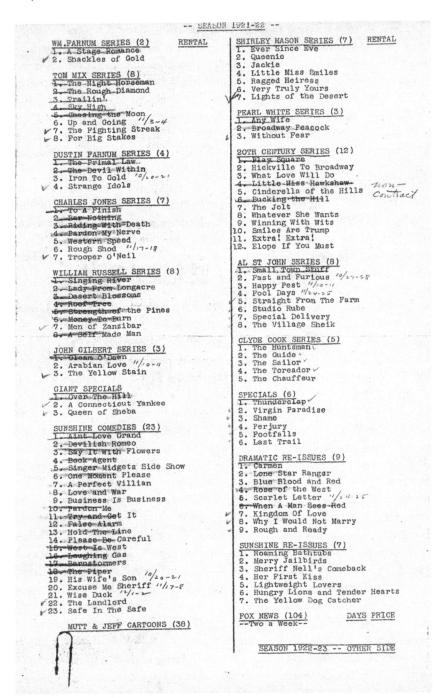

-- SEASON 1921-22 --

WM.FARNUM SERIES (2)   RENTAL
1. A Stage Romance
2. Shackles of Gold

TOM MIX SERIES (8)
1. The Night Horseman
2. The Rough Diamond
3. Trailin'
4. Sky High
5. Chasing the Moon
6. Up and Going 11/3-4
7. The Fighting Streak
8. For Big Stakes

DUSTIN FARNUM SERIES (4)
1. The Primal Law
2. The Devil Within
3. Iron To Gold 10/20-21
4. Strange Idols

CHARLES JONES SERIES (7)
1. To A Finish
2. Bar Nothing
3. Riding With Death
4. Pardon My Nerve
5. Western Speed
6. Rough Shod 11/17-18
7. Trooper O'Neil

WILLIAM RUSSELL SERIES (8)
1. Singing River
2. Lady From Longacre
3. Desert Blossoms
4. Roof Tree
5. Strength of the Pines
6. Money To Burn
7. Men of Zanzibar
8. A Self Made Man

JOHN GILBERT SERIES (3)
1. Gleam O' Dawn
2. Arabian Love 11/10-11
3. The Yellow Stain

GIANT SPECIALS
1. Over The Hill
2. A Connecticut Yankee
3. Queen of Sheba

SUNSHINE COMEDIES (23)
1. Aint Love Grand
2. Devilish Romeo
3. Say It With Flowers
4. Book Agent
5. Singer Midgets Side Show
6. One Moment Please
7. A Perfect Villian
8. Love and War
9. Business Is Business
10. Pardon Me
11. Try and Get It
12. False Alarm
13. Hold The Line
14. Please Be Careful
15. West Is West
16. Laughing Gas
17. Barnstormers
18. The Piper
19. His Wife's Son 10/20-21
20. Excuse Me Sheriff 11/17-8
21. Wise Duck 12/1-2
22. The Landlord
23. Safe In The Safe

MUTT & JEFF CARTOONS (38)

SHIRLEY MASON SERIES (7)   RENTAL
1. Ever Since Eve
2. Queenie
3. Jackie
4. Little Miss Smiles
5. Ragged Heiress
6. Very Truly Yours
7. Lights of the Desert

PEARL WHITE SERIES (3)
1. Any Wife
2. Broadway Peacock
3. Without Fear

20TH CENTURY SERIES (12)
1. Play Square
2. Hickville To Broadway
3. What Love Will Do
4. Little Miss Hawkshaw   non-
5. Cinderella of the Hills Contract
6. Bucking the Hill
7. The Jolt
8. Whatever She Wants
9. Winning With Wits
10. Smiles Are Trump
11. Extra! Extra!
12. Elope If You Must

AL ST JOHN SERIES (8)
1. Small Town Stuff
2. Fast and Furious 10/27-28
3. Happy Pest 11/10-11
4. Fool Days 11/24-25
5. Straight From The Farm
6. Studio Rube
7. Special Delivery
8. The Village Sheik

CLYDE COOK SERIES (5)
1. The Huntsman
2. The Guide
3. The Sailor
4. The Toreador
5. The Chauffeur

SPECIALS (6)
1. Thunderclap
2. Virgin Paradise
3. Shame
4. Perjury
5. Footfalls
6. Last Trail

DRAMATIC RE-ISSUES (9)
1. Carmen
2. Lone Star Ranger
3. Blue Blood and Red
4. Rose of the West
5. Scarlet Letter 1/14-15
6. When A Man Sees Red
7. Kingdom Of Love
8. Why I Would Not Marry
9. Rough and Ready

SUNSHINE RE-ISSUES (7)
1. Roaming Bathtubs
2. Merry Jailbirds
3. Sheriff Nell's Comeback
4. Her First Kiss
5. Lightweight Lovers
6. Hungry Lions and Tender Hearts
7. The Yellow Dog Catcher

FOX NEWS (104)   DAYS PRICE
--Two a Week--

SEASON 1922-23 -- OTHER SIDE

Figure 5.1. *Fox Dating Form, 1921. Wisconsin Historical Society, WHI-157858. "Season 1920-21," ca. October 1921, Box 8, Folder 20.*

income. In either case, distributors usually exercised their right to dictate a film's playdate, whether that date was open in an exhibitor's schedule or not. Distributors who chose to do this typically sent the film to the exhibitor cash-on-delivery (a practice imported from mail-order merchandising). The COD was an escalation, because it forced the exhibitor to either accept the film and pay the rental at the time of the film's delivery or refuse the film outright, in violation of the terms of the exhibition contract.

Any point along the chain of actions prompted by overbuying might result in a lawsuit, which exacerbated the wider climate of distrust between distributors and exhibitors. Such conflicts led to the rise of local exhibitor relations boards in the 1910s. Because these boards provided a mechanism for distributors and exhibitors to settle contract disputes over playdate refusal or other symptoms of overbuying through arbitration instead of resorting to expensive legal proceedings, they were generally favored (and often controlled) by distributors. Arbitration was a key development in film distribution in the late 1910s. Kia Afra notes that as early as 1916, distributors established Film Boards of Trade that acted in conjunction with a collections agency, the Hoy Reporting Service, to protect their interests against default from broken exhibition contracts. The so-called Film Boards would later be replaced by six-person arbitration boards that ostensibly represented both distributors and exhibitors on an equal basis, although Afra rightly notes that they continued to overwhelmingly favor distributors.[6] For Afra, arbitration's fundamental purpose was to be an instrument of industrial collusion and vertical integration: "Standardizing practices in film distribution was essential at a time when the MPPDA members were investing more and more in their theatrical divisions."[7]

Richard Maltby examines arbitration in the more specific context of the problems caused by overbooking. He argues that the MPPDA's establishment, as well as its 1923 adoption of the Uniform Exhibition Contract, was meant to address the "reputational hazard" posed by "the extreme contractual instability of the distribution industry." Citing statistics given by Will Hays in a 1929 lecture on arbitration, Maltby claims that "in 1920 and 1921, as many as 35 or 40 percent of pictures contracted for were not played and therefore not paid, so that [quoting Hays] 'the producer with $10 million worth of orders on his books did not know whether they might result in $5 million or $6 million worth of completed transactions.'"[8] Of course, we should be skeptical of these numbers, given that they originate from the producer-distributors' chief lobbyist—and in the context of an explicit argument for exhibitor arbitration. A more likely figure was cited by Robert Swaine, Paramount's lawyer at the Federal Trade Commission trial, who claimed that 20 percent of the contracts made with exhibitors in nine Famous Players–Lasky exchanges for the 1920–1921, 1921–1922, and 1922–1923 seasons went unplayed.[9] According to L. E. Harrington, the Dallas exchange manager for the distributor Film Booking Offices, 90 percent of all the exhibitors in the Southeast overbooked in the early 1920s.[10]

More important than the precise frequency of overbooking—which was clearly high from distributors' perspective—are the actual booking practices used by distributors and exhibitors in the early 1920s that encouraged overbuying in the first place. Afra and Maltby focus on overbuying as a problem in exhibition that gave rise to producer-distributors' attempts to control the industry through arbitration, collusion, and vertical integration. If we attend to overbuying as a symptom of specifically temporal problems in feature distribution, however, a slightly different picture emerges. As William A. Johnston pointed out in *Motion Picture News* in 1922, overbuying was not purely the fault of unscrupulous exhibitors, nor was it necessarily discouraged by distributors.[11] Rather, it actually benefited both the distributor and the exhibitor in the short term, which is one reason why distributors were slow to combat it. Exhibitors had a strong incentive to fill their playing time with the best product quickly, before their competitors gained access to it. Distributors, for their part, had always encouraged their sales representatives and exchange managers to sell aggressively, not only to meet sales quotas, but also to dominate screens with their product—and reach audiences before their competitors did.[12] The fevered energy of the national distribution market for cinema in the early 1920s was essentially a scaled-up version of the "excited gesticulation" of the negotiations between agents and bookers on the floor of vaudeville's United Booking Offices; the only difference was that the distributors could not all work under the same roof to coordinate the tens of thousands of film rental contracts signed across the nation every season.

Though overbuying certainly occurred under the program system in the 1910s, it was less of a problem then than it became in the 1920s. As smaller packages of distribution, such as the star series and individual films, became more common at the end of the 1910s, and average run lengths increased, distributors and exhibitors had more leeway in their mutual struggle for control of the one resource in film distribution that was available in strictly limited quantity: exhibitors' playdates. Longer runs not only increased the profitability of individual films in distribution, but also made feature production much more speculative, because of increased competition for playing time. Overbuying—or, as exhibitors called it, overselling—was the result, and it caused substantial unpredictability in the distribution market. Distributors responded to this unpredictability by reworking film booking and packaging in a fundamental way. Understanding the logic of that reworking requires a deeper examination of the causes and effects of overbuying in the early 1920s.

The year 1921 saw constant warnings in the trade press that overbuying was making the distribution market increasingly unpredictable.[13] Distributors' in-house publications began emphasizing to exhibitors the importance of providing timely playdates. Over the course of the 1921–1922 season, the *Associated First National Franchise*, a periodical published by First National and aimed at exhibitors, contained frequent appeals from company founder J. D. Williams on the subject: "Remember that First National Pictures are your pictures. You own them. You've got to set in play dates and play them."[14] Every issue of the paper also listed the distributor's releases with a proclamation: "An UNPLAYED Picture is an Unwelcome Guest at Your Table of Dividends. How Much Do You Owe Yourself in Delayed Dates on This List of Features?"[15] Selznick's *Brain Exchange* expressed the problem to workers selling its special *The Greatest Love* (Henry Kolker, 1920) by illustrating the large disparity between the number of contracts signed for the film and the number of contracts with paid playdates (figures 5.2.1 and 5.2.2).

First National and Selznick were not the only distributors facing overbuying from exhibitors. *Exhibitors Herald* publisher Martin Quigley, responding to reports that many producers were planning to shut down production in the summer of 1921, claimed that the reason was "a vast amount of unplayed business on the books of practically all the distributors of pictures" and argued that overbuying caused overproduction and unpredictability for producers.[16] Quigley's claim is supported by broader trends in production during this period. Feature production reached a quantitative peak in the United States at 854 films in 1921, but these numbers would fall 12 percent (to 748) by 1922, and more than 30 percent by 1923, when only 576 features were produced.[17] While there is no way to attribute this shift directly to changes in the frequency of overbuying, the decrease does neatly correlate with the adoption

"GREATEST LOVE" RENTALS AND CONTRACTS

One Dollar in the Till
'S Worth Ten to Get Still

*What Does it Avail a Man to Contract his
Whole Territory if the Play dates
Are Not Forthcoming*

The Graphic Chart Occupying the Opposite
Page is Very Encouraging as Regards
Contracts, But When We Consider Ac-
tual Rentals it is "Not so Good."

In order to Keep the Ratio Between Rentals
and Contracts at the Proper Percentage
it is Necessary to Get Your Big Contracts
Disposed of Early.

Figures 5.2.1 *and* **5.2.2.** The Brain Exchange, *March 22, 1921, 6–7. Harry Ransom Center, The University of Texas at Austin.*

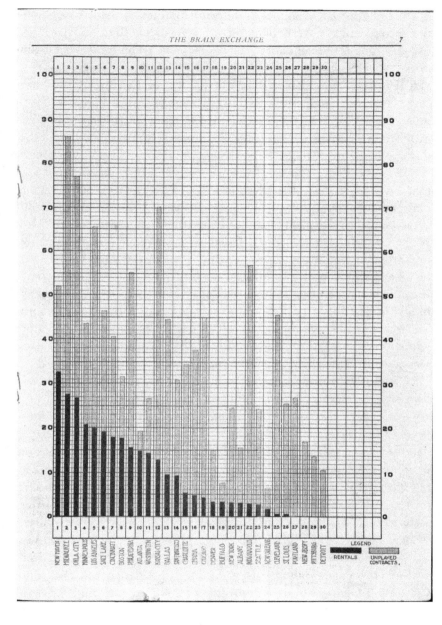

THE BRAIN EXCHANGE

of distribution blocks and the Uniform Contract, both of which were designed to combat overbooking. It also coincides with the move toward two-day runs as the standard in smaller theaters.[18] This meant that exhibitors were pickier about the quality of the films they played, since individual features now had to be profitable for longer runs. At the same time, overproduction encouraged overbuying, as distributors pushed the inflated stock of films they already had.[19] Thus, overbuying was not a problem in distribution or exhibition alone; it was a vicious cycle that distorted the entire process of planning, producing, and releasing films.

Evidence from Thomas Watson's papers further supports the idea that overbuying was a significant problem in the early twenties. Watson himself frequently withheld playdates or refused COD shipments, and his correspondence is explicit about the extent to which he overbought.[20] In a November 1922 letter to the W. W. Hodkinson company, then distributing through Pathé, Watson wrote to apologize for delaying the start date on an exhibition contract until after the first of the following year: "I am very sorry that I have to set you back again, but there are only 365 days in a year, and I have about 600 pictures (more or less)."[21] Watson typically changed his program three times a week, pairing a single feature with a short or two. Even if we assume his figure included shorts, Watson was contracting for at least 25 percent more product than he needed.

Watson was not an outlier in his overbuying; there is ample evidence to suggest that many exhibitors of a variety of sizes and in a variety of markets overbought. Distributors sent form letters to exhibitors urging them to provide playdates or to "clean up" previously delayed dates. Such appeals struck a variety of tones. One 1920 letter from the distributor Robertson-Cole began with a joke: "Gentlemen: There is an old legend about an exhibitor who was refused admittance to heaven on account of owing play dates on legitimate contracts."[22] Other letters were sterner. An example from Associated Exhibitors warned, "Gentlemen: FOURTH LETTER SENT TO YOU—PLAY DATES—THAT'S WHAT WE WANT!," with the undated titles listed in imposing red ink.[23] Still others vaguely threatened exhibitors with legal action: "Fox Film Corporation neither approves nor disapproves [lawsuits] on the part of any other distributor, but we have not nor do we desire to adopt any such action. We feel certain that exhibitors will reciprocate by immediately supplying sufficient dates to keep their contracts properly alive."[24] That these kinds of appeals were common enough to merit boilerplate letters addressed to exhibitors shows that the overbuying was not isolated, and that distributors had a set of standardized strategies for combatting it.

Why did exhibitors overbuy in the first place? After all, it would seem an expensive practice, given that exhibitors paid deposit money on their contracts and were legally required to play them through. One reason was overbuying's utility as a defensive strategy, as it enabled exhibitors to protect their schedules from the month-to-month contingencies of production. In contrast to program service, which supplied productions on a temporally regular basis, distributors' contracts for star series or branded sub-programs often could not guarantee an exact number of pictures. Watson's contract with Pathé for Hodkinson films in 1921, for example, specified only "a minimum of 24 features and maximum of 36 features"—hardly a reliable gauge for an exhibitor looking to set a booking schedule in advance.[25] Production output was never assured even when distributors sold films in smaller packages. If anything, the star series, which relied on the continued working output of a single person, was more unpredictable than larger branded sub-programs. Midway through the 1921–1922 season, Fox reduced the number of films in Dustin Farnum's star series from seven to four.[26] For Watson and other exhibitors with schedules to fill, this reduction amounted to a full week's worth of feature dates that would need late and potentially unprofitable spot bookings. Experienced exhibitors protected their schedules by overbooking, and distributors knew that occasional production problems were bound to occur—which is one reason why they treated overbuying somewhat more flexibly than we might expect.

Exhibitors also overbought because distributors made the practice more affordable than it seemed on paper. In their negotiations, distributor sales representatives tended to forgo the booking security of advance deposit money in return for exhibitors booking a greater volume of films. The standard deposit amount during this period was 25 percent of the total rental, but, as noted in chapter 2, small exhibitors often struggled to come up with sufficient cash to cover this cost.[27] They also needed a greater volume of films than urban theaters did, because of their shorter runs. As a result, distributors often substantially discounted deposits for exhibitors who booked in bulk. Watson's 1921 contract with Pathé for up to thirty-six features was worth around $2,500 in rentals, but it was secured by a mere $125 from Watson—an equivalent deposit of 5 percent.[28] Metro was even more generous, selling him thirty-seven pictures worth a total of $2,175 for a deposit of only $75 (just under

3.5 percent).[29] Such discounting reduced the extent to which exhibitors' cash was tied up in deposits, which gave them more liquidity—that they could then use to overbuy. Deposit discounts also reduced the monetary losses incurred by overbooking. If an exhibitor could net more in a spot booking by refusing a distributor a playdate than what he subsequently lost in deposit money, the strategy made perfect economic sense.

The legal risks to exhibitors of overbuying were further mitigated by the fact that distributors' local exchanges were often deficient in carrying out the coordination of bookings and the physical distribution of prints. This deficiency was particularly common in dealings with exhibitors that were more distant from an exchange, where the relatively low rental amounts involved often meant substandard service. In his study of correspondence between rural theaters and urban exchanges in this period, Martin Johnson noted numerous "complaints about missed deliveries, battered prints, and general incompetence."[30] Even Watson, whose Superba was located a mere one hundred miles from Chicago, was the frequent victim of scheduling, booking, and shipping mistakes on the part of the exchanges there.[31] Exhibitors had every reason to play up such incidents in their negotiations with distributors.

Another reason exhibitors overbought was that distributors often simply let them get away with it for fear of losing a theater to a competing service. Distributors often treated overbuying as a point of negotiation that could be used to force concessions from exhibitors. Letting delayed or delinquent bookings slide gave distributors the leverage to extract favorable terms from exhibitors in other areas, such as in the booking of bigger films on percentage.[32] When Watson booked Fox's special *A Connecticut Yankee* (1921) in 1922, the distributor was able to negotiate a whopping 60 percent of the gross from him, as well as requiring him to book a "lesser special," *Queen of Sheba* (1921).[33] Such distributor "solutions" to the problem of overbuying were often designed to extract as much information and playing time from exhibitors as possible.

The common historiographical impulse is to see distributors' conduct during this period as purely rooted in a collusive desire to control first-run theaters. Watson's correspondence, however, suggests a more complicated set of factors. Individual distributors did compete for a finite supply of exhibitor playdates, and that competition was motivated by a drive for temporal as well as spatial control of distribution. Because the most direct way for any one company to gain the upper hand in the play-date market was to oversell to exhibitors, distributors' rational conduct as individual companies had the collective effect of creating a market for playdates that they were increasingly losing control over. *Variety* cut to the core of the problem as it stood in January 1922: "Attempts have been made to compel exhibitors to make good on playing contracts, but distributor rivalry is too intense to make this possible. If one distributor undertook to cut off the service of every exhibitor who threw back a playing date, his distributor competitors would snap up the business, leaving him holding the bag."[34] Solving the problem posed by overbuying in the long term thus required distributors to cooperate.

Overbuying's Temporal Solutions: The Uniform Exhibition Contract, Block Booking, and Run Exhibition

As Afra and Maltby have shown in their respective discussions of arbitration, the consistent enforcement of exhibitor contracts was one of the driving forces behind the establishment of the MPPDA under Will Hays in the spring of 1922. Creating a Uniform Exhibition Contract was one of the earliest goals of the MPPDA, and, as *Variety* pointed out, it was a tall order: "Any agreement among the producers and distributors to outlaw defaulting exhibitors probably would be declared a conspiracy in restraint of trade."[35] Nevertheless, after six months of negotiations between the MPPDA and exhibitor organizations—most notably the New York State Exhibitors' League and the Theater Owners Chamber of Commerce (TOCC)—the MPPDA adopted the Uniform Exhibition Contract in February 1923.[36]

While the establishment of arbitration boards was an important part of the Uniform Contract, the contract also contained other provisions seeking to reduce friction between distributors and exhibitors. As Hays pointed out, "Each distributor had his own Exhibition Contract" before 1923, "each with varying terms and conditions."[37] Though the Uniform Contract did not completely standardize these conditions, it did encourage distributors to adopt new practices ostensibly meant to give exhibitors a fuller measure of information about the contracts they were signing. Contracted films now had to be "specially described and identified either by name or by the star who is to appear in them," and the exhibitor's rental was due only three days in advance of shipment instead of seven. Certain arbitrary distributor penalties were removed, and the only conditions under which distributors could terminate a contract with an exhibitor were failure to pay rentals or bicycling of film. Distributors also had to accept or reject an exhibitor's rental application within a reasonable time frame—they could no longer leave exhibitors in the lurch about a contract only to surprise them with COD deliveries. They also now had to leave a copy of the contract with the exhibitor for review.[38]

However, for the purposes of reducing overbuying, the Uniform Contract's stipulation of an exact procedure for selecting playdates was its most important provision. Earlier distribution contracts had simply reserved the distributor's right to dictate playdates, without specifying the mechanism or conditions under which that would happen. The playdate provision in Watson's 1920 contract with Pathé, for example, required that if the distributor was obliged to demand dates, the exhibitor had ten days to specify said dates or Pathé would simply dictate them. No provision was made for a deadline to come to an agreement about dates, nor were dates specified in the original contract: the Pathé sales representative who drafted the contract with Watson simply wrote, "Each feature to be played or paid for 60 days after its release" in the space on the contract for listing playdates.[39] Before the Uniform Contract, playdate determination was less a standardized process than another term of negotiation between the distributor and individual exhibitors.

The eighth paragraph of the Uniform Contract, by contrast, set forth a very specific procedure and timeline that distributors were to use in determining playdates for films that had not been dated in the initial stage of booking. First, distributors were obliged to give the exhibitor a written "notice of availability" at least four weeks before the "date of availability" of the film in question. Crucially, the date of availability was not necessarily the film's release date but an indefinite date left completely up to the distributor. Upon the mailing of the notice of availability, the exhibitor then had two weeks to select a playdate—which had to be within the two weeks commencing on the date of availability. If the exhibitor did not respond or refused to select a date within two weeks of the notice, the distributor could dictate the playdate by mailing another written notice at least three weeks in advance.[40]

In emphasizing a specific sequence for determining the playdates of individual films, the Uniform Contract sought to rationalize what had been a temporally haphazard process. Defining the boundaries of the exhibitor's choice when it came to playdates—within two weeks from the date of availability—helped to prevent backlogs of unplayed contracts. It also gave distributors incredible leeway to temporally manage distribution. The structuring of contracts around a film's "availability," rather than a specified release date, provided a cushion for any delays in production and time for holdovers of a film in previous runs, as well as time for prerelease engagements. At the same time, the Uniform Contract retained a certain measure of booking flexibility for exhibitors and contained other distribution provisions meant to appeal to small exhibitors. In contrast to previous practice, in which exhibitors who refused playdates were often denied clearance protection, the Uniform Contract ensured that exhibitors whose playdates were dictated by the distributor would still have any protection that had been negotiated in the original contract.[41] Most importantly, it stipulated that if an exhibitor did not have an open date during the period of availability, the distributor had to mail the exhibitor a new notice and date of availability. This measure prevented first-run exhibitors from holding back the playdate of a picture indefinitely and upsetting the schedules of subsequent-run exhibitors— although, importantly, it did nothing to prevent distributors from withholding films for general release for their own purposes.[42]

In general, the Uniform Contract was received positively in the trade press. Few writers claimed it was perfect, but the majority characterized it as a stark improvement from previous practice.[43] However, not all exhibitors were thrilled with it. *Moving Picture World* noted that Sydney Cohen, president of the Motion Picture Theater Owners of America (MPTOA), had been conspicuously absent from the contract negotiations, and only the New York branch of the organization had taken part in them.[44] Other MPTOA state branches condemned the Uniform Contract in various resolutions in the months following its adoption. Several exhibitors signed a resolution at the MPTOA's national convention in May 1923 decrying the contract's "cumbersome method of fixing play dates," among other provisions.[45] Some exhibitors recognized how the Uniform Contract strongly incentivized distributors to demand playdates at the time of initial booking, because a playdate specified on the initial contract released the distributor from the obligation of providing a notice of availability. "Lo and behold, this year [1923–1924] every other company wants immediate playdates on the signing of a contract," railed William Brandt, president of the New York State branch of the MPTOA, in August 1923. "It will close the market tighter than a clam. The independent producer won't have a chance to make pictures and find playdates."[46]

The Uniform Contract was thus a powerful tool for distributors to temporally manage the exhibition of their films. However, the exact form that the Uniform Contract should take was not obvious in the years leading up to its adoption. Its ideal terms and conditions from the perspective of distributors were framed by the success of other strategies of temporal management that had begun to be worked out in the release seasons prior to the Uniform Contract's adoption. Distributors realized that a general move away from the star series and selective booking and toward larger groups of films would be a necessary part of temporally managing distribution practice. As the recession of 1921 made the problem of over-buying impossible to ignore, distributors began to reverse the trend away from programmatic release formats that had defined the industry since the mid-teens. In place of the star series and the branded sub-program, they increasingly substituted a new format: block booking.

Before defining block booking as a specific format of programmatic distribution, it is worth repeating that the term is a particularly troubled one in the historiography of feature distribution. This is largely because of its imprecise meaning, which proliferated in the widespread trade press coverage of the Federal Trade Commission's case against Paramount in 1923. The FTC used "block booking" as a blanket term for *any* form of distribution that sold films in groups, the same way that some (though not all) of the witnesses giving testimony did.[47] Of course, this definition encompasses nearly all models of feature distribution used at the time except for specials. It obliterates the packaging distinctions discussed in chapters 3 and 4 between the program system, branded sub-programs, star series, selective booking, and mixed distribution blocks. To some extent, the FTC used the term as a rhetorical strategy, framing any method of selling films as a group as aberrant rather than acknowledging that many exhibitors needed programmatic packaging. Paramount's lawyers pushed back against that very rhetoric by constantly seeking to highlight the point that the sale of a group of films as a unit had been standard practice among all distributors at least since Paramount's initial feature program in 1914 and stretched back to shorts distribution.[48]

To further complicate the terminology at play, it is worth noting that from as early as 1916, and at least until 1922, "block booking" was used with some frequency in the trade press to refer not to American domestic distribution, but to the practice among American distributors of pre-selling full programs to sales and exhibition agents in the United Kingdom as much as a year before release.[49] The earliest trade press reference to block booking in a non-British context I have been able to find is from

August 1921, when Paramount announced that exhibitors would be able to "book in block and at an early date seven of Paramount's biggest fall releases."[50] Although I would not argue that the modern meaning of block booking was *never* used in an American context before 1921, it is clear that it was not a common term in the trade press before that point. Instead, writers referred to more specific practices, such as the "program system," "program booking," "brands," or "star series."

I refer to block booking in a much more restricted sense, as a specific format of distribution that was distinct from the program system, star series, and selective booking. The block system did not group feature films by star, genre, brand, or any of the other obviously marketable criteria that distributors had used with the star series and branded sub-programs. Rather, distributors using the system split their entire program into blocks that were defined purely *temporally*, with each block containing a few months' worth of a distributor's output for the season.[51]

For example, in the first season Paramount used block booking, 1920–1921, it divided its 93 releases into four blocks (of 26, 25, 22, and 20 films).[52] Each block was sold separately and successively across the span of the release season, one block at a time, and was composed of the films that would be available for the three-month period that followed the release of the first film in the block.[53] In the following season, when Paramount began using block selling exclusively, it released 73 films via three blocks (of 18, 23, and 32 films), with each block covering a four-month period.[54] Most distributors sold their yearly program in two, three, or four blocks, although some companies with smaller output released their entire program as a single block, as Goldwyn did with its 20 films in 1922–1923.[55] Blocks were generally envisioned as being roughly equal in size throughout the year, but one advantage of blocks to distributors was that they could adjust the size of the blocks to changes in the market as the release season progressed.

For exhibitors, block booking integrated the efficiency of the program system with the greater scheduling flexibility of selective booking. For frequent-change exhibitors, blocks packaged many films into a cost-effective unit of sale that did not gobble up their playing time to the extreme extent that programs had. Blocks were certainly a bigger package than star series, but the biggest were only for about 40 films—smaller than a one-a-week program, and certainly less than the 104 features the Paramount and Triangle programs had forced on exhibitors circa 1915. At the same time, blocks were not as inflexible as programs when it came to the specific playdates of individual films. Programs—and even some star series, such as those offered by Fox—had generally mandated that films be played in the order in which they were released from the distributor, without any skipping or rearranging of titles. Blocks were much more flexible while still giving distributors strong temporal control of playdates.[56] Distributors tended to mandate playdates in block contracts to combat overbooking, but the exact date that any one film from the block was played continued to be left up to the exhibitor, as long as *some* available film from the contract was played on the specified playdate.[57]

Blocks were also distinguished from programs and star series in allowing distributors to make more accurate promises to exhibitors about the quantity of films they were buying. Earlier distribution formats had locked in specific expectations about the output of individual stars or brands over the course of an entire year. Fox's announcements for the 1921–1922 season, for instance, promised series from William Farnum, Tom Mix, Pearl White, Buck Jones, Shirley Mason, and so forth in specific numbers at the very beginning of the release season in September 1921.[58] As we have already seen, promising a certain number of films from a specific star or brand so far in advance encouraged overselling, because neither the distributors nor the exhibitors had much confidence that production would actually live up to the anticipated totals. Fox's ad, for example, explicitly cautioned that films would be available only "in approximately the numbers listed."

Because blocks were sold in successive units one at a time, distributors could concentrate on selling only the films they were confident would be produced and thus were less likely to oversell. This new temporal organization of the distribution slate did not guarantee that any individual film would be released on time (or at all), but it did give exhibitors more confidence that the block as a whole would actually provide something close to the quantity of promised films, since any film whose timely completion was in doubt could be delayed until later in the block (or even until the subsequent block), and another substituted in its place. Blocks did not always work as planned, but exhibitors had much more certainty about them than they did about star series.

All of this gave distributors a significant amount of flexibility to adjust their production to suit the national market. With the introduction of block booking at Paramount, the number of films to be produced—as well as the number of blocks used to sell them—was no longer determined by the output capacity of particular stars, or by a programmatic release schedule of two "regular features" a week, as had been the case at the studio from 1914 to 1919. Instead, blocks allowed "market conditions" to guide these decisions, as Paramount's general manager of distribution, Sidney Kent, pointed out:

> The sales department first analyze[s] the market and determine[s] upon the number of pictures that we feel we should offer that year. . . . [Zukor] decides whether or not we are going through with a program that large. We then make whatever readjustments are to be made at that time, and we then definitely set out with any number of pictures from 40 to 70, according to what we decide to release. We then decide whether we split those into two blocks or four blocks, as we have done within that period from time to time according to the market conditions.[59]

These "market conditions" were not simply based on the instincts of Kent, Lasky, or Zukor. They were aided by the data that selective booking and percentage selling had enabled. As noted in chapter 4, by the early twenties, the sophisticated statistical division in Paramount's distribution department allowed for a much clearer picture about the value of individual productions than had been possible under the program system or the star series. Blocks enabled the studios to use a more flexible and granular *pricing* of individual films without having to go to the expense of selling those films individually via selective booking. As Kent pointed out, the star series gave "very little information upon which to base a schedule of prices other than the popularity of the star or director as best [sales personnel] could gauge it," so distributors were uncertain about the value of individual pictures. Block booking accounted not only for the value of individual films, but for the value of films in specific relation to the theater being booked.[60]

This data then dictated the negotiation process between the distributor and the exhibitor at the time of booking. In selling blocks to exhibitors, distributor sales personnel presented a price sheet (also known as a "work sheet" or "record routing sheet") to help work out a pricing schedule. This was similar to the previous practice used when exhibitors bought multiple series in a single contract, but instead of listing each film on the contract at the same price according to its star or brand, block contracts priced each title individually, just as selective booking had. The quoted price was based on the assumption that the exhibitor would rent the entire block as a unit. Exhibitors who selected individual films from the block paid a premium on the listed price, a practice that lay at the heart of the FTC's case against Paramount. The amount typically quoted in FTC testimony was a 50 percent increase per individual title, although Sidney Kent denied that figure.[61] Regardless of whether an exhibitor selected an individual film or rented the whole block, distributors got pricing information about—and based their initial pricing on—the valuation of individual films rather than stars or brands. Because this pricing scheme also provided information about individual theaters' valuation of particular titles, it was a crucial part of production planning. It allowed films to be more reliably budgeted on an individual basis rather than as part of an undifferentiated package of distribution.

This is not to suggest that the difference between sub-programs, star series, and blocks was always clear. Indeed, block booking was essentially a more temporally fine-tuned variation on the program-based methods that distributors had used since the mid-teens. Fox, for instance, continued to operate on the one-feature-a-week model as late as 1923–1924, when it released its program of 52 features in two blocks: 28 "star series" films (which, despite the name, it sold as a single block and not as several star series) and 24 "special features."[62] This combination of star series and blocks was not unusual in early block contracts. Metro put several star series, a pair of expensive Nazimova films, and a few individual titles together on a single block in 1921–1922.[63] On the whole, however, blocks tended not to be advertised as branded sales packages the way sub-programs had been and placed more emphasis on individual films. In fact, while blocks were nearly always advertised as having universally high quality ("All Big Ones," Goldwyn assured exhibitors), it worked to distributors' advantage for blocks to be as diverse as possible in terms of the quality of the films they included, based on the old feature program idea of selling many films based on the marketability of a few.[64] Advertising for blocks tended to combine appeals to program-minded exhibitors on the one hand—playing up the exact number of films in the block and emphasizing the uniformly high quality of the films—and pitches to a more idiosyncratic upscale market, on the other, with detailed advertisements for the individual pictures in the block that were closest to release.[65]

Why did block booking replace the star series and selective booking as the industry norm by 1924? One reason was that frequent-change exhibitors were more likely to give playdates for films on blocks up front because of their size. Distributors, for their part, were more likely to demand them. Some early block contracts in 1921 and 1922 were very similar to the program contracts of the mid-teens in their extraction of playdates from exhibitors. Firm control of playdates was a central part of the booking strategy of the Realart Pictures Corporation, a subsidiary of Paramount that had its own exchange network and marketed itself as a franchise distributor along the lines of First National.[66] The 1921–1922 contracts covering the planned production of 36 Realart films required exhibitors to allot three days a month in specific playdates at the time of signing.[67] This was effectively a return to the service model of the program system, as it forced exhibitors to choose playdates that landed on a predictably performing day of the week.[68] Realart also required exhibitors to pay their total rental in installments, "just as he does when he makes application for gas or electric light or telephone."[69] This was a way of enforcing the playdates allotted at signing, because payment was not linked to specific films but to regular service.[70]

While installment payments would not become the norm for block booking, explicitly defined playdates would, which further encouraged the industry-wide switch to blocks.[71] Watson's 1921–1922 contract with Metro for "approximately" 38 pictures, signed in June 1921, specified a start date of September 6, with the contract to run "at the rate of one picture each and every Wednesday and Thursday thereafter." Though this block booking was like a one-a-week program in the sense that it provided for regular releases and regular playdates, there were important differences. Some of the films and series on the contract had flexible runs of "2–3 days," with no additional payment required for a three-day run. Furthermore, it was still up to Watson to specify playdates for the individual films on the contract. When he did not—even after Metro sent a registered letter dictating those dates—the distributor sued him for $3,000.[72] Thus, blocks did not prevent exhibitors from withholding dates, but their clearer designation of playdates made overbuying much riskier. As United Artists' exchange manager for the Southeast testified at the FTC trial, "Those fellows that sell by blocks, they protect themselves. They take deposits and they take dates. At least, if you don't take specific dates they agree to play so many a week, one or two a week, [for] a certain time, or such a length of time, after the release of these pictures."[73] Thus, even before the adoption of the Uniform Contract, distributors were using blocks to take tighter control of exhibitors' playdates. By 1923, in conjunction with the leverage the Uniform Contract gave distributors, it was standard practice at Paramount to insert specific playdates in contracts at the time of initial booking.[74]

Distributors' use of block booking as a strategy of temporal management worked in concert with the development of run exhibition in the early 1920s. As we saw in chapter 3, distributors increasingly integrated specials and other high-budget films into the regular distribution system in the mid-teens through "rental-basis" runs, rather than handling them exclusively through roadshows or state rights. That system became more refined in the early twenties, as big films that were nevertheless not specials were given a dedicated model of non-roadshow prerelease exploitation. According to William Paul, run exhibition, as of the late twenties, took place in two different types of theaters. One was the "extended-run grind house" (also known as a "regular extended run" or "regular prerelease" house), a larger theater that ran both specials and promising films "verging on the special class" in continuous showings for six to eight weeks for "popular prices."[75] The other was the more exclusive roadshow house, also known as a "two-a-day" or "extended exploitation" house, which was typically a smaller converted legitimate theater. Two-a-days typically ran *only* specials (twice a day), charged higher prices, had reserved seating, and might run particularly successful films in prerelease for months.

Both types of venues were oriented around more idiosyncratic distribution—they emphasized the individual feature as the main attraction. By the late 1920s, this fact distinguished them from the more programmatic "presentation houses," the large picture palaces (typically seating three thousand or more) where the first run of general release began. Presentation houses generally changed weekly or biweekly (sometimes less often for big hits), and they highlighted the larger program of which the feature was only one part—in that sense they were effectively a continuation of the vaudeville program model. Paul argues that this bifurcation between run exhibition and presentation houses mirrored a "preexisting bifurcation in production." Whereas specials and other promising films premiered in run exhibition to drum up the value of films *before* they moved to presentation houses, program films typically premiered in presentation houses. The choice of whether to give a film a prerelease, as well as what kind of prerelease to give it, thus signaled a distributor's intentions for it. "Run pictures" enjoyed the attendant exploitation of prerelease distribution that films opening in weekly-change presentation houses did not, and two-a-day premieres designated higher confidence in a film than premieres in a regular prerelease house. As Paul shows in his examples of the distribution of *Life Begins* (James Flood, Warner Bros., 1932) and *The Crowd* (King Vidor, MGM, 1928), premiering a picture in the wrong type of theater could severely curtail its overall box-office potential.[76]

Paul's work delineates the form that run exhibition had taken as of about 1926. As he points out, the practice as it operated in New York originated with Vitagraph's 1914 acquisition of the Criterion Theatre for showcasing features.[77] The earliest theaters that were explicitly considered prerelease houses (and not presentation theaters) probably emerged around 1916 or 1917, in rough conjunction with the decline of the program system and the rise of open booking.[78] However, it was not until the industry's normalization of block booking around 1924 that run exhibition became a systematized practice. This was partly because run exhibition was planned and defined in direct relation to the regular release system—as a "prerelease"—and block booking (as well as the Uniform Contract) helped to bring about some consistency to that system. More importantly, block booking also synchronized run exhibition and the weekly release such that each maximized the returns of the other in an integrated form of distribution. An account of just how this happened will help to explain the convergence of factors that permanently changed the distribution market in the early 1920s.

In the late 1910s and the earliest years of the 1920s, prerelease exhibition was still a mostly separate tier of distribution associated with specials, despite the increasing integration of specials into the regular release system. One reason for this was length: because specials tended to be longer than six or seven reels, they were too long to play alongside live acts and shorts in presentation houses, which was why repurposed two-a-day legitimate theaters became the standard venue for long runs of such productions. Specials did play in dedicated film theaters after their initial prerelease, but they were often cut down to accommodate more shows (as *Fox's Over the Hill to the Poorhouse* was, from eleven to seven reels) and played on percentage contracts (demonstrated by Watson's 1922 bookings of *Over the Hill*, *A Connecticut Yankee*, and *Queen of Sheba*).[79] In small towns such as Freeport, Illinois, where Watson operated, this made them an occasional booking option. In larger cities, as we have seen, first-run theaters were much more likely to book a prereleased special—after all, that was the whole point of exhibition. However, the increasingly indefinite length of a special's prerelease run posed problems when it came to booking films for their rental-basis first runs.

Lea Jacobs and Andrea Comiskey's account of the roadshowing of *Over the Hill* provides an excellent example of the rather haphazard quality of run exhibition in the early twenties. After debuting in September 1920 in a three-and-a-half-week run at the Astor, a legitimate house, the film played for the next ten months in five separate theaters on or near Broadway—all of them also two-a-day legitimate houses.[80] The length of these runs varied greatly, from three weeks at the Astor, to a week at the Nora Bayes, to three weeks each at the Lyric and the Broadhurst, to three months at the Park. In late September 1921, almost two months after the conclusion of its Broadway prerelease, the film was booked at the Tivoli, a "good size" house on Eighth Avenue known for prices that were "cheaper than on Broadway," for its rental-basis first run.[81] The fact that *Over the Hill* kept jumping venues and playing them for uneven runs suggests the extent to which run exhibition in the early 1920s remained something of an ad hoc practice rather than a fully systematized model. This complicated not only a film's prerelease, but also the booking of its first run. As *Variety* pointed out, distributors ideally wanted a film's first run to follow the end of its Broadway prerelease after a relatively brief two-week clearance window, so that the prerelease exploitation would "edge into" the subsequent general release.[82] Jacobs and Comiskey's account of the 1927 distribution of another Fox Film, Frank Borzage's *7th Heaven*, points to its much more efficient run exhibition in contrast to *Over the Hill*: five months at the two-a-day Sam Harris on Broadway, two-week clearance, then two weeks' first-run presentation at the Roxy.[83]

The difference between the two films also suggests that New York and the other key cities were underseated in run houses in the early 1920s. Competition from legitimate theater was a major reason for this. While that industry was in decline nationwide, theater production had been booming in New York since the end of the war, peaking in the 1925–1926 season.[84] A tight market for extended playing time in New York theaters in the early 1920s resulted, even as legitimate houses outside of the city were closing or converting to cinemas during the same period. Increases in the average run length of films exacerbated this shortage of theater space. As selective distribution became more common after 1919 and distributors positioned more films as specials, the time available in two-a-days and prerelease houses was increasingly insufficient, as those productions garnered longer and longer runs. The industry's initial cycle of theater buying in 1919 and 1920 provided distributors with a more direct line to run exhibition less dependent on houses that also programmed live theater, but it is important to note that most of the acquired houses were likely devoted to program presentation or regular prereleases rather than extended exploitation. In mid-1922, *Variety* was still referring to the Criterion (a two-a-day) as Paramount's sole "run house" in New York, two years after the company had taken control of it.[85] FPL's two other Broadway theaters, the Rivoli and the Rialto, retained weekly changes, suggesting that they functioned as presentation theaters.

It is clear, however, that some presentation houses were *also* considered prerelease houses in the context of New York exhibition, as they often held films over for as many as four or five weeks.[86] Thus, weekly-change presentation theaters served a kind of dual function in the early twenties, before a clearer distinction between presentation and regular prerelease houses emerged. In any case, many "run houses" continued to be active legitimate theaters, which limited their run lengths and their potential for proper exploitation of specials. As Detroit's First National franchisee John Kunsky put it, "The large majority of legitimate houses are antiquated and poorly adapted to screen presentations, [and] runs of a picture are likely to be prematurely ended to make room for other bookings. The answer is more theatres, modern in construction and primarily devoted to the presentation of pictures."[87] Indeed, distributors and exhibitors had recognized the need for more run exhibition outlets as early as 1921. That year in Philadelphia, the Stanley theater company converted the Stanley, the presentation palace it had built in 1914, to serve as a two-a-day run theater, the Stanton.[88] The same year, one Nebraska exhibitor predicted that every city with a population of more than seventy-five thousand would have a two-a-day solely dedicated to motion pictures by 1923.[89] Before then, film-only two-a-days remained relatively rare, and those owned or otherwise directly controlled by distributors were even rarer.

Distributors in the early 1920s had also not yet fully realized that even films not intended for long-run exhibition needed to be carefully handled. This was particularly true for those films that were just below specials in the distribution hierarchy, which premiered in presentation houses during this period (sometimes for multiple-week runs). In the fall of 1921, after the particularly poor performance of the William S. Hart feature *Three Word Brand* at the Rivoli, Adolph Zukor explained the film's failure to *Variety* as the result of its prerelease placement.

[Had the film] been presented at the Rialto instead of the Rivoli, the result would surely have been entirely different. Elsie Ferguson's picture, *Footlights*, is a big draw at the Rivoli, because she attracts carriage trade, which is not so readily attracted to the Rialto. *Why Girls Leave Home* [a Warners film with Anna Q. Nilsson, based on a stage play] is doing a tremendous business at the Broadway [a run house], but the Ferguson feature wouldn't draw a nickel there. In the past the price of a feature had a good deal to do in deciding whether it would be played in the pre-release theaters on Broadway. The cheaper the producer or distributor made it, the better his chances of coming in. That means nothing today. We must have pictures that will draw, just as much as Mr. Erlanger or Mr. Shubert must have for their legitimate theatres.[90]

Zukor's statement suggests that the standard industry practice for distributing films to Broadway prerelease theaters was in flux as of 1921. The program-oriented distribution mentality of the teens had drawn sharp distinctions between specials (intended for legitimate houses) and programmers (intended for presentation theaters), but programmatic production was now of a quality to merit its tailoring around the considerations of individual features in individual theaters. The fact that all three of the films Zukor listed were seven- or eight-reel productions—not five-reel program films but also not obviously specials—suggests that the previous distinctions of price and film length that had guided those considerations in the teens were breaking down. Such films might not merit full extended-run prereleases in two-a-days, but they might clean up nicely in multi-week holdovers in the Rivoli, the Rialto, and similar theaters. By the late 1920s, these "pictures verging on the special class" (as Paul notes they were called by *Variety*) would be handled in regular prerelease grind houses.[91] In the early 1920s, however, distributing them was complicated by the factors discussed thus far, and the distinction between regular prerelease theaters and program-oriented presentation houses was somewhat ambiguous.

The 1922 run of Paramount's *Blood and Sand* on Broadway serves as a good example of all three of the issues complicating run exhibition in the early 1920s: haphazard run structure, the relative lack of run exhibition theaters, and the growing box-office potential of non-specials. When the nine-reel Valentino film began a scheduled two-week run starting August 6 at the Rivoli, it was an immediate hit, grossing $37,000 in its first week.[92] *Variety* estimated that the Rivoli was forced to turn away six times the number of patrons at the entrance as actually saw the film, and it was clear that *Blood and Sand* could easily be held over an additional four or five weeks. Complicating matters, the Loew circuit had booked the film solid for weeklong runs in all of its houses beginning the week of September 11, and Nick Schenck of Loew's "flatly refused" to push that date back an additional week.[93] As a result, *Blood and Sand* ended up running a total of four weeks at the Rivoli, with the last week playing simultaneously with the Rialto, enabling the latter to pick up the fifth week's worth of business.[94]

Although this arrangement worked out well enough for *Blood and Sand*, the holdovers of the film, combined with Metro's leasing of the Criterion for the Bessie Love film *Forget-Me-Not*, contributed to a significant backup in Paramount's New York prerelease bookings for September 1922. Once again, the Loew and Keith circuits—which, combined, controlled about two hundred days' worth of playdates—demanded that their subsequent runs start as contracted, and Paramount was deprived of valuable prerelease time for its upcoming films *Burning Sands* and *The Old Homestead*. Paramount—without question the most powerful distributor of the early 1920s—was caught flat-footed by the regular first-run release schedule in exploiting *Blood and Sand* and other films to their fullest extent. By the late 1920s, the company would be much better positioned to take advantage of the unexpected popularity of a film like *Blood and Sand*, either by premiering it for an indefinite run in a dedicated prerelease grind house in the first place or by moving it to a two-a-day, as MGM would with *The Crowd* in 1928.[95]

By 1923, the normalization of block booking and the Uniform Contract, along with the construction of more two-a-days dedicated to film, had begun to integrate run exhibition and programmatic distribution into a more rationalized and temporally flexible system. This system of temporal organization had important implications for distribution and production planning. The increased granularity of film pricing in distribution enabled a concomitant granularity in the classification of films in production. Paramount films were organized into four distinct production tiers by 1929, each defined not only by the films' budgets, but by criteria such as whether they were vehicles for stars or featured players, whether their scripts were selected far in advance or relatively close to the time of production, and whether the marketing for them emphasized their stars or their titles (in the case of adaptations).[96] These distinctions had operated in the minds of studio executives since the decline of the program system, but the developments of the early twenties allowed for more careful tailoring of pre-production decisions about individual films to specific channels of feature distribution. Films ceased to be planned simply as either specials or programmers according to their lengths or their stars. While the distinction between a special and a programmer remained important in a general way through the end of the 1920s, those categories became increasingly blurred when it came to actual production and distribution practices. Instead, the rise of block booking, run exhibition, and uniform contract terms made the crucial decision about how to handle a film—on the program in a presentation house, in a regular prerelease grind house for indefinite runs, or in extended release in a two-a-day—a function of its individual qualities above all else. At the same time, the temporal management of distribution meant that a film could be distributed much more actively and flexibly according to its *unexpected* qualities, even after it had been released.

We will now turn to Paramount as a case study of the development and implementation of these practices. In addition to more granular distinctions in production, Paramount developed more sophisticated methods of cost control and scheduling, moved toward mid-level management of production through supervisors, and experimented with a new form of prerelease "demonstration run" distribution. Through these practices, the company sought to temporally manage production and distribution more carefully than the program system had permitted.

Paramount and the Relationship between Block Booking and Production Planning, 1921–1924

In the late 1910s and early 1920s, Paramount instituted significant changes in its production and distribution organization. The following list of Paramount's distribution groups from the 1917–1918 to 1923–1924 release seasons, adapted from the 1927 FTC case against Paramount, shows not only the extent of these changes but also the degree to which production and distribution planning were interrelated practices at the studio.

Paramount Distribution Groups by Release Season, 1917–1924
Group 1 (1917–1918): 134 pictures in 23 star series

Group 2 (1918–1919): 123 pictures (93 Paramounts and 30 Artcrafts) in star series

Group 3 (1919–1920): 99 pictures (71 Paramounts and 28 specials) via selective booking

Group 4 (1920–1921): 93 pictures in four blocks (26, 25, 22, 20), sold in a combination of sales methods

Group 5 (1921–1922): 73 pictures released, three blocks (18, 23, 32)

Group 6 (1922–1923): 72 pictures released, two blocks (38, 34)—sold in blocks of 41 and 39 (the Famous Forty-One and Super Thirty-Nine)

Group 7 (1923–1924): 48 pictures released, three blocks (12, 19, 17)—first and third blocks sold normally, the first 10 pictures of the second block sold selectively through pre-demonstration[97]

Paramount's full-time switch to block booking for the 1921–1922 season began a new phase in the company's distribution policies.[98] However, this shift did not mean that Famous Players–Lasky had worked out a single optimal distribution strategy when it came to the specific use of blocks, or that its policies as of 1921 were identical in form to later distribution practice. The subsequent seasons saw an experimentation with and refining of the block model as well as related changes in production organization and planning. The company's changes to its distribution model ranged from variations in the number of blocks, to the overall size of blocks, to the way in which blocks were advertised to exhibitors. These changes demonstrate the constantly shifting terrain of the national distribution market in the early 1920s as Paramount tailored its blocks not only to suit the requirements of that market but also to accommodate production necessities. These years thus demonstrate the extent to which the relationship between distribution and production planning was mutually determined.

The 73 films of the 1921–1922 season were released in three blocks of 18, 23, and 32 films. Planning for this season at FPL was heavily structured by cost-cutting measures implemented after the industry-wide recession, including the temporary closure of the studio's plant in Astoria and salary reductions for a significant number of production personnel.[99] Keeping production costs to a minimum was thus a priority, but it was complicated by William Randolph Hearst's threat to remove the twelve films supplied by his Cosmopolitan Productions from the Paramount program because of a profit-sharing dispute. Lasky assured Zukor, "We can make up the twelve pictures [in Los Angeles]. I have already planned, on account of word received from Kent a week ago, to increase the number of [Jack] Holt and [Agnes] Ayres pictures from four to six each. . . . I feel that we can readily make up the twelve pictures that were to be supplied by Cosmopolitan provided you determine it is necessary to do so."[100]

Here, one of the advantages of the block system for production is evident. Some of the Cosmopolitans—most notably *The Bride's Play* (George Terwilliger, 1922), with Marion Davies—had already been prominently listed the previous spring as being part of the season's Paramount release. Despite this fact, Lasky clearly assumed that Cosmopolitan's prestigious vehicles could be at least partially substituted with program films from two reliable Paramount stars, demonstrating that blocks provided a measure of release flexibility that could accommodate changes in production.[101] Nevertheless, Zukor's reply suggests that achieving the season's quota of releases on the distribution program was preferable to adjusting production. After Hearst demanded an increase in Cosmopolitan's take of gross receipts to 60 percent, Zukor admitted, "Under the circumstances I felt it was advisable to agree to his proposition, particularly as we have made advances to him running over $400,000 on negatives which had not as yet been delivered, and if a controversy arose between us he might hold us up. We would then be obliged either to reduce the quota of releases, or, if we considered it necessary to release the original number decided upon, you would have to add more companies and this would mean an additional outlay of money, which I felt decidedly should be avoided."[102] Thus, though blocks did not necessarily remove the pressure to produce a particular quantity of films for distribution, they did allow for substitutions and delays in release.

Lasky and Zukor's correspondence from the beginning of this season also reveals that star-centered production units had a lasting impact on production organization at Paramount, even two years after the star series had been abandoned as a distribution format. According to Lasky, twelve star/director units were operating at his Los Angeles studios in mid-1921. Three of these units were specifically designated as handling specials and were organized around directors: Cecil B. DeMille, William DeMille, and George Melford. The other nine were all stars: Fatty Arbuckle (just before the Virginia Rappe scandal), Gloria Swanson, Betty Compson, Wallace Reid, Thomas Meighan, Jack Holt, Agnes Ayres, Ethel Clayton, and May McAvoy. In addition, four star units produced at the Realart Studio: Bebe Daniels, Wanda Hawley, Constance Binney, and Mary Miles Minter.[103]

In this organization, we can already see at least a tripartite distinction in production that mapped onto separate channels of distribution: specials that called for extended prerelease (the DeMilles and Melford), starring productions that might or might not garner prerelease exploitation (the other Lasky units) and films that were intended only for program release (the Realarts). While the Realart studio would be shuttered less than six months later, and stars would become less important as actual production units, production *planning* continued to be conceptualized according to stars or directors throughout the twenties.[104] In a 1923 letter to Lasky discussing production plans for the 1923–1924 season, Zukor divided the 41 pictures initially planned for the season into twenty-five different unit categories of one to three films each, only four of which were defined by an individual title rather than a director or a star.[105] According to Howard Lewis, by 1929 production at the studio would be divided into four distinct tiers: the Personality Pictures, the Commander Specials, the Leader Specials, and the New Show World Specials. The first two tiers were clearly intended for program release in presentation houses, with exceptional Commanders having slightly more leeway for prerelease handling. Leader Specials were given "extended run exhibition," by which Lewis meant that they were premiered in regular prerelease grind houses. The New Show Worlds went straight to extended release in two-a-days, at the $1.50–$2.00 scale.[106] Nevertheless, the Personalities continued to be subdivided by star, with each star producing three or four films across the season. Thus, even if distributors abandoned the use of stars as distribution brands after 1922 or so (depending on the studio), they continued to be an integral part of production planning practice.

In the following season Paramount introduced an innovation in block booking that was widely covered in the trade press. The 1922–1923 season films were sold in two blocks that were heavily promoted as the "Famous Forty-One" and the "Super Thirty-Nine," for a total of 80 films (only 72 of which would eventually be released). This was a departure from typical practice, which generally avoided the explicit branding of distribution blocks over the individual films on those blocks. However, the stipulations Paramount placed on the blocks called for special marketing. First, the distributor sold the blocks under a new policy that demanded playdates from exhibitors at the time of signing (this was almost a full year before the adoption of the Uniform Contract). Paramount's rental contract now "*absolutely reserved* [emphasis in original] for the Distributor the dates specified in the schedule." Even more boldly, Paramount explicitly reserved the right to "interchange" the dates of pictures "from time to time."[107] As mentioned above, studios had always reserved the right to dictate playdates, but the new policy blatantly admitted that Paramount wanted absolute control of those dates from the very beginning, in order to have the flexibility to delay certain films from general distribution. As *Variety* noted, this was not a reciprocal relationship: "It gives the distributor the right to change pictures and dates, and does not provide the same relief for the exhibitor."[108] Paramount's direct approach to the temporal management of distribution was soon adopted by the wider industry.[109]

What justified ironclad control over dates—at least in Paramount's estimation—was that more than half of the films on the first block of 41 either had been completed or were in production by May 1922, in time for the start of the annual booking season. This ostensibly meant that the distributor could offer exhibitors an unprecedented level of assurance about the films that would fill their dates for the first half of the 1922–1923 season.[110] Paramount sales personnel enticed exhibitors with a "beautifully illustrated" bound booklet that specifically outlined each production in detail and included a contract application for the block.[111] This was upgraded to a leather-bound book for the Thirty-Nine, which one Illinois exhibitor supposedly donated to his public library.[112] Paramount mounted a huge national advertising campaign for the Forty-One that included extensive promotion not only in the trade press, but also in fan magazines, newspapers, and popular publications, including the *Saturday Evening Post* and *Ladies' Home Journal*.[113]

The scale of the marketing was certainly impressive compared to the typical advertising of films sold on the block system, which tended to emphasize individual films rather than the block they were sold in. From the perspective of exhibitors, however, Paramount's willingness to state specific release dates for each picture on the Forty-One was more significant. Since the decline of the program system, distributors had been deemphasizing the release dates of individual features to encourage longer and more flexible runs, and earlier marketing of films on block contracts tended to give release dates for productions only a month or two ahead of time, as they were completed. In that respect, Paramount implicitly positioned the Forty-One and the Thirty-Nine as a return to the reliability of the program system; some exhibitors even described the blocks as programs.[114] Furthermore, the branding of the blocks emphasized the exactness of their quantity. These were the Famous Forty-One and the Super Thirty-Nine—not films that would be available in "approximately the numbers listed." Sidney Kent drove home the sales pitch: "These pictures are not promises—they are all set, established, and backed by an organization which has led the world in the high-grade consistency of its product."[115]

Indeed, Paramount's promises were not simply marketing; the company had made important changes to its production organization to produce the 1922–1923 season further in advance. The first of these was a more extensive system of production scheduling, which had been instituted at the Lasky plant beginning in the summer of 1921, following Zukor and Lasky's efforts to economize production across the slate. Lasky seems to have left the specifics of the task to Frank E. Woods, the former "supervising director" at Lasky who had recently been promoted to chief supervisor of all Paramount production activity.[116] Woods—who as a screenwriter had collaborated with D. W. Griffith, and later became production manager at Fine Arts—focused his efforts around "non-special productions." He also brought in a pair of managers from the shuttered Astoria plant, H. H. Barter and Victor H. Clarke.[117] In 1927, Woods recalled their system: "They were system men, introducing system into the studio, and they started in by giving us schedules, not only from the time the story was given to the director and the writer to concoct, but right on down the line. There were dates fixed when a story had to be assigned and the treatment had to be ready. There was a further date fixed when the continuity had to be ready; there was a further date fixed when the shooting should commence."[118]

Woods's emphasis on pre-production here suggests that the primary function of Barter and Clarke's scheduling system was less about managing the in-process details of shooting than it was about producing a finished script that could be started on time and finished without delay—a "schedule for all stages of operation," as Woods put it. Applied to non-special productions, the system was a macro-level production control strategy, because it scheduled productions in relation to each other according to the studio's temporal resources as a whole. Specific strategies of communication and coordination sought to minimize the drain of any one picture on those resources. For example, the system mandated that writers consult with the art and construction departments, so that they could write each script with an eye toward the specific studio resources that would be available at the time of shooting.[119]

This temporal management of production was made possible by the second major change Woods instituted at Paramount: a reconfiguration of the studio's supervisor system of production control. The title of "supervisor" had a somewhat ambiguous meaning during this period. It was commonly used to refer to any mid-level figure who reported to a studio's central producer but had authority over a film's director and writers.[120] Jesse Lasky, who credited Woods and himself with the designation, described the role as "the eyes of the management."[121] A supervisor might be a film's scenario editor or a former director and might go by the titles of "representative to the producer" or "associate producer," though the latter was increasingly becoming the standard term by the late 1920s. In the early 1920s, regardless of any other title they might have held, supervisors generally supervised one film at a time and would be assigned to a particular director- or star-centered unit of production. At Lasky—perhaps because of Woods's background—supervisors were effectively glorified scenario editors who had the authority to "settle difficulties" between the director and the writer by making final decisions about the script.[122]

Woods expanded this role in 1922, giving supervisors charge over three or four pictures at once: "from the moment the scenario is turned over to the director to the completion of the editing and titling."[123] This expansion of the role of the supervisor operationalized production control at a scale larger than the individual film, but smaller than the level of the entire program. Unlike the later producer-unit system of the 1930s, in which producer units were defined by the type of picture, the decision as to which films a particular supervisor worked on at a time was a direct function of the new scheduling system.[124] Woods explicitly described that system as an "elaboration" of the older function of the supervisor, as supervisors were now able to budget studio time and resources across three or four films rather than just one.[125] Producing films according to the advanced schedule that would be required by the "Famous Forty-One" thus necessitated careful "mid-level" temporal management of production resources, and block booking undoubtedly helped to facilitate that management.

Paramount's strategy worked well, if not perfectly, for the first block of 41. By the time of its completion on February 7, 1923, 38 films had been released on block 1. The three-picture shortage was the result of Cosmopolitan withdrawing two of its productions from the program and Paramount failing to produce one picture originally slated for January. Block 2, however, fell even shorter: only 34 pictures of the "Super Thirty-Nine" had been released by June 1, 1923. This time, the blame was primarily Paramount's, but not because of production problems. Rather, Paramount intentionally withdrew three very successful specials—*The Covered Wagon, Hollywood,* and *Bluebeard's 8th Wife*—from the block to give them extended prerelease runs.[126] Because these runs ran into the subsequent season, it was impossible for Paramount to continue selling them on block 2—in fact, most exhibitors did not get access to *The Covered Wagon* until the fall of 1924.

According to *Variety*, exhibitors "howled" over the decision, and they had good reason to: the move was yet another example of a strategy Paramount had used since 1916, when it removed Mary Pickford from the program and put her on the premium Artcraft brand.[127] Exhibitors were especially miffed that the original sale of the specials been largely based on the promise of specific release dates for general distribution.[128] While exhibitors did not necessarily expect to get a specific film on a given date, their surrender of playdates to Paramount was based on the expectation that all the company's films would eventually be available that season. Paramount's withdrawal effectively rendered a number of dates worthless for exhibitors that had reserved the block—anywhere from one to five weeks' worth of films, depending on expected run times. Some exhibitors even threatened legal action, which held up the road-show of *The Covered Wagon* in some areas.[129] Despite the problems it caused exhibitors, Paramount did not suffer any significant consequences, and the practice of withdrawing specials from blocks would continue at least for the next two seasons. In the 1925–1926 season, for instance, *The Vanishing American* (George B. Seitz, 1925) was removed from its initial block of 40 films so that it could be roadshowed. As the owner of the Stanley Theatre in Bensonhurst, Brooklyn, put it, "That's the only trouble with block-booking. Essentially, the idea is great, and a god-send

for most exhibitors . . . [but then] they show a picture that surpasses all
expectations in its Broadway release, and then delay the national release
until it suits their own devices."[130]

The 1922–1923 season was an important one for Paramount's conceptualization of the relationship between block booking and production
planning. Making productions far enough in advance to convince exhibitors to give up their playdates was an effective sales strategy to a point,
but it was a risky and inflexible way to make big features that could
perform exceptionally at the box office. In April 1923, as distribution
planning for the 1923–1924 season was in full swing, Lasky wrote a
letter to Zukor:

> I am quite convinced that we must find some way of adapt-
> ing our selling methods to the making of productions. As it is,
> we are trying to make our product to accommodate the selling
> plan, which I feel has a lot of faults. In a word, we are forcing
> ourselves to make hasty decisions, through working too far in
> advance. . . .
>
> When the time comes for the [sales] book to go to press,
> you and Mr. Kent can check up and see how many productions
> are listed, and how much information the book can contain.
> I still hope you can find a way of listing only four months, or
> better yet, three months in advance. This means extra selling
> cost, I know, but it has so many compensations that it is worthy
> of the most serious consideration. . . .
>
> Our competitors are making the best pictures of their
> careers. Many of them have abandoned the so-called "star"
> pictures, and are making only specials, and all of them spend-
> ing money lavishly. I never saw such active competition, and
> there never was a period of such high salaries—inflated sala-
> ries you will call them—as exists right now. Naturally we must
> keep abreast of the times, and I have keyed up our production
> organization to the very limit. Regardless of how we name our
> productions they will all actually be "specials," in a sense, from
> now on.[131]

Lasky's letter highlighted fundamental tensions in both distribution
and production. As productions grew more and more ambitious, greater
flexibility in distribution was required to sell them; at the same time,

distributors needed a certain amount of predictable output, not only to keep up a steady cash flow, but to convince exhibitors to buy their product both in bulk and in advance. Block booking offered the most obvious middle ground in its combination of programmatic organization and flexible scheduling, but the production-in-advance approach of 1922–1923, combined with the two-block distribution strategy, was still too inflexible for Lasky's purposes. Simply selling big films in distribution blocks was not enough; those blocks had to be flexible enough for the most promising films to develop to their fullest potential in production, as well as to accommodate prerelease presentation in a more systematic way. Furthermore, Lasky's distinction between "star pictures" and specials pointed to another significant development. In the late 1910s, stars had been differentiated from the more modest production of the regular program, but as the 1920s went on, they increasingly became associated with the program rather than with special productions. Lasky's distinction anticipates the more explicit production distinctions that, by 1929, would place star-centered features at the bottom two levels of the production hierarchy.[132]

Lasky's proposals in this letter, along with the box-office success of *The Covered Wagon*, would shape much of Paramount's sales policy for 1923–1924. That season was organized into three blocks instead of two, and the number of features produced for the season was drastically reduced, to an anticipated output of only 50 films, in an effort to concentrate on Lasky's "specials."[133] The three blocks would eventually be made up of 12, 19, and 17 films, respectively, for a total of 48 pictures actually distributed—the fewest number of features Paramount had ever released in a single year up to that point. Paramount's distribution planning for this season seems to have been delayed; little fanfare or certainty accompanied the initial sale of the first block in the late spring of 1923, certainly as compared to the marketing of the Famous Forty-One a year earlier. As late as June, the company was still making decisions about how to sell the new season: "For the benefit of the exhibitor who books Paramount's new product for 1923–1924 it has been deemed advisable not to reveal plans and details on [more than 14 pictures] at this time."[134] The first block of 12 films—Paramount's first to be distributed according to the terms of the Uniform Exhibition Contract—was sold on the typical model.[135]

The second block of the 1923–1924 season brought about yet another major change accompanied by trade press fanfare. Paramount announced that beginning on November 1—the start of block 2—its features would be released on a "demonstration plan," whereby "no exhibitor will be asked to sign a contract for the future Paramount Pictures until he has witnessed an actual demonstration of their box-office value."[136] The demonstration policy was effectively a return to the selective booking policy of 1919–1920, as pictures were now sold on an individual basis, but with the added twist of giving every feature on the Paramount program a regional prerelease. Exhibitors could only book films *after* they had finished a run in one of one hundred (mostly Paramount-controlled) pre-demonstration theaters, the idea being that any film could conceivably turn into the next *Blood and Sand* or *Covered Wagon* and that exhibitors would benefit from the exploitation.[137]

In a deviation from the contemporary practice of prereleases, Paramount would demonstrate each production not only in New York, but in *every* key city, so that exhibitors would have an accurate demonstration of how the film would fare in their particular territory: "You will not be asked to accept a Broadway showing alone as a basis of value."[138] This was an important change, because it nationalized the practice of run exhibition and decreased the relative importance of the Broadway prerelease in determining the exhibition value of Paramount's films. Paramount had already experimented with this concept in the 1922–1923 season, when it prereleased at least 7 films across both blocks in cities other than New York.[139] However, it became an official distribution policy in 1923–1924.[140]

As it turned out, exhibitors hated the new policy. According to FPL's Dallas exchange manager, "they did not have any assurance of product; they didn't know when they were going to get the next picture; they didn't know how to set their bookings in. As a whole, it proved very unsatisfactory to the average exhibitor."[141] Because it denied exhibitors the ability to buy in bulk or in advance, as well as the assurance of specific release dates or pricing, the demonstration plan had the opposite effect from what Paramount had ostensibly intended: it actually reduced the rental prices of most individual features. This was because the company's exchanges often did not have release dates for exhibitors until three or four months after the beginning of the initial demonstration run, by which time the exhibitors had set in their bookings with product from other distributors. Exhibitors had been annoyed with Paramount's removal of specials in the 1922–1923 season, but its programmatic blocks were at least reliable enough that many exhibitors used the distributor as their "backbone" or "rib" program, scheduling the product of other companies around the playdates they had reserved for Paramount in advance. The 1923–1924 pre-demonstration policy lost the distributor much of that assured playing time. On top of that, sales costs were much higher under pre-demonstration, because each film now required a separate sales call (just as had been the case with selective booking in 1919–1920). Paramount quickly retracted the policy; though they had planned to apply it to a total of 31 films in the second block of the 1923–1924 season, the company ended up selling only 10 pictures through pre-demonstration. The rest of the season was reorganized and sold in traditional blocks.[142]

Paramount's brief pre-demonstration policy in the 1923–1924 season highlighted block booking's primary advantage as a strategy of temporal management: its ability to reserve exhibitors' playdates in advance. Building the exploitation value of films through prereleases and delayed runs meant little if exhibitors did not have free dates on which to book those films once they were finally available. Exhibitors might complain about successful films being delayed or removed from the program, but after 1923, the Uniform Contract's playdate and arbitration provisions gave them almost no control over when they were entitled to actually play specific features. We also should not discount the possibility that Paramount expected the pre-demonstration policy to be unsuccessful to some extent. The company, then embroiled in the FTC case, had every reason to mount a publicized, full-throated move to individual sales of pictures. If exhibitors didn't *want* to buy pictures individually—which certainly must have crossed the minds of the sales department—Paramount's lawyers could then point to the policy's failure as an argument for block booking, which they did. Regardless of whether this was the case, pre-demonstration did help to solidify the national key city pre-release as a standard practice in film distribution during the classical period. Paramount and the other distributors increasingly prereleased their pictures in all the key cities as a standard practice after 1924.[143]

In the first half of the 1920s, distributors reasserted their temporal control over exhibitors' playing time in response to the problem of overbooking. Mixed distribution blocks, by emphasizing the playdate rather than the star or the program as the fundamental unit of transaction in film sales, enabled distributors to release their product more flexibly while still pricing films individually. Although the transition to sound would see important changes to the pricing structure of the block system—most notably the systematic integration of percentage-based rentals—the superiority of block booking as a programmatic but flexible distribution format was obvious throughout the industry by the end of the 1923–1924 season. After 1923, uniform contract terms defined a more explicit practice of playdate determination, which only solidified block booking's utility as a tool of temporal management.

Both of these developments enabled distributors to integrate run exhibition more systematically into the regular release system, which allowed for a tiering of distribution that mirrored distinctions among individual films in production. Films continued to be planned for specific channels of distribution, but those channels were no longer as predetermined or totalizing as they had been under the program system. Features could now be handled more easily in distribution, *after* their release, according to their individual characteristics. However, as the failure of Paramount's pre-demonstration policy indicates, programmatic distribution continued to be important, and studios refined their production control practices as a consequence. These refinements involved new methods of controlling costs across the program as a whole as well as greater attention to the temporal management of "mid-level" production resources. By giving supervisors authority over three or four films at once, Paramount enabled them to temporally manage individual films with an understanding of their larger place within the distribution hierarchy. By the mid-twenties, distributors had developed a refined sense of how to plan a program made up of individually distinguished features—features that could nevertheless be distributed flexibly and profitably.

6 PRICING

What Price Sound?
Selling the Percentage Exhibition Contract, 1919–1930

By the mid-1920s, the practices of film packaging, centralized marketing, and production planning at the Hollywood studios had reached a level of sophistication that starkly contrasted with the practices of both the General Film Company and the early feature program distributors. Certainly, overbuying and overselling, unplayed contracts, and other conflicts with theaters continued throughout this period. These would not disappear even at the height of the studio oligopoly. However, by 1926 distributors had gathered nearly twenty years of increasingly granular market and price signals from American exhibitors. This information did not always extend to theaters' actual box-office receipts, but it certainly gave them a strong sense of the income potential and relative power of the independent houses within their local markets. Along with the settling of the distribution market in the aftermath of mixed block packaging and more uniform contracting, this was one factor in the "second wave" of Wall Street's investment in the industry in the mid-1920s. As Lee Grieveson notes, film industry executives knew both that distribution was "integral to profitability and control" and that the studios had ostensibly achieved that control at a global scale. They constantly communicated this understanding to financiers and Wall Street investment firms.[1]

It was obvious that movies were now big business. Yet just as the struggle between distributors and exhibitors over film packaging was turning decisively in favor of the studios in late 1923—the beginning of the first full season under the Uniform Contract—a long-standing question about the pricing of films to exhibitors began to take on new relevance. Since the beginning of the industry, exhibitors who bought film service programmatically had generally paid flat rental fees for it. This was largely a result of the packaging developments covered in chapter 2. Since cinema distribution eventually came to be organized around the programmatic rental of films alone rather than complete, idiosyncratic packages of exhibition, the default pricing model followed that of vaudeville and the early exhibition services: a flat "salary" paid to the act for each day of performance. Percentage-priced ("sharing") contracts, where box-office receipts were split between venue and production, were reserved for situations where the producer-distributor brought something of unusual value to the booking, such as an idiosyncratic characteristic of the attraction itself or extensive exploitation through an advance manager. This is why legitimate theater had used sharing arrangements since the earliest star benefit performances, and why percentage pricing to exhibitors was the norm for the state rights feature and the roadshow.[2]

Picture theaters, by contrast, generally paid all the expenses for local advertisement, and the continued short runs of most films—two or three days in 1922—meant that the majority of films were priced according to the assumption that they constituted routinely changed programming rather than something special. Almost all the exhibition contracts Thomas Watson signed were for flat fees. Pricing is explicitly mentioned in his papers for roughly 150 films booked at the Superba between 1918 and 1924, either on contracts or in correspondence. Of these, only four—all big specials that had previously been roadshowed—were priced via a percentage of box office paid to the distributor.[3] Thus, though it was not unusual for even small exhibitors to book an occasional special production for which they shared receipts with the distributor, percentage pricing was the exception rather than the rule for most exhibitors in the 1920s.

Yet with the growing tendency among the studios to package "selectively booked" films into programmatic distribution blocks while pricing them individually, distributors sought to capitalize on individual films more directly. In part, this was because they realized just how much money exhibitors were bringing into their box offices. Though the total yearly intake of the 5 percent admissions tax instituted in May 1919 covered all forms of theatrical entertainment, not just motion pictures, it gave distributors some sense of what this aggregate amount was and how much more money there was to be made via percentage booking as opposed to flat rentals. In November 1923, *Exhibitors Trade Review* did some rough math. Assuming that about half the intake of the previous year's admissions tax was for movies specifically, the paper estimated that total box-office receipts for 1923 were on track to total about $700 million. A similar calculation for the distributors' rentals amounted to $150 million—suggesting that distributors were collecting roughly 20 percent of the total box office. The *Review* explicitly counterposed these numbers to the typical percentage contracts in legitimate theater, where anywhere from 35 to 80 percent of the box office went to the producer.[4] From the *Review*'s perspective, distributors had a strong incentive to push for more percentage booking.

Starting in 1919, percentage pricing in exhibition contracts became a frequent topic at all levels of industry discourse, from the individual small exhibitor negotiating with a distributor, to performative trade press editorials, to internal industry discussions. Since the emergence of multireel feature films as the industry's standard product in the mid-1910s, distributors had waged a mostly fruitless campaign for percentage rentals to become the norm in programmatic exhibition contracts, particularly in large theaters. Although percentage rentals would become standard among large urban exhibitors by the mid-1920s, most exhibitors continued to pay for the bulk of their product via flat fees. This changed with the transition to sound, which would prove an advantageous moment for shifting the industry's distribution pricing toward a model that was anchored around percentage rentals—not just from the biggest first-run houses, but from nearly all exhibitors.

Exhibitors in the 1910s and 1920s preferred flat fee rentals for several reasons. First, they were a conservative and familiar pricing strategy for exhibitors who had been paying for film service at flat rates since the nickelodeon days. Flat fees were less about gathering all the box-office take of hit films than about keeping rental costs consistent and predictable, which for small houses was the most direct means to ensure regular profits. Second—and this was a point constantly reiterated in the exhibitor-oriented trade press—percentage rentals revealed box-office data to distributors, giving them a powerful point of leverage in later negotiations over rental pricing with the exhibitor or their competitors. Independent exhibitors thus tended to avoid them as a rule, certainly for program films that would have given distributors particularly revealing numbers about a typical night's box office.

Even for distributors, who benefited more obviously from a shared stake in their film's ticket sales, flat fees had some advantages. For one, percentage booking depended in part on the assumption that exhibitors were going to be honest in reporting their ticket sales. Distributors sometimes hired representatives known as "checkers" to verify a theater's box-office intake, but generally only in large, independently owned theaters and markets. It made very little economic sense to hire checkers for small theaters, as the cost of employing the checker could be more than the likely meager additional profit to be made from a percentage rental in those situations. Furthermore, percentage booking was itself not without risk, particularly if it was not accompanied by a so-called guarantee—a flat rental fee due to the distributor in addition to some percentage split. For distributors dealing with small and independent exhibitors, flat rentals eliminated much of the uncertainty of film booking by sacrificing potentially higher profits. Especially in the silent era, these additional profits were likely to be marginal anyway.

Nevertheless, percentage rentals would be a standard part of exhibition contracts in the 1930s. The changes that the transition to sound brought about in the standard pricing of exhibition contracts in smaller markets are apparent when we compare two sets of contracts from similarly sized theaters. First, consider the June 1921 contract Thomas Watson signed with Metro sales representative Edwin M. Booth for the 1921–1922 season (figure 6.1).

Each of the approximately thirty-eight films in the contract is priced at a particular flat rental rate according to the star: Nazimova's two features are priced at $75 each, and Viola Dana's six films are $60 for each two-day run. Four individual titles are also included as part of the contract, at a higher price per film than any of the star series films; these are Metro's six- and seven-reel "special releases" for the 1921–1922 season. Most programmatic contracts signed between distributors and small exhibitors in the early 1920s likely resembled this mixed package of programs, series, and individual films priced at a flat rate according to picture. Though the contract includes films labeled as "specials," these were not really Metro's specials but the kind of interstitial upmarket films *Variety* would later describe as "verging on the special class"—A films, put in the language of the 1930s.[5] When Watson did book specials, they

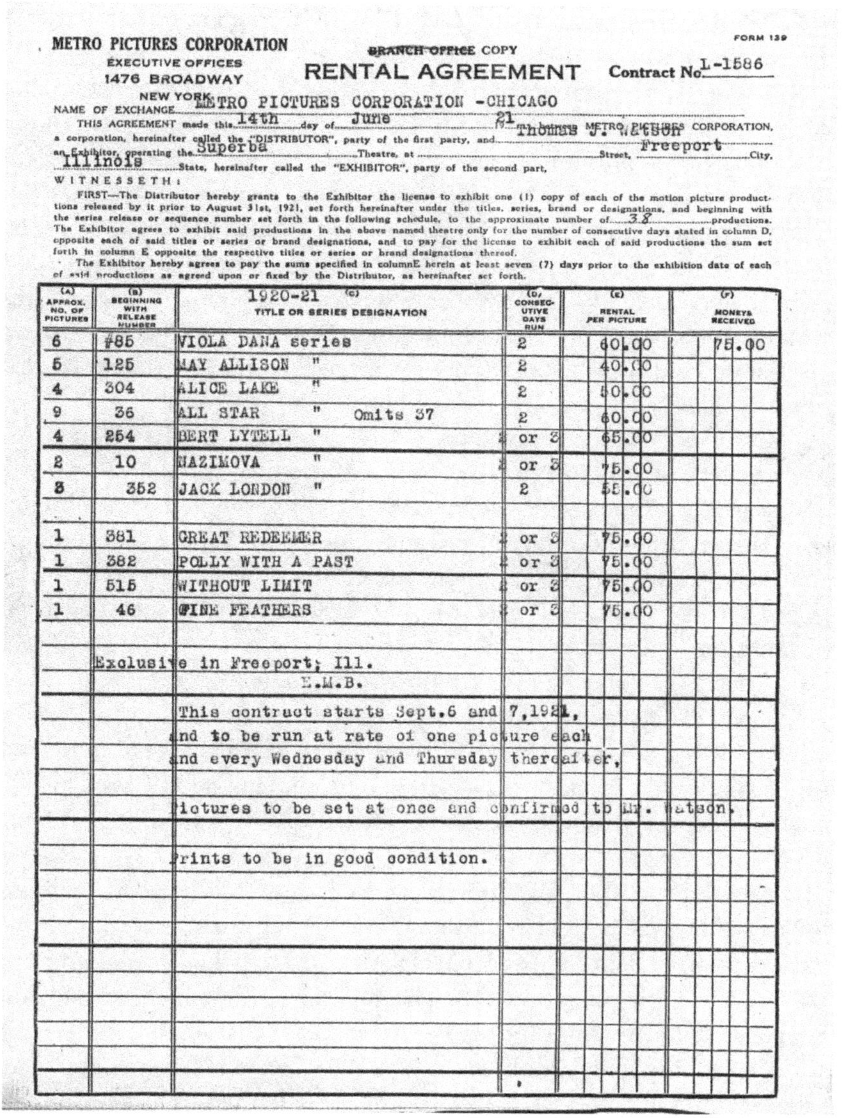

METRO PICTURES CORPORATION
EXECUTIVE OFFICES
1476 BROADWAY
NEW YORK

~~BRANCH OFFICE~~ COPY

RENTAL AGREEMENT

FORM 139

Contract No. L-1586

NAME OF EXCHANGE METRO PICTURES CORPORATION -CHICAGO

THIS AGREEMENT made this 14th day of June 19 21 between METRO PICTURES CORPORATION, a corporation, hereinafter called the "DISTRIBUTOR", party of the first party, and Thomas J. Watson an Exhibitor, operating the Superba Theatre, at .... Street, Freeport City, Illinois State, hereinafter called the "EXHIBITOR", party of the second part,

WITNESSETH:

FIRST—The Distributor hereby grants to the Exhibitor the license to exhibit one (1) copy of each of the motion picture productions released by it prior to August 31st, 1921, set forth hereinafter under the titles, series, brand or designations, and beginning with the series release or sequence number set forth in the following schedule, to the approximate number of 38 productions. The Exhibitor agrees to exhibit said productions in the above named theatre only for the number of consecutive days stated in column D, opposite each of said titles or series or brand designations, and to pay for the license to exhibit each of said productions the sum set forth in column E opposite the respective titles or series or brand designations thereof.

The Exhibitor hereby agrees to pay the sums specified in columnE herein at least seven (7) days prior to the exhibition date of each of said productions as agreed upon or fixed by the Distributor, as hereinafter set forth.

(A) Approx. No. of Pictures	(B) Beginning with Release Number	(C) 1920-21 Title or Series Designation	(D) Consecutive Days Run	(E) Rental per Picture	(F) Moneys Received
6	#85	VIOLA DANA series	2	60.00	75.00
5	125	MAY ALLISON "	2	40.00	
4	304	ALICE LAKE "	2	50.00	
9	36	ALL STAR " Omits 37	2	60.00	
4	254	BERT LYTELL "	2 or 3	65.00	
2	10	NAZIMOVA "	2 or 3	75.00	
3	352	JACK LONDON "	2	55.00	
1	381	GREAT REDEEMER	2 or 3	75.00	
1	382	POLLY WITH A PAST	2 or 3	75.00	
1	515	WITHOUT LIMIT	2 or 3	75.00	
1	46	FINE FEATHERS	2 or 3	75.00	

Exclusive in Freeport; Ill.
E.M.B.

This contract starts Sept.6 and 7,1921, and to be run at rate of one picture each and every Wednesday and Thursday thereafter,

Pictures to be set at once and confirmed to Mr. Watson.

Prints to be in good condition.

Figure 6.1. *Thomas J. Watson's 1921 contract with Metro. Wisconsin Historical Society, WHI-157857. Metro Pictures Corporation Rental Agreement with Watson, June 30, 1921, Box 9, Folder 13.*

were always on a separate contract, as with a booking of Paramount's *The Covered Wagon* in 1924 (figure 6.2).

The settlement statement for this contract indicates that the booking covered a weeklong run and was priced on percentage: 50 percent of the box-office gross, plus a flat rental guarantee of $600. These were exceptional terms for Watson. Through the guarantee, he paid the equivalent of $85 a day plus half of his box office for *The Covered Wagon*, as opposed to a flat $20 or $30 a day for the Metro films in the previous contract. Of course, *The Covered Wagon* was the top-grossing film of 1923, and this would have been the premiere of the film in Freeport, Illinois. Thus, while percentage contracts were not unheard of in the early 1920s, they tended to be handled separately and reserved for the biggest films.

Compare Watson's contracts to those signed by Mrs. Daniel M. Shaver of Shavertown, Pennsylvania (1940 population: 4,000), for her 350-seat theater in advance of the 1939–1940 season, recorded in congressional testimony on the Neely anti–block-booking bill (figure 6.3).[6] Shaver's contract with Paramount covers forty-seven features and is priced across five different tiers. Most are still sold for flat fees, but seven of the films, amounting to 15 percent of the contracted features, have been priced as a percentage of gross receipts: six at 35 percent and one at 40 percent. This was only Shaver's contract for features; she signed three others with Paramount covering, respectively, the Fleischers' animated special *Gulliver's Travels*, sold at 40 percent; six Hopalong Cassidy westerns, sold for flat fees; and a season's worth of Paramount shorts, also for flat fees.

The terms and organization of Shaver's contracts are corroborated by accounts elsewhere in the testimony collected for the Neely bill, as well as in other sources describing 1930s contracts that integrated both sharing and flat pricing brackets. The government's 1950 Amended and Supplemental Complaint for the *Paramount* case characterized as typical a block contract for forty films in which *half* were sold on percentage: "four features at 35%; six at 30%; ten at 25%; ten at $200.00 flat rental; and ten at $100.00 flat rental."[7] The much higher flat pricing of this average contract compared to Shaver's—ten times the $12 to $15 she paid for B films—suggests that the income of her theater was quite marginal indeed. This indicates how common percentage was within the pricing structure of block contracts by the end of the 1930s, even for very small exhibitors. By that point, percentage pricing was used not only for specials that, like *Gulliver's Travels*, were packaged separately from the rest

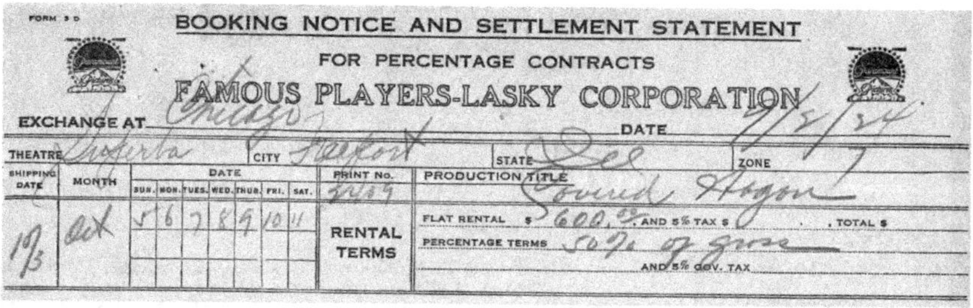

FORM 5 D

BOOKING NOTICE AND SETTLEMENT STATEMENT

FOR PERCENTAGE CONTRACTS

FAMOUS PLAYERS-LASKY CORPORATION

EXCHANGE AT Chicago DATE 9/2/24

THEATRE Liberta CITY Freeport STATE Ill ZONE

SHIPPING DATE	MONTH	SUN.	MON.	TUES.	WED.	THUR.	FRI.	SAT.	PRINT NO.	PRODUCTION TITLE
10/3	Oct	5	6	7	8	9	10	11	2209	Covered Wagon

RENTAL TERMS

FLAT RENTAL $ 600.00 AND 5% TAX $, TOTAL $

PERCENTAGE TERMS 50% of gross

AND 5% GOV. TAX

Figure 6.2. *Thomas J. Watson's contract for* The Covered Wagon. *Wisconsin Historical Society, WHI-157557. Booking Notice and Settlement Statement for Percentage Contracts, Box 8, Folder 16.*

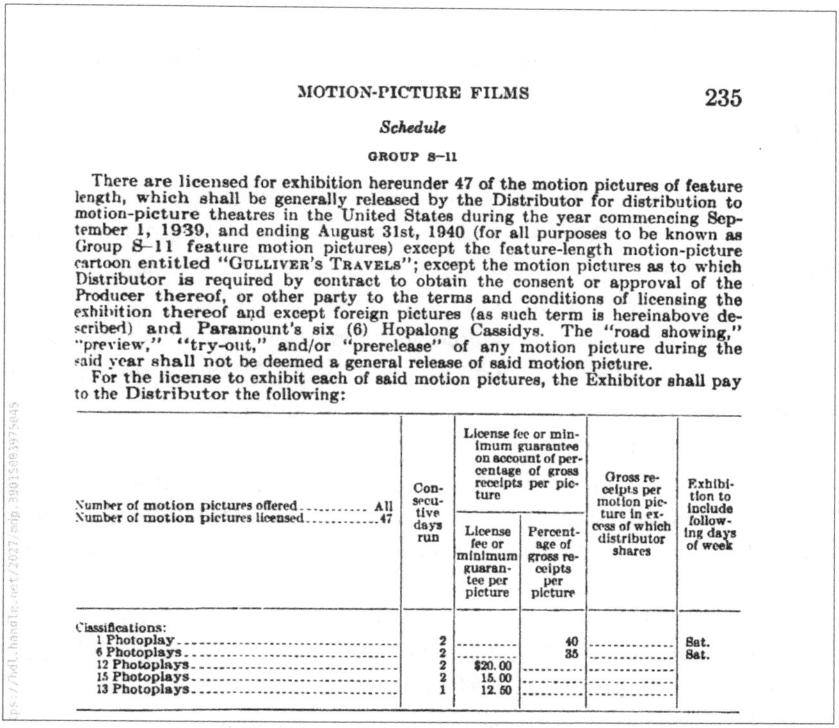

MOTION-PICTURE FILMS 235

Schedule

GROUP S–11

There are licensed for exhibition hereunder 47 of the motion pictures of feature length, which shall be generally released by the Distributor for distribution to motion-picture theatres in the United States during the year commencing September 1, 1939, and ending August 31st, 1940 (for all purposes to be known as Group S–11 feature motion pictures) except the feature-length motion-picture cartoon entitled "GULLIVER'S TRAVELS"; except the motion pictures as to which Distributor is required by contract to obtain the consent or approval of the Producer thereof, or other party to the terms and conditions of licensing the exhibition thereof and except foreign pictures (as such term is hereinabove described) and Paramount's six (6) Hopalong Cassidys. The "road showing," "preview," "try-out," and/or "prerelease" of any motion picture during the said year shall not be deemed a general release of said motion picture.

For the license to exhibit each of said motion pictures, the Exhibitor shall pay to the Distributor the following:

Number of motion pictures offered .... All Number of motion pictures licensed 47	Consecutive days run	License fee or minimum guarantee on account of percentage of gross receipts per picture: License fee or minimum guarantee per picture	License fee or minimum guarantee on account of percentage of gross receipts per picture: Percentage of gross receipts per picture	Gross receipts per motion picture in excess of which distributor shares	Exhibition to include following days of week
Classifications:					
1 Photoplay	2	....	40	....	Sat.
6 Photoplays	2	....	35	....	Sat.
12 Photoplays	2	$20.00	....	....	
15 Photoplays	2	15.00	....	....	
13 Photoplays	1	12.50	....	....	

Figure 6.3. *Mrs. Daniel M. Shaver's contract with Paramount. House Committee on Interstate Commerce (for S. 280, the "Neely bill"),* Motion-Picture Films (Compulsory Block Booking and Blind Selling*) (1940), 235.*

of the features, but also for the higher-level program features that were now commonly referred to as A films.[8]

The economist F. Andrew Hanssen has made perhaps the most compelling case for the ubiquity of percentage exhibition contracts through the 1930s, showing that at seven West Coast theaters (most of them Warners affiliated) during the 1930–1931 season, 95 percent of the bookings for Warner Bros. films were priced on percentage. The average percentage charged also steadily increased: Fox and Paramount charged Warners-owned theaters an average of 23 percent for their 1931–1932 films and 32 percent for their 1942–1943 films. This pattern obtained not only between the major distributors and their affiliated theaters, but for independent bookings as well. At a selected group of independent theaters renting Warners films in and around Philadelphia and northern New Jersey, the average percentage rental paid to Warners increased from 18 percent (1931–1932) to 25 percent (1939–1940) to 38 percent (1947–1948).[9]

Why did percentage pricing become the norm over the course of the years separating Watson's and Shaver's respective contracts? Scholars have generally pointed to the transition to sound as the moment when percentage-based terms became standard in nearly all exhibition contracts. Howard Lewis, writing in 1933, argued that sound pictures, because of their "unknown worth," presented an "opportunity for experimentation with percentage pricing" beginning in the 1928–1929 season.[10] Donald Crafton has argued that distributors offered sound films on percentage in part simply to exploit anticipation of the new technology, but also as an effort to "poach" the significant economic value produced by stage and radio entertainers for exhibitors' live prologue presentations. According to Crafton, percentage contracts encouraged exhibitors to cut their expenses on prologues, moving that value onto the screen itself.[11]

Hanssen offers an explanation similar to Crafton's, based in the economic principle of "shirking": the tendency to do less work when the promise of a return on that work is lower. He argues that because sound films eliminated any economic return from providing the sonic aspects of the moviegoing experience (accompanying musicians, stage performances, etc.), exhibitors no longer risked those costs and were more willing to accept sharing contracts with distributors. Distributors, in turn, were less threatened by the risk of exhibitor shirking that percentage contracts had presented during the silent era: "Postsound," according to Hanssen, "the films were the reason that patrons visited a cinema. This was not true during the silent film years, when the exhibitor's own live shows often surpassed the film in their attractiveness to audiences."[12] Hanssen's argument amounts to the idea that sound transformed presentation-oriented exhibitors from contributing producers of cinema as an experience—through their provision of live music and theater alongside films—into mere agents of the distributors, the final point of sale for a mass-market supply chain.

All these arguments situate the change in pricing terms to exhibitors as the result of what Hanssen terms the "technology shock" presented by sound. However, as proximate explanations for the transition to percentage pricing, they mostly ignore distribution practices, situating the change either in production (the new supply of sound films) or exhibition (the decline of live presentations in theaters). They also buy into an assumption that the period 1928–1930 saw a clear break, with percentage contracts rare before then and dominant afterward. Hanssen's own data complicates this assumption. In his survey of nine mostly Warners-affiliated West Coast theaters, the two lowest-revenue houses—the California (revenue: $997/week) and the Forum ($1,238/week), both in Los Angeles—reversed the pattern of the other seven, paying flat fees rather than a percentage rate for nearly all of their contracts.[13] Though Hanssen assumes from their revenues that these two theaters were "smaller," they were in fact the two largest houses of the nine, with the California seating 1,900 and the Forum 2,000.[14] Hanssen's data also troubles any correspondence between theaters' affiliation with a major distributor and the use of percentage rentals. As of 1933, the Forum was Warners affiliated and the California independent.[15] While the broad pattern Hanssen and Crafton lay out still holds, given the other evidence presented above, it is clear that the exhibition-related aspects of the transition to sound cannot entirely explain why the American film industry shifted to a percentage pricing model.

The "technology shock" explanation is further complicated by the fact that other shocks to exhibitors in the earliest years of the 1930s could reasonably explain why theaters reduced their weekly outlays for film rental—the beginning of the Great Depression being the most obvious. The distribution practices examined in the previous chapters must also be taken into consideration as causal factors—particularly the advance deposit system, which made a kind of reappearance with sound. As we will see later in this chapter, the percentage contracts offered in 1928 and 1929 relied on guarantees to the distributor and additional charges for sound that presented real cash-flow issues for many exhibitors. As a result, they were not well liked, eventually prompting distributors to move toward "straight percentage" pricing, which was much more common in the contracts of the mid- and late 1930s. If not for the Great Depression, it is possible that this antipathy toward percentage booking would have continued and the practice not have been as widely adopted in the industry. Perhaps most importantly, percentage booking was not necessarily assumed to be ideal even among distributors, as suggested by their internal discussions. Since the decline of the program system, percentage booking had been a much-written-about topic in the trade press, and it was not always viewed in a favorable light. The coming of sound presented a new opportunity to reframe these debates as an appropriate response to technological change. Beginning in 1927, the Motion Picture Producers and Distributors of America (MPPDA) waged a campaign in the trade press, at exhibitor organization conventions, and at regional Film Boards of Trade that inevitably situated percentage booking as the solution to renting sound film. This rhetoric came out of preexisting discourses in the 1920s that situated the same method as the solution to *other* problems of film distribution.

The role of sound in selling to exhibitors on a percentage basis must thus be understood not simply as the result of a technological shock, or as an inevitable result of the laws of economics, but also as an outgrowth of developments in film distribution. Ultimately, sound was just one part of a larger long-term effort among distributors to turn the 20 percent of box-office receipts that flat rentals were ostensibly yielding in the early 1920s into something more lucrative—or, at the very least, something over which they could exert greater control.

The "Percentage Plan," Exhibitors, and the Trade Press, 1919–1926

The earliest sustained discussions of reconfiguring film pricing around percentages in the trade press came about as a response to the emergence of United Artists and the subsequent move among distributors toward "selective" booking in the spring selling season of 1919. Most authors at the time tended to frame percentage pricing not as a replacement for flat rentals, but as a kind of modification of them through guarantees ("first money"), allowances for house expenses ("second money"), and other hedging strategies. *Exhibitors Herald* and *Motography* saw percentage contracts as an equitable way to "force longer runs and consequently better profits" but thought it "inconceivable" that distributors would not also include a flat guarantee "of an amount equivalent to the old rental."[16] *Variety* reported that Famous Players–Lasky's sales plan for 1919–1920 would integrate percentage booking at 50 percent, with a guarantee to Paramount set at half the amount of the former flat rental, but without any charges for "overhead and exploitation."[17] By August 1919, it was clear that Paramount was marketing this plan only for twelve "special film subjects" within the distribution slate, but *Variety* thought it noteworthy that percentage pricing was being offered not only to the picture houses playing the company's "regular weekly features," but also to legitimate theaters.[18]

This percentage plan was thus part of an early attempt to integrate run exhibition into the broader release system. *Variety* emphasized that a feature sold on the plan was "not limited in its stay and may endure as long as the box office says it is advisable," but doubted that the picture theaters running Paramount service programmatically would alter their change policy for these specials (the first of which was *The Miracle Man*). Legitimate theaters had the subsequent option to book the films. Paramount's percentage strategy for 1919–1920 actually extended to its broader program as well. In Washington, DC, exhibitor Tom Moore accepted an arrangement giving him his pick of forty program films from Paramount at the same 50 percent terms as the specials. While Marcus Loew's Columbia retained the first run in Washington, Moore's second-run booking with Paramount was significant: "It is believed to be the first time a picture exhibitor has entered into an agreement of this kind with a distributor to play percentage under weekly releases (no specials) continuously," said *Variety*.[19]

Despite these early attempts at integrating percentage pricing into both legitimate and picture houses in the key cities, percentage booking was difficult to systematize, in part because of the wider changes in the market that open and selective booking had created. *Motion Picture News* noted, in September 1919, that the extreme prices first-run flat rentals were reaching in cities obviously called for a wider adoption of percentage booking, but the individuated nature of the films involved made the question of what constituted a "fair return to the producer" extremely complicated.[20] This was one reason why distributors set exhibition scales for their films in this period; endless negotiation over idiosyncratic sharing contracts threatened to whittle away the profitability of the program as a whole.

In response to *Motion Picture News* editor William A. Johnston's claim, in a widely read pro-percentage editorial, that distributors' rentals collectively amounted to only 12 percent of the national box office—a definite underestimate—Omaha exhibitor "A. H. Blank" insisted that when factoring in the amount of advertising material exhibitors paid distributors for, the amount was closer to 30 percent.[21] Some distributors, including Louis B. Mayer, defended Johnston's claims, situating percentage booking as the solution to high prices for program features according to the "fewer and better pictures" logic discussed in chapter 3.[22] None other than Robert W. Priest, now president of the state rights firm The Film Market, predicted that all films would someday be booked on percentage, "exactly as theatrical attractions are now played." A more accurate and strategically ambivalent view was offered by Milwaukee exhibitor and First National franchisee Thomas Saxe, who noted that percentage booking would likely encourage producers to dictate admission prices: "Although I earnestly believe this is coming to pass and expect some day to probably sell First National Pictures on that basis, still I regret it."[23]

Small exhibitors were less torn over the percentage system and generally preferred flat rentals. Illinois exhibitor Maurice Rubens characterized any manager willing to book on a percentage basis as a "jelly-fish," reflecting a common belief that percentage contracts simply gave distributors too much information and bargaining power.[24] Wisconsin exhibitor J. P. Gruwell argued that percentage booking would never resolve the more fundamental cultural differences between distributors and small exhibitors that lay at the heart of the industry's troubles: "Called 'hicks' and 'rubes' by astute (?) willy-boys from Gotham's slop-over, who are wished onto branch offices by home-office desk warmers, these 'small time' exhibitors are usually in a state of bitter revolt, ready to take every possible advantage; justifying themselves with the belief that the exchanges are always ready to take every possible advantage of them."[25]

The glut of trade press editorials and counter-editorials offering commentary on percentage booking continued through 1920 and 1921, prompted by related developments in selective distribution and subsequent organization among exhibitors. This was despite the fact that actual contracts using percentage pricing for programmatic releases were few and far between; some exhibitors claimed, not without merit, that the distributors were mounting an "agitation" campaign in the trade press.[26] Indeed, distributors barely disguised their attempts to normalize percentage booking in the trade press, writing stories with grossly exaggerated headlines, such as "2,200 Houses Now Playing Percentage" and "Percentage Opponents Harming Selves."[27] Metro took a stance of public ambivalence, promising that it would not "force the percentage system of booking upon exhibitors, but [would] adopt it if they desire[d] it."[28] Louis B. Mayer's sales manager Paul Mooney took a subtler approach when he spoke to the *Motion Picture News* after arranging "special percentage presentations" of the Anita Stewart drama *In Old Kentucky* (Marshall Neilan, 1919) for First National: "I had expected considerable opposition to the percentage idea, but was agreeably surprised by the opinion of a majority of leading first-run exhibitors, to the effect that they would welcome a percentage policy backed up with pictures big enough to warrant it."[29]

Exhibitors certainly responded to any distributor campaign for percentage in kind, most effectively via the Motion Picture Theater Owners of America (MPTOA), which emerged as the dominant exhibitors' trade organization in the spring of 1920. President Sydney Cohen fired numerous broadsides against the percentage system in the lead-up to the organization's convention in Cleveland that June, where the MPTOA adopted a resolution declaring its absolute opposition to all forms of percentage booking.[30] "All" here really meant all; there was vocal exhibitor opposition even to the idea of booking specials by percentage. In February, the newly formed Theater Owners Chamber of Commerce (TOCC) accused United Artists of using *Pollyanna* (Paul Powell, 1920) as a "wedge for the furtherance of percentage distribution," even writing to Mary Pickford directly (her lawyer sent a polite response referring TOCC to UA head Hiram Abrams).[31] TOCC made similar objections regarding Fox's *Over the Hill* and certain Metro specials in September 1921, prompting William Fox, Winfield Sheehan, and Marcus Loew to make amends in person.[32]

Despite distributors' push in the trade press, organized exhibitor resistance, coupled with the wider unsettledness of the distribution market (examined in chapter 5) and the beginning of the FTC's investigation of Paramount in 1920, generally limited the uptake of programmatic percentage booking through the mid-1920s. Flat fees remained the norm, even among first-run picture-only houses. Percentage booking continued to be common in idiosyncratic situations, particularly at the legitimate theaters that were serving as run houses for distributors' biggest specials. However, as we have seen, prerelease exhibition in the early 1920s, especially in New York, was a crowded space. Even those distributors who had direct affiliations or close relationships with the live-theatrical industry in the city had to work around the scheduling of the legitimate houses. A 1921 telegram exchange between Lee Shubert and Goldwyn chairman F. J. Godsol illustrates this problem. Godsol wired Shubert on April 21:

> We have two big pictures that absolutely require legitimate runs beginning September first—As you are so strongly averse to giving the company a years [sic] lease on the Astor Theatre I will renounce this but I do ask you to reserve a limited time[,] say ten weeks at the same rental as you can get from anyone else.[33]

Shubert replied the next day:

> Have booked [the operetta] *Little Dutch Girl* at Astor to open August first which you are interested in[.] [T]hat is only reason I cannot give you time for the Goldwyn but have been able to get [Marc] Klaw to postpone *Dutch Girl* until November seven[.] This enables us to give the Goldwyn the time from middle of August to November fifth[.] If this is satisfactory[,] wire answer[.] Terms to be same as *Four Horsemen [of the Apocalypse]* [Rex Ingram, Metro, 1921].[34]

Godsol agreed to Shubert's percentage rental terms at the Astor for the two Goldwyn specials: 60/40 in favor of the house, with a guarantee to the house of $4,750 out of the distributor's 40 percent share. Shubert additionally specified that this price covered only the house, "lighted and heated," and three stagehands—"no advertising, no orchestra."[35]

For distributors, reserving time for extended-run exploitation (six weeks for each film, in this case) was expensive, because it required specific scheduling and sometimes involved modifying existing live-theatrical bookings. As noted, the "all specials" model had put a premium on this kind of exhibition, which gave the owners of legitimate houses a superior position in negotiating percentage terms with distributors. On Broadway, this often meant a guarantee paid to the house rather than the distributor (the reverse would be common later in the 1920s). Likely because of their preexisting relationship, the terms Shubert offered Godsol were reasonable compared to some others. For distributors attempting to break into the market for Broadway prerelease exhibition, percentage and guarantee terms could be outrageous. In June 1922, *Variety* reported that "a certain releasing company" booked three of its pictures in a Broadway first-run theater for percentage terms, at a guarantee to the house of $19,000. None of the films grossed above that amount, and the distributor made nothing.[36]

While these terms were likely exceptional, they demonstrate one reason why distributors were so interested in vertical integration—owning theaters directly obviated pricing and scheduling negotiations with impresarios like Lee Shubert. They also demonstrate why it was so difficult to force exhibitors at the more programmatic end of the industry to accept percentage pricing for non-specials in the early 1920s. If scheduling extended runs of five or ten weeks on percentage in New York was a tricky business, then scheduling runs of two or three days on percentage in a small-town theater was even trickier. For program films, it simply wasn't worth the effort.[37] Even in idiosyncratic booking circumstances where distributors were able to get a percentage booking from a small exhibitor, such as in Watson's contracts for *The Covered Wagon*, *Over the Hill*, and other specials, they generally demanded a large guarantee, assuming that it would amount to most or all of their rental income for the booking.

Nevertheless, there were exceptions, and percentage pricing gradually became more common in the mid-1920s. This was especially true for circuits. In October 1922, First National struck a deal with Stephen A. Lynch to book all of its films to his 150 theaters on an 80/20 sharing basis, with 20 percent of box office going to First National.[38] Smaller circuits, such as the Cooney Brothers' National Theater Corporation, which comprised four subsequent-run houses in Chicago, also signed programmatic deals partially on percentage.[39] Despite continuing concerns about revealing their box-office receipts, exhibitors of all stripes became more likely to book the occasional special, typically under 50/50 or 60/40 terms with a guarantee to the distributor. By the end of 1923, *Exhibitors Trade Review* was opining that the fear of revealing accounts had become largely meaningless, because distributors were now quite able to accurately assess any theater's average business.[40]

In early 1924, *Exhibitors Herald* asked theater owners to write in with their thoughts on percentage and other booking matters, asking whether they favored it, and if they did, what they thought the fairest percentage arrangement would be.[41] Of the 105 mostly small exhibitors who responded, 21 percent wrote that they favored the percentage system, 29 percent said they favored it "in some cases," and 50 percent reported that they did not favor any kind of percentage booking. Small exhibitors were effectively split evenly regarding the basic principle of percentage booking. Exhibitors' responses to the question of the most favorable arrangement, however, revealed the extent to which roadshows likely influenced expectations about percentages. The question was open ended, and exhibitors responded with a variety of answers. Several suggested percentages ranging from 20 to 35 percent to the distributor; one insisted that it "depends on the length of runs"; and another rejected percentages entirely, writing, "Booking film on percentage would be like selling overalls on commission." The most repeated answer was some variation on the typical percentage used for the roadshow: 50/50. For exhibitors who were open to percentage booking in principle but objected to it in practice, objections were rarely based in the breakdown of the percentage itself. Rather, exhibitors resented concrete, predictable losses, such as required guarantees or arrangements that failed to account for their house expenses. Thus, although at least half of the exhibitors writing in to the *Herald* were somewhat willing to share their box office, they were generally not willing to let the distributor directly have those amounts. Put another way: flat rentals could be justified as an investment, but guarantees were an extraction.

Distributor editorials and planted stories advocating the percentage system continued in the mid-1920s, albeit not at the same frequency as in 1919 and 1920.[42] Exhibitor organizations and their representatives likewise continued to oppose percentages, although by the end of 1924 it was clear that percentage-sold specials such as *The Covered Wagon* were simply too much of a draw for all but the most stubborn exhibitors to pass up.[43] Much of the discussion surrounding percentage booking from 1924 to 1926 revolved not around any talk of industry-wide adoption, but around the mechanics of checking receipts and resolving disputes through arbitration. Paramount was especially zealous about enforcing an honest accounting of exhibitors' box offices. In February 1926, Famous Players–Lasky sued the Cooney Brothers for $25,000 after discovering that they had kept two sets of books for their percentage contracts. A week earlier, the company had taken exhibitor Harry Dembow in front of the Philadelphia arbitration board for understating his takings on *The Ten Commandments* (Cecil B. DeMille, 1923). Based on the testimony of the distributor's checker, the board awarded Paramount their claim: $62.[44] Such situations highlighted the risk of the percentage system for distributors. While Dembow's location in the outskirts of Philadelphia made hiring a checker a worthwhile investment, the extra expense was simply not feasible outside of cities. The question of exhibitor honesty would continue to factor into strategies surrounding percentage booking even after the transition to sound.

Sound and Percentage, 1926–1930

We might assume that the successful October 1927 release of the first part-talking Vitaphone feature, Alan Crosland's *The Jazz Singer*, was a turning point in the wider move toward percentage pricing. Warner Bros. sales manager Sam Morris (having moved on from Selznick) ensured that Vitaphone's initial contracts for the film required special terms, including sliding-scale percentage bookings and a week-to-week holdover clause once the film took in a certain gross.[45] Morris's approach was of a piece with Warners' wider strategy for selling Vitaphone as a technology, which was rooted in the booking and pricing conventions of the mid-1920s. That strategy began to take shape as early as April 1926, when Warner Bros. signed a contract with Western Electric giving the studio exclusive rights to the company's synchronized sound-on-disc technology. The deal, which was signed just in time for the 1926–1927 selling season, called for a distribution strategy that simultaneously sold Vitaphone as a novelty and hedged the risks of investing too wholeheartedly in the new technology.

The emergence of sound puts into sharp relief just how effectively Hollywood's distribution practice had integrated programmatic and idiosyncratic approaches to booking by 1926. We might assume that the novelty of sound would have required mostly idiosyncratic distribution by definition, just as multireel features had in 1912, or cinema itself had in 1896. Yet Warner Bros.' campaign for Vitaphone employed both an idiosyncratic component that positioned the new technology as a special attraction *and* a programmatic component that sought to carefully institutionalize sound technology as an integral part of the exhibition program.

The idiosyncratic component involved the marketing of nine new specials for 1926–1927: *Don Juan*, *The Better 'Ole*, *Manon Lescaut* (later retitled *When a Man Loves*), and numerous unnamed (i.e., unproduced) others. All would be released with Vitaphone soundtracks and sold "individually and on [their] own merits" alongside the company's twenty-six "Warner Winner" program films.[46] The initial plan was to give *Don Juan* the full idiosyncratic prerelease treatment: a Broadway premiere at the Warner Theater followed by a roadshow tour made up of multiple companies.[47] After the success of the film's premiere—it would eventually run thirty-six weeks at the Warner—Warners canceled the roadshow plan and put the film into extended run exhibition wherever they could find a theater to lease.[48] Donald Crafton suggests that the company made this change to delay the beginning of the film's "popular price" release through the programmatic distribution system, so that first-run theaters had time to install Vitaphone equipment.[49] *Don Juan* would not begin its "first run" in New York until August 1927, when it opened at the Roxy.[50] By that point, the film had been playing at "pop" prices in Chicago for nearly six months (figure 6.4).[51]

The programmatic component of Warners' Vitaphone distribution strategy involved the release of short subjects of musical acts to be packaged with each of the "Warner Winner" programmers. Warners saw this as a potential way to replace live presentation acts in theaters, in an approach Crafton has termed "virtual Broadway." After the success of the premiere of *Don Juan*, the strategy expanded to include the program films themselves, which would also be made available with optional Vitaphone soundtracks. However, there were still only a handful of theaters wired for the Vitaphone by the end of 1926, and these programmers played mostly silently for the 1926–1927 season. Before Warner Bros. committed itself more fully to Vitaphone in production in early 1927, its program feature strategy was thus meant to reassure exhibitors already using Warners films that business would continue as usual. They continued to be sold as normal via flat fees, and the company's marketing of the program films did not articulate them to Vitaphone in any meaningful way. Conceptually, this suggests that Warners' aspirations for Vitaphone in distribution were not purely idiosyncratic, even though the company was releasing its first sound feature according to existing norms of special distribution. Rather, the Vitaphone was primarily meant to disrupt the live-performance acts *within* the typical exhibition program, and not necessarily the silent features that made up its bulk. A conceptualization

Figure 6.4. *Ad for* Don Juan, Moving Picture World, *February 19, 1927, 566.*

of sound as an addition or partial replacement to the program would be taken up industry-wide in 1927.[52]

Whether Warners had any kind of percentage-based pricing strategy to go along with its planned reconfiguration of the program remains unclear, but neither the announcement of Vitaphone nor the success of *Don Juan* produced much new editorializing about percentage booking in 1926. Instead, percentage booking seems to have become prevalent among urban first-run theaters largely independently of the technology shock of sound. Run exhibition houses (both two-a-days and regular prerelease theaters) had rented films on percentage since the late 1910s, in keeping with their role in idiosyncratic distribution, and presentation houses tended to be rented or owned directly by distributors. Although some sound films played in New York theaters for long runs (thirty-six weeks for *Don Juan* and twenty-three weeks for *The Jazz Singer*, for example), demonstrating the significant promise of sound films, they were not especially impressive performers compared to exceptional super-specials, such as *The Covered Wagon* (1924, fifty-nine weeks), *The Ten Commandments* (1923, sixty-one weeks), and *The Big Parade* (1925, ninety-five weeks).[53] The increasing costs of specials, the growing power of distributors in key exhibition markets, and even the marketing and drawing power of individual stars all helped to normalize percentage booking in first-run houses well before it was clear that sound would permanently change the industry. Paramount's advertising for Harold Lloyd's *The Kid Brother* (Ted Wilde and J. A. Howe, 1927) urged exhibitors to "play it like a road show" (i.e., on percentage), and in May 1927 the general manager of Lloyd's production company announced that all of the star's films for the 1927–1928 season would be sold on percentage.[54] *Exhibitors Herald* noted the significance of the move as a test for percentage booking, because Lloyd's films "[came] as near being universal attractions as anything on the market": "They are wanted by every type and kind of theatre and their attraction value is such as to govern a theatre's receipts during an engagement."[55] Percentage pricing, which had been largely exclusive to specials, roadshows, and run exhibition in 1920, was increasingly unavoidable. By November 1927, *Film Daily* was reporting that "most first runs in cities now buy pictures on percentage, if only because they can't get them any other way."[56]

Thus, the last segments of the exhibition market not already accustomed to percentage contracts before the transition to sound were subsequent-run, independent, and small theaters. However, there was little consensus that percentage rentals were a good idea when dealing with such exhibitors. A spring 1927 exchange of letters between various industry executives and MPPDA officials reveals both the importance of and uncertainty surrounding percentage pricing.[57] Paramount general manager Sidney Kent initiated the discussion, writing MPPDA chairman Will Hays about dishonest box-office reporting practices among exhibitors:

> There is no doubt but that incorrect reporting is rampant on pictures played on percentages. . . . I have some very definite information involving some outstanding exhibitors of the country, but for political reasons we have never yet made an example of these people. However, the time is coming when we will have to take a definite stand and do something to protect ourselves, inasmuch as the vogue of playing pictures on percentage is coming more and more to the front.[58]

Kent's intimation that even big exhibitors cheated was enough to rouse Hays's attention, and he tasked MPDDA general counsel Gabriel Hess with investigating the wider implications of percentage booking. Hess consulted major figures in distribution and exhibition, including MGM sales executive Felix Feist and longtime theater manager Arthur Mayer of the Paramount-affiliated chain Balaban and Katz. Feist suggested a copyrighted ticketing system to curb cheating.[59] Mayer's response to Hess emphasized that concerns about exhibitor dishonesty in reporting rentals were, if not unfounded, at least only minor:

> I do not think that as far as the circuits are concerned, any distributor needs feel anxiety over the reliability of the statement of gross receipts. . . . I enclose a copy of a typical percentage contract such as we worked out this year with Famous, First National, and Metro, and which I think proved satisfactory to both parties concerned. I think percentage should apply to all pictures purchased by the exhibitor and not merely to a few specials. . . . No exhibitor would in my opinion ever dare to steal as much as the difference which he would pay on the flat rental of a picture like "The Way of All Flesh," and the percentage which it would yield on a deal such as the one which I enclose.[60]

The contract Mayer included, for the booking of D. W. Griffith's *Sorrows of Satan* (1926) at the Belpark Theater in Chicago, specified a 25 percent rental to Paramount on a sliding-scale basis that eventually increased to 50 percent after grossing specified amounts.[61] In referring to *The Way of All Flesh* (Victor Fleming, 1927), then in the middle of a twelve-week premiere run at the popularly priced Rialto in New York, Mayer emphasizes the opportunity presented by *programmatic* percentage bookings of films that were not specials. His theory that such films now typically grossed too much at the urban box office for exhibitors to risk cheating may help to explain the uptake of percentage in 1926 and 1927. Mayer was less definite about small exhibitors, but he believed they would accept percentage contracts if the terms were "fundamentally equitable."

This exchange took place in the spring and summer of 1927, well before sound film's impact on the industry was obvious. The major studios had just adopted an all-for-one agreement giving a committee of technicians and distributors' representatives, chaired by Sidney Kent, one year to determine which sound technologies merited wide adoption. This largely delayed any sound-related changes in distribution practice beyond idiosyncratic releases.[62] When a new Standard Exhibition Contract went into effect in May 1928, it made no mention of sound.[63] However, in the spring of 1928, the studios signed consolidated licensing agreements with Electrical Research Products, Inc. (ERPI) to manage the installation of sound systems. The number of wired theaters subsequently grew, reaching around four hundred by that summer. As it became clear by the end of the 1927–1928 season that sound films would require at least some programmatic handling, a whole host of booking- and pricing-related questions confronted distributors. Some of these, such as the question of paying public performance rights for synchronized music heard in wired theaters, had been sorted out through ERPI in late 1927, through an arrangement with the American Society of Composers, Authors, and Publishers (ASCAP). But how would sound films be priced and packaged? What changes to the Standard Exhibition Contract would sound require? And would small exhibitors rent sound films on percentage?

Each distributor approached these questions of distribution practice separately in advance of the 1928–1929 season, the first to involve substantial programmatic sales and bookings of sound film. The newly programmatic emphasis on sound sales in this season was evident from studio marketing. In contrast to its program film ads in 1926 and 1927, which made no mention of sound, Warner Bros.' copy for the eighteen "Warner Winners" of 1928–1929 emphasized each film's availability in both silent and synchronized versions (figure 6.5). Essentially every distributor did something similar. Film Booking Offices' (FBO) ads for the season took additional care to soothe the nerves of exhibitors, emphasizing films' sound *and* silent box-office performance in presentation houses while at the same time urging, "Don't be panicked by sound!" (figure 6.6).

A sound-related matter more pressing than marketing for distributors in the spring and summer of 1928 involved specifying the license fees for each film's soundtrack in sales contracts. Because the Standard Exhibition Contract of 1928 was so new, most distributors specified fees and licenses through an attached rider. In the case of contracts with the Western Electric–aligned distributors, riders also granted exhibitors ERPI-managed sub-licenses for ASCAP music.[64]

Sound synchronization presented distributors with an opportunity to charge exhibitors new fees beyond their standard rentals and to reconfigure old fees for new purposes. The most notorious of these was the "score charge." As a practice, score charges predated sound; distributors levied them whenever they supplied exhibitors with sheet music for a film's musical accompanists.[65] Thus, when feature rental fees for Paramount's 1928–1929 exhibition contracts were divided into three columns— one for silent rentals, one for synchronized rentals, and a third column labeled "score charge"—most exhibitors probably thought little of it.[66] But the score charge would become one of the most hotly contested practices in early sound distribution, as studios repurposed it to charge exhibitors for any number of supposed sound synchronization costs. The cost to manufacture physical discs was the most common distributor explanation, as in the case of Vitaphone contracts, but vaguer responses, including "arrangements," "synchronized prints," or simply "royalties," were common as well.[67] Even sound-on-film features sometimes had score charges—though shorts, tellingly, did not. Vitaphone's Ralph Wilk summed up the distributors' disingenuous position when he told *Exhibitors Herald-World*, "Production and synchronization are two separate departments and must be paid separately."[68]

For distributors, score charges became a kind of additional premium for sound feature bookings in the absence of a percentage rental. They could be quite hefty: a sample weekly report from an accounting manual for Publix Theater managers lists a flat rental of $2,500 for a booking

Figure 6.5. *Ad for* State Street Sadie, Motion Picture News, *September 8, 1928, 765.*

Figure 6.6. *Ad for* The Perfect Crime, *Variety, August 15, 1928, 23.*

of *The Desert Song* (Warner Bros., 1929) with a score charge of $250, or 10 percent.[69] *Variety* claimed that some larger exhibitors were being charged up to $1,000 for the discs accompanying a single film.[70] Smaller exhibitors complained frequently and bitterly in the trade press about the charges, which were in addition to the much higher rentals for synchronized film. In the rush to sign contracts for sound films, many exhibitors had not factored in the additional cost of these fees, which distributors continued to claim was separate from the "film" rental. Amounts varied, but one unnamed exhibitor claimed that he paid an average of $75 flat rental plus a $20 score charge for his sound films, as compared to $17.50 total rental for silents.[71] Score charges often equaled or exceeded the cost of silent film, which meant that flat rentals for sound film among small exhibitors ran anywhere from two to four times silent rates.[72] One California exhibitor complained that it wouldn't take long for his score charges to equal what he spent to wire his theater for sound.[73]

The score charge issue first began to percolate about halfway through the 1928–1929 season, as many independent theaters began paying for their first sound films. By June it was a constant topic in the trade press. The fact that score charges and increased flat rental costs affected smaller and independent exhibitors disproportionately, including even some theaters in the now largely distributor-dominated MPTOA, presented a major exhibitor relations issue for the MPPDA. Though distributors attempted to frame score charges and increased rental costs as temporary effects that would eventually resolve themselves, they were really an acute manifestation of long-standing objections to trade practices in the industry. A renewed government push to rein in these practices was emerging in 1927. In July, the FTC issued a mostly toothless cease-and-desist notice to Paramount, ordering it to end its block-booking and theater-buying activities. The commission would organize a trade conference a few months later, which eventually resulted in the new Standard Exhibition Contract of 1928. In December 1927, US Senator Smith Brookhart, a Republican from Iowa, introduced an anti–block-booking bill that brought even greater attention to the practice.[74] The coming of sound now threatened to escalate the situation.

For distributors, the Brookhart bill and similar legislative proposals were the greatest long-term threat posed by exhibitor agitation over sound. A more immediate threat, however, was the unraveling of the arbitration system—which they saw as having stabilized both the distribution market and the industry as a whole. The Allied States Organization, an association of independent exhibitors led by former FTC chairman Abram F. Myers, led the charge against the industry's arbitration practices.[75] In early July 1929, the Texas branch of the exhibitors association withdrew its members from arbitration; exhibitors in Iowa later followed suit.[76] Something clearly needed to be done about sound film rentals.

In response to the outcry, the MPPDA mounted a campaign in the trade press, at exhibitor organization conventions, and with regional Film Boards of Trade to encourage the nation's eight thousand independent exhibitors to adopt a ready-made solution to the problem of crushing sound rentals: book their sound films on percentage. Throughout the spring and summer of 1929, articles and editorials in the trade press proclaimed that percentage pricing would be the order of the day for the 1929–1930 season.[77] In part, the campaign was a specific effort to ensure that the public fight over score charges and sound film pricing was conducted on the producer-distributors' terms, and, in particular, that the proposed solutions came from members of the distributor-controlled MPTOA, rather than independent exhibitor associations such as Allied States. Indeed, the MPTOA attempted to upstage the Allied States convention in Washington on July 2, 1929, by holding a rival meeting to discuss the problems of sound rentals.[78] More generally, however, MPPDA officials recognized that the confusion over sound presented both an opportunity to increase the prevalence of percentage rentals and useful cover for their practices. As William A. Johnston put it in *Motion Picture News*, "Sound pictures have knocked block booking into a cocked hat."[79]

The MPPDA's campaign started in earnest at meetings between representatives of the major distributors and the MPTOA-dominated Exhibitors' Committee at the Union League Club in New York beginning July 9.[80] At those meetings, the Exhibitors' Committee proposed that all future contracts with independent exhibitors be made at least partially on a percentage basis. The distributors, represented primarily by Sidney Kent, put forth an additional proposal for a so-called National Board of Adjustment. Exhibitors unsatisfied with their sound rentals could appeal to this board through their local Film Board of Trade and, upon inspection of their books, could have their already signed, legally binding flat-rate contracts amended to percentage contracts. Crucially, this included the score charge, as the text of the MPPDA's declaration for the board emphasized.

Inherent in the production of pictures with sound, because of the royalties that must be paid, is some addition to the rental of the picture, commonly called score charge. This score charge should not be based on an arbitrary figure as a result of negotiation to see who will pay the most but should be fixed and determined by an agreed percentage of the rental price of the picture. There should be material reduction of this score charge in such cases where pictures are played on a percentage basis, because of the quasi-partnership relation between distributor and exhibitor.[81]

The distributors were essentially proposing to use score charges, which were an arbitrary fee in the first place, as a point of leverage to induce independent exhibitors to book on percentage. The rhetoric of distributor-exhibitor "quasi-partnership" was a common turn in distributors' discourse on percentage booking, but it was a crucial part of the strategy. The Board of Adjustment was pitched as a kind of exhibitor relief organization both rhetorically and in its mechanics; the MPPDA took pains to emphasize that the total rental costs of any contracts that were switched over to percentage should not "in any event exceed the [flat] rental specified in the contracts for such pictures."[82]

The goal of the National Board of Adjustment, at least in the short term, was not to increase income to the distributors. Rather, it was to shift wider industry discourse away from competitive negotiations between exhibitors and distributors over flat fees and score charges and toward percentage as the fairest and most cooperative form of film pricing. The MPPDA attempted to foster this discourse not only among exhibitors, but also among the distributors themselves. As reflected in the internal communications surrounding the meeting, not all distributors were happy with giving exhibitors the idea that their contracts were "adjustable." Warner Bros. distribution head Sam Morris was particularly opposed to the proposed Board of Adjustment:

I have been hearing about the public in relation to the motion picture industry for 20 years. We don't give a blank about the exhibitor agitation and we think the talk about public interference with this business is all bunk. What counts in the world is money—money—and the money of the country is in chain banks. Chain banks, chain stores, and chain theatres are here to stay and if the little exhibitor has to go to the wall, that is his hard luck. If it is a choice between his buying a picture at a loss or us selling it without a profit, we are in favor of his buying it at a loss. Our contracts with our exhibitors are our business and nobody else's.

Initially, Harry Warner concurred with Morris, worrying that adopting the plan "would lead exhibitors to believe that we had committed wrong against them."[83] Eventually, after a series of phone calls between Will Hays and Harry Warner and further collaboration between Morris and Sidney Kent, Warner Bros. fell in line with the other distributors and participated in the Board of Adjustment. Nevertheless, Morris's tirade illustrates the extent to which the priorities of distributors did not necessarily match the priorities of the MPPDA when it came to relationships with exhibitors and the public. Agreement over percentage as the future basis of film pricing in the sound era was not inherent; it had to be forged. Absent the MPPDA, some distributors would have been more than happy to continue with a flat fee system when dealing with independent exhibitors.

By July 26, the distributors had reached an agreement over the Board of Adjustment's policies and the wording of the press release, which was sent out the next day.[84] The *New York Herald-Tribune* and *Film Daily* gave the announcement positive front-page coverage, and the National Board of Adjustment was put into effect on July 29.[85] Among exhibitor organizations, reaction was tepid. Abram Myers responded to reports of the adjustment plan by describing it as a meaningless gesture, "eleventh hour relief for the exhibitor who has been gouged until he can no longer meet his obligations."[86] Individual theater owners in sound-related financial straits did avail themselves of the board, however, and the MPPDA archive includes extensive correspondence with individual distributors instructing them to cooperate with exhibitors—if grudgingly—in revising their contracts. Nevertheless, even as the costs of sound rentals became more manageable, as both distributors and exhibitors adjusted to sound as part of the process of sales, score charges did not entirely go away until the 1940s.[87]

As an actual instrument for moving exhibitors to the percentage system, the National Board of Adjustment was always intended as a temporary measure. Yet the campaign surrounding the establishment of the board set the stage for further developments in negotiations over trade practices. This included a revision of the Standard Exhibition Contract in April 1930 that built percentage pricing into the distribution system more systematically by clarifying several percentage-related provisions. These included a 65 percent penalty on the last day's gross if percentage-payable pictures were not given their full contracted run in exhibition, as well as checking and auditing measures intended to reduce the understating of box-office grosses.[88] Nevertheless, the "evil" of percentage cheating only persisted, if only because the number of shared rental contracts continued to expand.[89] In early 1930, *Variety* reported that among the major distributors, percentage contracts now accounted for more than half of total rentals, with MGM collecting 50 to 60 percent of its rentals via percentage and Paramount 60 to 65 percent.[90]

Resistance by Allied States and other exhibitor organizations to percentage booking continued in the early 1930s, especially after the October 1929 US district court ruling in *United States v. Paramount Famous Lasky*, which neutered the compulsory arbitration clause of the Standard Exhibition Contract. Negotiations over arbitration and the distribution problems it was intended to solve would continue in the 1930s, all the way up to the 1940 consent decree issued by the Department of Justice that limited block sales by the studios to packages of only five features. Nevertheless, by 1932 only a handful of local exhibitors' organizations, in markets such as Cleveland, Baltimore, and Detroit, continued to specifically hold out against percentage rentals.[91] By 1932, MGM had so much leverage over exhibitors that some contracts for *Grand Hotel* were priced at 85 percent of gross rentals to the distributor.[92] By that time, as the Depression deepened, independent exhibitors were increasingly likely to accept percentage deals—particularly if they did not include score charges, guarantees, or any other charge that required them to put their scarce cash into contracts.

If sound opened up the room to percentage arrangements like the ones in Mrs. Shaver's contract, the Depression invited independent exhibitors in and closed the door. For distributors, percentage exhibition contracts certainly bolstered income. But the MPPDA's negotiations in forming the National Board of Adjustment demonstrate that percentage rentals were valuable to the studios for political and rhetorical reasons as well, as they helped them weather the significant changes brought about by sound production. Percentage booking had been the norm in legitimate theater for a reason: it gave both the production and venues a stake in the economic value of live performance in situations where that performance was the sole unit of value. Before sound, cinema had often been a programmatic, vaudeville-modeled grab bag of mechanically reproduced visual entertainment, musical performance, and live presentation. As Crafton notes, sound did not completely end that model, but it did marginalize it.[93] The transition gave distributors an unusual opportunity to recast the nature of film as a product—and, more importantly, to change how most theaters paid for it. By actualizing the discursive ideal of a cooperative industry through pricing structures, percentage booking played a major role in forging Hollywood's oligopoly in the 1930s.

Epilogue

On August 7, 2020, the US Federal Court for the Southern District of New York terminated the *Paramount* decrees. Since 1948, the decrees had prohibited film distributors from owning exhibitors and restricted contract practices that had been common in the 1930s and 1940s. These included block booking, single-contract circuit dealing, and ticket price minimums. In a press release issued in the immediate aftermath of the court's decision, Makan Delrahim, head of the US Department of Justice's Antitrust Division—and a former lobbyist for Comcast[1]—praised the decision and described the decrees as "outdated":

> As the Court points out, *Gone with the Wind*, *The Wizard of Oz*, and *It's a Wonderful Life* were the blockbusters when these Decrees were litigated; the movie industry and how Americans enjoy their movies have changed leaps and bounds in these intervening years. Without these restraints on the market, American ingenuity is again free to experiment with different business models that can benefit consumers. . . . The conspiracy and practices that existed decades ago no longer exist. New technology has created many different movie platforms that did not exist when the Decrees were entered into, including cable and broadcast television, DVDs, and streaming and download services.[2]

234 | PLAYING THE PERCENTAGES

Putting aside the various appeals to nostalgia for the Golden Age of Hollywood and the dubious description of the famously money-losing *It's a Wonderful Life* as a "blockbuster," Delrahim's argument contradicts itself. Somehow, the *Paramount* decrees were "restraining American ingenuity" and preventing "different business models that can benefit consumers"—while also being made completely obsolete by ingenious new business models such as TV, home video, and streaming services. The implicit assumption at work in Delrahim's rhetoric, of course, is that there is some fundamental difference between the film industry of the 1930s and 1940s and the industry of the 2020s. At first glance, this seems reasonable—why should a government agency ostensibly dedicated to antitrust issues care about block booking and first-run theater ownership when the cinema industry of 1939 that was so utterly defined by those practices is long gone?

As I hope to have shown in this book, distribution practices in Hollywood have never had the primary goal of "benefiting consumers." They have always been about controlling and extracting as much value from markets as possible. It is no accident that in the aftermath of the *Paramount* decision, the studios chose to divest from their theater chains rather than their distribution networks. Distribution is the fundamental economic engine of the media industries; film—indeed, "content" of any kind—has no purely economic value if it is not available. The greater the scale of availability, the greater the value—but only if that availability is controlled. The distribution of mechanically or digitally reproduced media presents something of an economic paradox: the more it succeeds in its function of circulation, the more it fails in its function of maximizing value. *Regulating* availability in such a way that a production's value is maintained has been the fundamental goal of nearly every commercial media distribution practice since the beginning of cinema, from film rental and the run/zone/clearance system to the Standard Exhibition Contract and staggered release windows. Distributors' control of first-run exhibition certainly helped them to regulate the availability of their product and to extract immense value from it. But this income was only possible in conjunction with a distribution system that spatially and temporally maximized the value of films at every stop along their journey through the theater hierarchy, from the studio-controlled picture palaces to the thousands of smaller theaters dotting the United States. The historical quantity and geographic diversity of exhibition outlets seem to have been completely missed by the Justice Department, which in a description of the *Paramount* decision on its website bizarrely claims that "unlike seventy years ago, most metropolitan areas today have more than one movie theatre."[3]

Attending to the historical and material practices of film distribution is not simply an academic exercise; it has real implications for public policy. Antitrust in the media industries must move beyond technological determinism and neoliberal assumptions about our "choices" as media consumers, and media historians have a responsibility to provide policymakers with the context necessary for such a move. In this book, I have attempted to provide that context by concentrating on specific practices at a nearly season-by-season level of analysis. From these details, a broader pattern of continuity emerges that helps to illuminate media distribution as a set of deeply ingrained practices and assumptions. That pattern, of ever greater consolidation around a handful of distributors from the 1910s to the 1930s, repeated after the decline of the studio system in the 1950s, and especially after the deregulation of the 1980s. Even as the *Paramount* decree continued to be enforced, the media distribution practices and "antitrust" policies that have obtained since then have helped to create a market where, as of 2019, 40 percent of domestic theatrical box-office revenue was going to a single distributor—Disney—and an additional 50 percent was going to just four other companies. Considered in this light, the oligopoly control of exhibition identified with the studio system of the 1930s and 1940s is really a historical aberration. Commercial media companies have historically tended toward more targeted strategies of consolidation and control operating at the level of distribution. This is no accident—control over media availability is a more consistent source of profit than exhibition or transmission, particularly as technological shifts change the ways that entertainment media are consumed. Matters related to new forms of media distribution have formed the basis of many (if not most) of Hollywood's labor disputes since the decline of the studio system. As this book was going to press in July 2023, both the Writers Guild of America (WGA) and the Screen Actors Guild–American Federation of Television and Radio Artists (SAG-AFTRA) were on strike, in part over the system used by distributors to structure residual payments from streaming media services.

While the studio system of 1939 is obviously no longer with us, its distribution practices continue to be deployed, if in modified form, in the media industries of today. A full account of what the Hollywood studios taught today's media conglomerates will have to wait for another book; this one is too long already. But as one example, consider streaming services, which function much in the way that program booking did in 1915. By packaging lots of indifferent material on the back of a handful of coveted films or shows, streamers sell customers a "service" of entertainment that often functions less as a way of connecting viewers with something compellingly idiosyncratic than as familiar nightly programming. This idea of content consumption as a comforting ritual is not a new one—today's binge-watching was once simply "going to the show"—and it was created through distribution practice. The pricing of distributed media packages still works the same way as well. Ad-free versions of streaming services made available at a higher price, or bundles of related services sold at a group discount, might be thought of as the 2020s version of the "open" or "selective" booking of the 1920s. Even the distinction between programmatic and idiosyncratic distribution still stands, although it encompasses much more than just the movies. Contemporary media distribution practices provide audiences with various programmatic channels for regular consumption of audiovisual entertainment—Netflix, Disney+, YouTube, Twitter, Facebook, Instagram, TikTok—while framing the theatrical moviegoing experience as an idiosyncratic, specially marketed product available only at advanced prices.

I do not wish to overstate my point; certainly, these comparisons are largely rhetorical, and of course there are important distinctions between the media distribution practices of 1920 and those of today. Streaming's over-the-top distribution model reaches consumers directly, whereas Hollywood could reach audiences only through the intermediary of the theater. This seems to be the implicit thrust of Delrahim's point—the government need no longer regulate film distributors' practices, because consumers can now supposedly connect "directly" with the content producers. But even if theaters were historically the only available outlet for the programmatic distribution of entertainment, distribution practices— whether they were related to booking, circuiting, or packaging—were never fundamentally about controlling theaters. Rather, they sought to control the availability of entertainment. This was as true in the live-theatrical industries of the nineteenth century as it was for film and is for streaming—even if performers could not be mechanically reproduced, they could be booked, circuited, or packaged by distributors such that their availability was regulated and appropriately priced. This is the fundamental through-line of industrial (and postindustrial) entertainment distribution: control over packaging, pricing, and temporal windows of availability to obtain maximum profitability at minimum risk.

Periodization always carries with it the risk of teleology, and I do not wish to imply by ending this story in 1930 that Hollywood had reached a "fully mature" distribution practice by then. There remains much work to be done on the study of Hollywood's distribution practices. One potential follow-up to this project would attend more closely to the role of local and regional entities in the development of early forms of national feature distribution, from state rights distributors and local exchanges to franchisees. First National deserves a much closer examination in this regard. Further work on the history of the film industry's use of statistical data, both as market research and as a pricing strategy, would help us to see any through-line between Paramount's statistical department and Netflix's algorithm, for example. Whatever direction that subsequent work takes, I hope that this book has given media scholars both historical context and a set of conceptual tools for approaching distribution beyond its circulatory functions.

Acknowledgments

No reasonably sized acknowledgments section would be enough to allow me to thank everyone who had a hand in the making of this book or to accurately express the extent of my gratitude. Nevertheless, here is my attempt. In reflecting on the decade I have spent completing this project, I am truly humbled by the professional and personal support of so many colleagues, friends, and family members. In those ten years, I moved from Atlanta to Wisconsin to Illinois; made research trips to Los Angeles, New York, and Texas; and experienced no small number of life changes. Throughout that time, the "distribution book" was an object that loomed, for lack of a more appropriate verb, over my life. The following people—and likely others whose absence I apologize for in advance—made this work not only possible but fulfilling.

The conceptual and methodological training I needed for this book began at Middlebury College, where, as an undergraduate, I took Chris Keathley's freshman seminar on the New Hollywood of the 1970s. His class introduced me to film studies and inspired in me a lifelong habit of thinking about cinema historically. Also at Middlebury, I met Jason Mittell, whose professional guidance has helped me countless times since then. Middlebury's history faculty, including Louisa Burnham, Bill Hart, Paul Monod, Amy Morsman, and James West, taught me how to work with sources and build an argument. Perhaps more importantly, they taught me how to find joy in doing historical work—a practice that has helped me to sustain my research.

My professional training in film history began at Emory University. I could not have asked for a better adviser and mentor there than Matthew Bernstein, whose work inspired me to specialize in the economic history of Hollywood. I must also thank David Pratt, whose historiography seminar found me—like so many historians who had come before—sitting in front of a microfilm reader, scanning through *Variety* and fighting glazed-over eyes. After the perverse pleasure of that experience, I knew I was meant to be a film historian. Michele Schreiber, Dana White, Eddy von Mueller, Annie Hall, John Smith, Kristen Grade, Danica Leigh, Marten Carlson, and Murphy and Katherine Davis also have my heartfelt thanks for making the two years I spent in Atlanta so formative for this work. Special thanks to Josh Gleich for suggesting I submit my work to the University of Texas Press.

This book emerged out of my dissertation research at the University of Wisconsin–Madison, where I had the immense privilege to be part of a fantastic community of cinema and media historians in the Department of Communication Arts. No one deserves more credit for inspiring me to work on film distribution than my dissertation director, Lea Jacobs. Her methodological rigor, precision of argumentation, and ability to ask just the right questions shaped the direction of this book more than anything else. The other members of my committee, Jeff Smith, Vance Kepley, Eric Hoyt, and Wyatt Phillips, gave invaluable feedback that pushed this book toward its final form. Ben Brewster deserves special thanks for sharing his expertise on the workings of the program short system.

Among the faculty of the Department of Communication Arts, I would like to thank David Bordwell, Kristin Thompson, Kelley Conway, Ben Singer, Maria Belodubrovskaya, J. J. Murphy, Michele Hilmes, Jonathan Gray, and Derek Johnson for their support throughout my time in Madison. I was so lucky to work with wonderful colleagues there, including Amanda McQueen, Eric Dienstfrey, Leo Rubinkowski, Drew Zolides, Megan Boyd, Booth Wilson, Matt Connolly, Chelsea McCracken, Brandon Colvin, Nora Stone, Jonah Horwitz, Kit Hughes, Tony Tran, Colin Burnett, Zach Zahos, and Matt St. John, whose friendship and expertise all shaped this book in one way or another. I owe a special debt to fellow distribution scholars Andrea Comiskey and Maureen Rogers, whose work was essential to my own. However, no Badger deserves more credit for blazing the film distribution trail than Michael Quinn, without whose dissertation this book could not have been written.

Perhaps no other single person has done more to shape the scope of this research than my friend and mentor Eric Hoyt. I cannot thank him and David Pierce enough for co-creating the Media History Digital Library (MHDL), or for involving me in various digital initiatives in media history. This book would not have been possible without the work of Eric and the MHDL team to provide searchable open access to the media industries' trade press. Beyond his scholarly contributions, Eric's generosity, encouragement, and enthusiasm bring out the best in all his students and collaborators. Throughout graduate school and my early career, I left every conversation I had with him feeling better about my work and myself.

As I began my career at the University of Illinois Urbana–Champaign and the final form of this book started to take shape, I could not have asked for more supportive colleagues on campus and in the Department of Media and Cinema Studies. Julie Turnock, CL Cole, James Hay, Rob Rushing, Lilya Kaganovsky, Victor Font, Angela Aguayo, Josh Heuman, Amanda Ciafone, Anita Chan, and Jonathan Knipp all made this book what it is. Special thanks to Will Helmke, whose research assistance was crucial for chapters 2 and 3.

I would like to thank the anonymous reviewers who shared their helpful comments on previous versions of this manuscript. Other colleagues from the film and media studies community have my additional thanks for their feedback on various iterations of this project throughout the years, both in written form and at conferences. These include Gregory Waller, Charlie Keil, Ross Melnick, Paul S. Moore, Rob King, Dimitrios Latsis, Deb Verhoeven, Valentine Robert, Brad Schauer, Tanya Goldman, and Martin Johnson.

This work was possible thanks to professional archivists and librarians. I thank all those who assisted me with primary material. Special thanks to Sylvia Wang and her staff at the Shubert Archives, who culled nearly all the Shuberts' film-related material for me. I am still making my way through it five years later. At the Harry Ransom Center, Michael Gilmore spotted *The Brain Exchange* in an unprocessed part of the Lewis Selznick collection; chapter 4 exists thanks to him. Many other special collections professionals provided indispensable help with my research, including Mary Huelsbeck and Amy Sloper at the Wisconsin Center for Film and Theater Research; Jenny Romero at the Margaret Herrick Library; and Brett Service and Sandra Garcia-Myers at the University of Southern California Warner Bros. Archives. My work on distribution and the transition to sound would also not have been possible without the MPPDA Digital Archive at Flinders University.

The research in this book was funded by grants from several entities, including the Institute for Museum and Library Services, the Canadian Social Sciences and Humanities Research Council, and especially the University of Illinois Urbana–Champaign Campus Research Board, which deserves special acknowledgment. An Arnold O. Beckman Research Award enabled me to travel to New York for my research in chapter 1; numerous travel grants allowed me to present this work at conferences; and a Humanities Release Time award afforded precious writing time to help me complete the manuscript. I was very privileged to receive their support.

At UT Press, I am indebted to my editor, Jim Burr, whose guidance, thoughtfulness, and boundless patience kept this project moving throughout the review and production process. Special thanks to publishing fellow Laura Fish, who was an enthusiastic advocate for work on film distribution and shepherded the early review process. Thanks as well to Lynne Ferguson, Mia Uribe Kozlovsky, and the rest of the UT Press team, who made the production and publication process an absolute pleasure, as well as Kathy Streckfus, who did a masterful job copyediting this book.

I wrote much of this book during the COVID-19 pandemic while other profound changes were taking place in my life. These challenging times highlighted the extent of my family's incalculable contributions to this work. Of all the people mentioned here, my mother, Ursula, deserves the most credit for this book's completion. Sadly, she passed away as I was writing the manuscript. She never once wavered in her love and support for her sons, and we all miss her profoundly. Immense thanks go to my father, Ron; my brothers, Stuart and Victor; and my stepparents, Christine and Don, whose love and encouragement kept me on track. The other major life change that took place as I wrote this book was the birth of my son, Henry. My thanks to him for being an endless source of joy—and for learning how to sleep through the night (usually). Special thanks to my parents-in-law, Bernie and Monique, who read and shared comments on the final manuscript. They also provided a priceless gift as I completed the book one hot Illinois summer: room, board, and child care after mice destroyed our home's air conditioning.

Finally, this book would never have been finished without my partner and best friend, Jenny. If she'll permit me, I'd like to thank her with a brief historical aside. Film exhibitors had a name for the group of films they would prioritize during a given season: their "rib program." The rib program was so steadfast and attractive that it formed the basis of a theater's schedule. An exhibitor's booking decisions rested on the strength of the rib program; it was the foundation of their business and the key to its success. Through the joys and travails of all the years it took to write this book, Jenny was my rib program. She has my eternal love and gratitude.

Glossary of Distribution Terms

One of the challenges of understanding film-distribution-related material, both in primary documents and in the trade press, is the specific vocabulary that exhibitors, exchange managers, distributors, and trade press journalists used to refer to distribution practices. Here are some basic terms that distributors and exhibitors understood by convention. Some of these came out of the live-theatrical distribution industry, while others were film specific. While I define most of these terms as they arise in the main text of this book, I also offer this glossary for the reader's reference.

Block booking: As traditionally used by film historians, any form of booking that required exhibitors to buy films in batches rather than individually. This meaning became common only after about 1921, when the Federal Trade Commission began investigating Paramount and distributors began using temporally based methods of organizing and selling their yearly release programs. Before then, the industry-standard practice of selling multiple films in a single package was referred to according to various models, including the "program system," "program booking," "brands," and "star series," among others. The more specific definition of block booking used in this book refers to the block *system* of booking, which divided a distributor's yearly output into multiple blocks that were sold successively, as a unit, at regular points throughout the release season.

Booking: The process by which distributors (live-theatrical and film) sold attractions to venues. In the standard model of feature booking that emerged in the 1910s, it occurred in two stages: the actual booking, in which an exhibitor promised to play a certain film or group of films and often secured that promise with a deposit, and "dating," in which the exhibitor specified an exact playdate for the purchased attraction.

Branded program (aka *brand* or *sub-program*): A subdivision of a distributor's complete yearly program into tiers that were more flexible as a unit of distribution than full service. Brands might be defined by genre, star, length, prestige, or some other factor of distinction. When grouped purely temporally (rather than by some defining characteristic), branded programs are effectively synonymous with blocks.

Clearance (aka *protection*): The temporary period after the conclusion of a particular run during which distributors made a film or program unavailable for playing in a zone. It "protects" the value of an exhibitor's run by discouraging theatergoers from simply waiting for the film to appear at a cheaper price in a subsequent run.

Dating: See **Booking.**

Exchange: A local film distribution office. Early exchanges were generally independent businesses. As the industry consolidated, exchanges increasingly became either franchisees or fully controlled local offices for national distributors based in New York. Exchanges managed the physical circulation of film prints and served as bases of operation for local sales personnel.

Exhibition value (or *scale*): The specific amount a particular film was expected to earn in a local market. This was often set by the distributor to determine sales quotas for local exchanges.

Feature: Initially, any "special" film of unique or idiosyncratic interest, regardless of length. In the mid-1910s, it came to refer more specifically to *multireel features*—films of four or more reels, and thus longer than the one- and two-reel program films that had been commonly distributed between 1905 and 1915. These longer films would become the dominant production format by the end of the 1910s.

Flat fee vs. percentage (sharing-contract) booking: Films were sold to exhibitors through a variety of pricing mechanisms. The most common in the 1910s and 1920s was the exhibitor's payment of a flat fee for a program, series, or individual film. Flat fees (also referred to as *license fees* on contracts) depended on the unit of booking and the frequency of an exhibitor's change of bill. *Percentage booking* (or *sharing-contract booking*), which came primarily out of legitimate theater and became widespread around the transition to sound, entitled the distributor to a percentage of ticket sales. A variety of arrangements structured percentage contracts; some split the percentage only after a film grossed a particular amount, while others built in *guarantees*—flat amounts paid to the distributor or exhibitor before subsequent proceeds were split.

Full-service program: A single program that could provide exhibitors with all of their film service for the year. It was a holdover from the variety shorts system, where exhibitors who signed up via standing order for service would get all their programming from that service until they stopped. Paramount's two-features-a-week program, which debuted in the fall of 1914, was the first successful full-service feature program.

Guarantee: See **Flat fee vs. percentage (sharing-contract) booking.**

Holdover: The extension of a booking past its originally scheduled run.

Open booking: A fluid term that generally referred to alternatives to the program system in the late 1910s. In the early 1920s, it often came to mean *selective booking* (aka *open-market* or *wide-open* booking), whereby distributors marketed a policy of allowing exhibitors to book films individually from within their program.

Percentage booking: See **Flat fee vs. percentage (sharing-contract) booking.**

Playdate: The exact date(s) reserved by the exhibitor for the screening of a distributor's film. Playdates were not necessarily specified at the time of booking.

Prerelease: The idiosyncratic distribution of a film to theaters before it entered the more programmatic system of first, second, and subsequent runs.

Program: In exhibition, the showing of multiple films together as a whole evening's entertainment. In distribution, a unit of sale comprising multiple films. In the absence of further specification, a distributor's program included all the films on its slate for a particular release season. Depending on context, this could either include or exclude its special releases.

Program booking (aka the *program system*): A format of feature distribution whereby exhibitors purchased a distributor's entire yearly output (program) in advance. The dominant form of feature distribution from 1914 to about 1918.

Program film (aka *programmer*): A film sold as just one alongside others on a distribution program. These contrast with **specials,** which tended to be sold, distributed, and marketed more idiosyncratically. By the 1930s, the term "programmer" took on the more specific meaning of a mid-budget film that could be flexibly sold as either an A- or a B-film for the purposes of double features. "Program film" sometimes referred to program *shorts* of one to three reels, the dominant film production format in the United States before the mid-1910s.

Protection: See **Clearance.**

Release season: The season around which distribution activity was generally organized. It began in August or September and ended the following July or August, with the exact date varying by distributor. Film release seasons followed the traditional live-theatrical release season, which did not match the calendar year because business was generally much slower in the summer. The release season dictated the timing of booking activity; exhibitors generally booked their first films for the subsequent release season about three months ahead, in the late spring. Booking and sales continued throughout the season.

Rental: The price paid by an exhibitor to a distributor for the right to exhibit a film.

Run: A term, partially derived from the length of a play's booking in live theater, that came to define the temporal structure of film distribution. Early on, the term had a mechanical connotation, referring to the run of a film print through the projector. An exhibitor booking a print's "first run" was assured both of high technical quality in the image and the economic advantage of a completely new attraction. As distribution practices rationalized, "run" increasingly came to define the hierarchical temporal status of a particular booking within a local distribution zone, and, by extension, the theater playing that booking. For distributors, runs organized a film's *national* circulation, with first runs typically defining the earliest "regular" (i.e., not prerelease) distribution of a film within the major theaters of key cities, and subsequent (third, fourth, fifth, etc.) runs defining decreasingly lucrative venues in central neighborhoods, smaller cities, and rural areas. Exhibitors, by contrast, tended to define runs only in the context of their local market. Thus, an exhibitor with "first-run" status in a small town might play a particular film for the first time in that town, but almost always *after* it had played in the nearest big city.

Run exhibition: The practice of playing a particular film for an extended run of many weeks in one or more key cities to promote its drawing power prior to entering the normal release system.

Selective booking: See **Open booking.**

Sharing contract: See **Flat fee vs. percentage (sharing-contract) booking.**

Special (aka *special release*): A film, typically of higher budget and prestige, that is sold and marketed individually rather than as just one part of a wider release program. Specials often merited more idiosyncratic, targeted distribution. Specials contrasted with **program films.**

Star series: A **branded program** (typically of two to twelve films) featuring the same star or director.

Sub-program: See **Branded program.**

Zone: The geographically defined area within which a film played exclusively for a particular run. Theaters within the same zone were generally competitors for the same run of a film or program. Zones were determined by distributors, who organized them to their own advantage according to the local exhibition market.

Notes

INTRODUCTION

1. Tino Balio, ed., *The American Film Industry* (Madison: University of Wisconsin Press, 1985), 253.

2. Thomas Schatz, *The Genius of the System: Hollywood Filmmaking in the Studio Era* (New York: Henry Holt, 1988).

3. David Bordwell, Janet Staiger, and Kristin Thompson, *The Classical Hollywood Cinema: Film Style and Mode of Production to 1960* (New York: Columbia University Press, 2016).

4. Kristin Thompson, *Exporting Entertainment* (London: BFI, 1985).

5. Shelley Stamp, *Lois Weber in Early Hollywood* (Oakland: University of California Press, 2015); Mark Garrett Cooper, *Universal Women: Filmmaking and Industrial Change in Early Hollywood* (Urbana: University of Illinois Press, 2010); Erin Hill, *Never Done: A History of Women's Work in Media Production* (New Brunswick, NJ: Rutgers University Press, 2016).

6. Michael Quinn, "Early Feature Distribution and the Development of the Motion Picture Industry: Famous Players and Paramount, 1912–1921" (PhD diss., University of Wisconsin–Madison, 1998); William Paul, *When Movies Were Theater: Architecture, Exhibition, and the Evolution of American Film* (New York: Columbia University Press, 2016).

7. Janet Wasko, *Movies and Money: Financing the American Film Industry* (Norwood, NJ: Ablex, 1982); Lee Grieveson, *Cinema and the Wealth of Nations: Media, Capital, and the Liberal World System* (Oakland: University of California Press, 2018).

8. Alfred D. Chandler Jr., *The Visible Hand: The Managerial Revolution in American Business* (Cambridge, MA: Harvard University Press, 1977).

9. Robert C. Allen and Douglas Gomery, *Film History: Theory and Practice* (New York: McGraw-Hill, 1985), 138–143; Richard Caves, *American Industry: Structure, Conduct, Performance* (Englewood Cliffs, NJ: Prentice-Hall, 1972).

10. Eric Smoodin, "As the Archive Turned: Writing Film Histories without Films," *The Moving Image* 14, no. 2 (Fall 2014): 96–100.

11. Mark Lynn Anderson, "The Historian Is Paramount," *Film History* 26, no. 2 (2014): 3–7.

12. Joel Frykholm, *George Kleine and American Cinema: The Movie Business and Film Culture in the Silent Era* (London: Palgrave, 2015), 3.

13. Grieveson, *Cinema and the Wealth of Nations*, 75, 248.

14. Gerben Bakker, *Entertainment Industrialized: The Emergence of the International Film Industry, 1890–1940* (New York: Cambridge University Press, 2008).

15. Robert C. Allen, *Vaudeville and Film, 1895–1915: A Study in Media Interaction*, Dissertations on Film 1980 (New York: Arno Press, 1980).

16. Jean Giraud, *Lexique française du cinéma des origines à 1930* (Paris: CNRS, 1958), 105; Frank Kessler, "Distribution—Preliminary Notes," in *Networks of Entertainment: Early Film Distribution, 1895–1915*, ed. Frank Kessler and Nanna Verhoeff (Bloomington: Indiana University Press, 2007), 1–3.

17. Julia Hallam and Les Roberts, eds., *Locating the Moving Image: New Approaches to Film and Place* (Bloomington: Indiana University Press, 2014). See also Santiago Hidalgo, ed., *Technology and Film Scholarship: Experience, Study, Theory* (Amsterdam: Amsterdam University Press, 2018), and Ramon Lobato, *Shadow Economies of Cinema: Mapping Informal Film Distribution* (London: Palgrave, 2012).

18. Richard Maltby, "New Cinema Histories," in *Explorations in New Cinema History: Approaches and Case Studies*, ed. Richard Maltby, Daniel Biltereyst, and Philippe Meers (Malden: Wiley-Blackwell, 2011), 3.

19. Mae D. Huettig, *Economic Control of the Motion Picture Industry: A Study in Industrial Organization* (Philadelphia: University of Pennsylvania Press, 1944).

20. Benjamin B. Hampton, *A History of the Movies* (New York: Covici-Friede, 1931).

21. Huettig, *Economic Control*, 138–139, 114.

22. Wyatt Phillips, "'A Maze of Intricate Relationships': Mae D. Huettig and Early Forays into Film Industry Studies," *Film History* 27, no. 1 (2015): 136.

23. Aimee-Marie Dorsten, "'Thinking Dirty': Digging Up Three 'Matriarchs' of Communication Studies," *Communication Theory* 22 (2012): 30–31.

24. Kessler and Verhoeff, *Networks of Entertainment*, 1.

25. Ross Melnick, *Hollywood's Embassies: How Movie Theaters Projected American Power throughout the World* (New York: Columbia University Press, 2022).

26. Huettig, *Economic Control*, 115.

27. Contract between Triangle Film Corporation and Ernest A. Fenton, December 27, 1915, Aitken Papers, Wisconsin Historical Society, Box 11.

28. See Lea Jacobs and Andrea Comiskey, "Hollywood's Conception of Its Audience in the 1920s," in *The Classical Hollywood Reader*, ed. Steve Neale (New York: Routledge, 2012), 94–109.

1 | PRECURSORS: *The Circuits of Show Business*

1. See Robert C. Allen, "The Movies in Vaudeville: Historical Context of the Movies as Popular Entertainment," in *The American Film Industry*, ed. Tino Balio (Madison: University of Wisconsin Press, 1985), 57–82.

2. Alfred Bernheim, *The Business of the Theatre* (New York: Actors' Equity Association, 1932), 50.

3. Barnard Hewitt, "'King Stephen' of the Park and Drury Lane," in *The Theatrical Manager in Britain and America: Player of a Perilous Game*, ed. Joseph W. Donohue Jr. (Princeton, NJ: Princeton University Press, 1971), 91.

4. John Frick, "A Changing Theatre: New York and Beyond," in *The Cambridge History of American Theatre*, vol. 2, *1870–1945*, ed. Don B. Wilmeth and Christopher Bigsby (New York: Cambridge University Press, 1999), 198–199.

5. Rosemarie Bank, *Theatre Culture in America, 1825–1860* (Cambridge: Cambridge University Press, 1997), 4.

6. Douglas McDermott, "Structure and Management in the American Theatre," in *The Cambridge History of American Theatre*, vol. 1, *Beginnings to 1870*, ed. Don B. Wilmeth and Christopher Bigsby (Cambridge: Cambridge University Press, 1998), 196.

7. Frick, "A Changing Theatre," 199; Bruce McConachie, "American Theatre in Context, from the Beginnings to 1870," in Wilmeth and Bigsby, *Cambridge History of American Theatre*, 1:148; Calvin L. Pritner, "William Warren's Financial Arrangements with Travelling Stars, 1805–1829," *Theatre Survey* 6, no. 2 (November 1965): 84–85.

8. See McDermott, "Structure and Management," 197–210, for case studies of different engagements of traveling stars at a wide variety of theaters.

9. Bernheim, *The Business of the Theatre*, 34, 27.

10. Bank, *Theatre Culture in America*, 93.

11. Pritner, "William Warren's Financial Arrangements," 87.

12. St. Vincent Troubridge, *The Benefit System in the British Theatre* (London: Society for Theatre Research, 1967), 11.

13. McDermott, "Structure and Management," 211.

14. John Gaisford, *The Drama in New Orleans* (New Orleans: J. B. Steel, 1849), 52–54, quoted in Bernheim, *The Business of the Theatre*, 28–29.

15. McDermott, "Structure and Management," 195.

16. Frick, "A Changing Theatre," 199; Rosemarie Bank, "Antedating the Long Run: A Prolegomenon," *Nineteenth Century Theatre Research* 13, no. 1 (Summer 1985): 33–36.

17. Frick, "A Changing Theatre," 199–200.

18. Bank, "Antedating the Long Run," 35.

19. Frick, "A Changing Theatre," 200–202.

20. Jack Poggi, *Theater in America* (Ithaca, NY: Cornell University Press, 1968), 6–7.

21. William Paul, *When Movies Were Theater: Architecture, Exhibition, and the Evolution of American Film* (New York: Columbia University Press, 2016), 122–128.

22. Poggi, *Theater in America*, 6.

23. Marlis Schweitzer, *When Broadway Was the Runway* (Philadelphia: University of Pennsylvania Press, 2009), 16.

24. Bernheim, *The Business of the Theater*, 33–35; Arthur Frank Wertheim, *Vaudeville Wars: How the Keith-Albee and Orpheum Circuits Controlled the Big-Time and Its Performers* (New York: Palgrave Macmillan, 2006), 95.

25. Bernheim, *The Business of the Theater*, 35, 36.

26. Bernheim, *The Business of the Theater*, 36–37.

27. Frick, "A Changing Theatre," 204; Bernheim, *The Business of the Theater*, 39–40.

28. Bernheim, *The Business of the Theater*, 37–39.

29. Bernheim, *The Business of the Theater*, 42.

30. Frick, "A Changing Theatre," 210.

31. Bernheim, *The Business of the Theater*, 42–45.

32. Bernheim, *The Business of the Theater*, 52.

33. Frick, "A Changing Theatre," 213.

34. Bernheim, *The Business of the Theater*, 49–50.

35. Hartley Davis, "The Business Side of Vaudeville," *Everybody's Magazine* 17 (October 1907): 528.

36. Herbert Lloyd, *Vaudeville Trails through the West* (Philadelphia, 1919).

37. Bernheim, *The Business of the Theater*, 67, 69.

38. Marian Spitzer, "The Business of Vaudeville," *Saturday Evening Post* 196, no. 47 (May 24, 1924): 18; Don B. Wilmeth, *Variety Entertainment and Outdoor Amusements: A Reference Guide* (Westport, CT: Greenwood Press, 1982), 132–133; David Monod, *Vaudeville and the Making of Modern Entertainment, 1890–1925* (Chapel Hill: University of North Carolina Press, 2020), 165, 189.

39. Nicholas Economides, "Bundling and Tying," in *The Palgrave Encyclopedia of Strategic Management*, ed. Mie Augier and David J. Teece (London: Palgrave Macmillan, 2018), 140–145.

40. Charles Musser, "Another Look at the 'Chaser' Theory," *Studies in Visual Communication* 10, no. 4 (1984): 24–52.

41. Brett Page, *Writing for Vaudeville* (Springfield, MA: Home Correspondence School, 1915), 6–12.

42. Spitzer, "The Business of Vaudeville," 130.

43. Spitzer, "The Business of Vaudeville," 130.

44. Monod, *Vaudeville and the Making of Modern Entertainment*, 156–157; David Nasaw, *Going Out: The Rise and Fall of Public Amusements* (New York: Basic Books, 1993), 20.

45. Wertheim, *Vaudeville Wars*, 101; Monod, *Vaudeville and the Making of Modern Entertainment*, 154–155.

46. Monod, *Vaudeville and the Making of Modern Entertainment*, 157, 154–155, 163.

47. Monod, *Vaudeville and the Making of Modern Entertainment*, 157.

48. Nasaw, *Going Out*, 30.

49. John E. DiMeglio, *Vaudeville, U.S.A.* (Bowling Green, OH: Bowling Green University Popular Press, 1973), 183.

50. Monod, *Vaudeville and the Making of Modern Entertainment*, 176–182.

51. DiMeglio, *Vaudeville, U.S.A.*, 174.

52. Examination of Daniel F. Hennessy, March 27, 1919, in *Federal Trade Commission vs. Vaudeville Managers' Protective Association et al.* [Stenographic transcript], 902, HathiTrust Digital Library, https://babel.hathitrust.org/cgi/pt?id=uc1.c3092502.

53. Wertheim, *Vaudeville Wars*, 96.

54. Robert Snyder, *The Voice of the City: Vaudeville and Popular Culture in New York* (New York: Oxford University Press, 1989), 36.

55. The Vaudeville Managers Association was referred to by a variety of names during this period. I'll refer to it here simply as the VMA.

56. Wertheim, *Vaudeville Wars*, 103–105.

57. Monod, *Vaudeville and the Making of Modern Entertainment*, 166.

58. Spitzer, "The Business of Vaudeville," 125.

59. Monod, *Vaudeville and the Making of Modern Entertainment*, 168.

60. Wertheim, *Vaudeville Wars*, 117, 103–104, 121.

61. Wertheim, *Vaudeville Wars*, 122–123.

62. Monod, *Vaudeville and the Making of Modern Entertainment*, 167–168, 165.

63. Davis, "The Business Side of Vaudeville," 530.

64. Wertheim, *Vaudeville Wars*, 118–133.

65. Spitzer, "The Business of Vaudeville," 18.

66. Spitzer, "The Business of Vaudeville," 18.

67. Wertheim, *Vaudeville Wars*, 157–158.

68. Wertheim, *Vaudeville Wars*, 159; Examination of Samuel K. Hodgdon, February 3, 1919, in *FTC vs. Vaudeville Managers' Protective Association et al.*, 522–523.

69. Wertheim, *Vaudeville Wars*, 157.

70. Examination of Hodgdon, 520, 522.

71. Wertheim, *Vaudeville Wars*, 157.

72. Examination of Hodgdon, 520.

73. Examination of Hodgdon, 514; Examination of Hennessy, 911–923.

74. Examination of Hennessy, 912–913.

75. Examination of Hodgdon, 525; Examination of Hennessy, 920, 928.

76. Erin Hill, *Never Done: A History of Women's Work in Media Production* (New Brunswick, NJ: Rutgers University Press, 2016), 19.

77. Examination of Hodgdon, 526–527.

78. Samuel Backer, "The Informational Economy of Vaudeville and the Business of American Entertainment," *Business History Review 95*, no. 3 (Autumn 2021): 427–428, 435–436, 437; Examination of Hennessy, 930.

79. Davis, "The Business Side of Vaudeville," 528.

80. Bernheim, *The Business of the Theater*, 64.

81. Bernheim, *The Business of the Theater*, 66, 70–71.

82. Brooks McNamara, "Popular Entertainment," in *The Cambridge History of American Theatre*, vol. 2, *1870–1945*, ed. Don B. Wilmeth and Christopher Bigsby (New York: Cambridge University Press, 1999), 75.

83. Poggi, *Theater in America*, 30.

84. Kevin Lewis, "A World across from Broadway: The Shuberts and the Movies," *Film History* 1, no. 1 (1987): 39–51; McNamara, "Popular Entertainment," 74–80.

85. Letter from Adolph Zukor to Lee Shubert, December 21, 1911, Shubert Archive, Moving Pictures Collection, Moving Pictures General Series, Box 3.

86. "A Few Facts about the Shubert Feature Film Booking Company," undated pamphlet (likely 1914), Shubert Archive, Moving Pictures Collection, Moving Pictures General Series, Box 2.

87. "Priest to Handle 'Civilization,'" *Motography*, September 2, 1916, 530.

88. "Ince Appoints Priest Publicity Director for 'Civilization,'" *Motion Picture News* (hereafter *MPN*), September 2, 1916, 1393.

89. André Gaudreault and Philippe Gauthier, "De la nouveauté des Passions filmées du cinéma des premiers temps. Ou: comment faire du neuf avec du vieux . . . ," in *Jésus en représentations: De la Belle Époque à lapostmodernité*, ed. Alain Boillat, Jean Kaempfer, and Philippe Kaenel (Gollion, Switzerland: Infolio, 2011), 184–188. Thanks to Valentine Robert for pointing to and translating this reference.

90. Letter from F. L. McGovern to Robert W. Priest, March 30, 1914, Robert W. Priest General Correspondence, Shubert Archive. All subsequently cited Priest correspondence and archival material related to *The Life of Our Saviour* comes from this collection.

91. Roy Kinnard and Tim Davis, *Divine Images: A History of Jesus on the Screen* (New York: Carol Publishing Group, 1992), 29–30.

92. List of bookings of *The Life of Our Saviour*, March 31, 1914.

93. Letter from Priest to Ed Smith, April 18, 1914.

94. Letter from Priest to Jules Murry, April 6, 1914.

95. Letter from Priest to J. J. Shubert, March 24, 1914.

96. Blank and undated Memorandum of Agreement (rental contract) for *The Life of Our Saviour*.

97. Letter from Priest to Joseph G. Weimer, March 23, 1914.

98. Letter from Priest to Weimer, March 26, 1914.

99. Sheldon Hall and Steve Neale, *Epics, Spectacles, and Blockbusters* (Detroit: Wayne State University Press, 2010), 2–5, 26–28. See also Michael Quinn, "Distribution, the Transient Audience, and the Transition to the Feature Film," *Cinema Journal* 40, no. 2 (2001): 35–56.

100. See letter from Priest to Harry E. Allen (manager of Company #5), April 2, 1914.

101. Letter from Priest to Ed Smith, April 18, 1914.

102. Letter from W. Fred Mason to Priest, April 7, 1914.

103. Letter from Fred Harding to Priest, March 30, 1914.

104. Hall and Neale, *Epics, Spectacles, and Blockbusters*, 28–31.

105. Letter from Henry Pierson to Priest, April 22, 1914.

106. Telegram from Tom Morrow to Priest, April 5, 1914; letter from Henry Pierson to Priest, March 29, 1914.

107. Letter from M.R.T. [Pathé] to Priest, March 30, 1914.

108. "'Saviour' Film Falls Down," *Variety*, April 17, 1914, 19.

109. Hall and Neale, *Epics, Spectacles, and Blockbusters*, 12.

110. Letter from Priest to E. S. Thorp, April 16, 1914.

2 | THE PACKAGE, PART I: *Programming the Studio System*

1. Charles Musser, with Carol Nelson, *High-Class Moving Pictures: Lyman H. Howe and the Forgotten Era of Traveling Exhibition, 1880–1920* (Princeton, NJ: Princeton University Press, 1991), 58–59.

2. Musser and Nelson, *High-Class Moving Pictures*, 117–121, 160–161, 192–199, 94–95, 110–111.

3. See Derek Long, "From Program Shorts to Mutual Masterpictures: Cost Control as a Macroscale Production Strategy at 4500 Sunset Boulevard, 1914–15," *Film History* 29, no. 3 (2017): 76–104.

4. Nico de Klerk, "Program Formats," in *Encyclopedia of Early Cinema*, ed. Richard Abel (London: Routledge, 2005), 533; Richard Abel, "Early Film Programs: An Overture, Five Acts, and an Interlude," in *A Companion to Early Cinema*, ed. Andre Gaudreault, Nicolas Dulac, and Santiago Hidalgo (Oxford: Wiley, 2012), 334–359.

5. Max Alvarez, "The Origins of the Film Exchange," *Film History* 17, no. 4 (2005): 431–433.

6. Charles Musser, *The Emergence of Cinema: The American Screen to 1907* (New York: Scribner's, 1990), 366–368.

7. Paul S. Moore, "'Bought, Sold, Exchanged, and Rented': The Early Film Exchange and the Market in Secondhand Films in *New York Clipper* Classified Ads," *Film History* 31, no. 2 (2019): 4.

8. Alvarez, "The Origins of the Film Exchange," 433; Moore, "Bought, Sold, Exchanged, and Rented," 10–13.

9. Musser, *The Emergence of Cinema*, 433–439.

10. Alvarez, "The Origins of the Film Exchange," 434–435; Musser, *The Emergence of Cinema*, 367.

11. Testimony of Albert E. Smith, November 14, 1913, *United States v. Motion Picture Patents Company*, 225 F. 800 (1915), 1702–1703.

12. Testimony of J. A. Schuchert, 2 December 1913, *U.S. v. MPPC*, 2036.

13. Musser, *The Emergence of Cinema*, 81–82.

14. Ben Brewster, "Periodization of Early Cinema," in *American Cinema's Transitional Era*, ed. Charlie Keil and Shelley Stamp (Berkeley: University of California Press, 2004), 67.

15. Musser, *The Emergence of Cinema*, 111–115.

16. Dan Streible, *Fight Pictures: A History of Boxing and Early Cinema* (Berkeley: University of California Press, 2008), 72–73, 77–83.

17. Streible, *Fight Pictures*, 80–83.

18. See Gregory Waller, *Main Street Amusements: Movies and Commercial Entertainment in a Southern City, 1896–1930* (Washington, DC: Smithsonian Institution Press, 1995), 49.

19. Brewster, "Periodization of Early Cinema," 66–75.

20. "Future of Pictures," *Variety*, December 22, 1916, 12, quoted in Michael Quinn, "Distribution, the Transient Audience, and the Transition to the Feature Film," *Cinema Journal* 40, no. 2 (2001): 42.

21. Quinn, "Distribution, the Transient Audience, and the Transition to the Feature Film," 42.

22. Robert C. Allen, "The Movies in Vaudeville: Historical Context of the Movies as Popular Entertainment," in *The American Film Industry*, ed. Tino Balio (Madison: University of Wisconsin Press, 1985), 80–82.

23. Moore, "Bought, Sold, Exchanged, and Rented," 21–23.

24. Alvarez, "The Origins of the Film Exchange," 435.

25. Eileen Bowser, *The Transformation of Cinema, 1907–1915* (Berkeley: University of California Press, 1990), 27–28.

26. Bowser, *The Transformation of Cinema*, 32, 33.

27. Robert Anderson, "The Motion Picture Patents Company: A Reevaluation," in Balio, *The American Film Industry*, 133–152.

28. Michael Quinn, "Early Feature Distribution and the Development of the Motion Picture Industry: Famous Players and Paramount, 1912–1921" (PhD diss., University of Wisconsin–Madison, 1998), 57–58, 75–77.

29. Quinn, "Early Feature Distribution," 55.

30. Bowser, *The Transformation of Cinema*, 33.

31. Bowser, *The Transformation of Cinema*, 81, 83–84.

32. Bowser, *The Transformation of Cinema*, 78.

33. *Moving Picture World* (hereafter *MPW*), April 15, 1911, 827; *MPW*, June 24, 1911, 1466.

34. Bowser, *The Transformation of Cinema*, 84.

35. "Limits Five Cent Program to Three Reels," *MPN*, December 19, 1914, 32; "Campaign for Higher Prices Is Being Pushed in New Haven," *MPN*, July 11, 1914, 34.

36. "Three Reels for 5 Cents, Or Not?," *MPN*, March 28, 1914, 61; *MPN*, July 11, 1914, 42–49.

37. "The Motion Picture News Review of Film Trade Conditions in America," *MPN*, July 11, 1914, 29–64.

38. Anderson, "The Motion Picture Patents Company: A Reevaluation," 150.

39. Quinn, "Early Feature Distribution," 60–77.

40. "Limit on Chicago Programs," *MPN*, January 18, 1913, 61.

41. Jas. S. McQuade, "Chicago Letter," *MPW*, September 20, 1913, 1269.

42. *MPN*, July 11, 1914, 45–46.

43. "Chicago Letter," *MPN*, September 27, 1913, 37.

44. *Reel Life*, September 20, 1913, 30.

45. Quinn, "Early Feature Distribution," 76.

46. The 1908 rental schedule for Edison films did not even have a pricing tier for contracts above seven days. See *U.S. v. MPPC*, 350.

47. Quinn, "Early Feature Distribution," 61–62.

48. Ben Brewster, "*Traffic in Souls*: An Experiment in Feature-Length Narrative Construction," *Cinema Journal* 31, no. 1 (Autumn 1991): 37; "'Slaver' Films Hurried," *Variety*, December 12, 1913, 13; "'Square' Shows a Profit," *Variety*, February 13, 1914, 22.

49. Derek Long, "From Program Shorts to Mutual Masterpictures," 90–97.

50. Quinn, "Early Feature Distribution," 141, 134.

51. Waller, *Main Street Amusements*, 117.

52. "Industry Answers 'News' Appeal for Longer Runs," *MPN*, February 17, 1917, 1035–1036.

53. Richard Koszarski, *An Evening's Entertainment: The Age of the Silent Feature Picture, 1915–1928* (Berkeley: University of California Press, 1990), 34–35.

54. See *MPW*, July 29, 1916, 755.

55. See Petitioner's Exhibit no. 98, *U.S. v. MPPC*, 431–437.

56. "Maritime Protest Against Deposit," *MPW*, November 11, 1916, 886.

57. *MPW*, July 29, 1916, 753; Sam Spedon, "Deposits or No Deposits: That's the Question," *MPW*, February 17, 1917, 986.

58. "Brooklyn Triangle Exhibitors in Deposit Mix-Up," *MPN*, March 10, 1917, 1521; "Exchange Fails—Ties Up Deposits," *MPW*, March 10, 1917, 1542.

59. W. Stephen Bush, "Abuses of the Deposit System," *MPW*, September 16, 1916, 1805.

60. "Don't Like Cash Deposits," *Variety*, April 21, 1916, 24.

61. *MPW*, March 18, 1916, 1800.

62. *MPW*, July 29, 1916, 755. *Photoplay* (July 1917, 65) claimed that a certain "eminent film manufacturer of brief name"—presumably William Fox—"is alleged to have conducted his entire screen operations on loans made by banks wherein he had deposited a total of $600,000 in exhibitors' money."

63. F. J. Rembusch, "Need of Economy in Picture Business," *MPW*, December 2, 1916, 1323.

64. *Motography*, July 8, 1916, 61.

65. As more open contracts for smaller groups of films became prevalent, the norm for deposits was increasingly 25 percent of the total rental cost. Exhibitors who booked in bulk often paid much less. By the 1920s and 1930s, 10 percent of the rental was a common amount.

66. Quinn, "Early Feature Distribution," 179.

67. "Selznick Branches Out," *MPW*, April 8, 1916, 272.

68. Advertisement for Clara Kimball Young Film Corporation, *Variety*, July 21, 1916, 23.

3 | THE PACKAGE, PART II: *Reprogramming the Studio System*

1. Michael Quinn, "Early Feature Distribution and the Development of the Motion Picture Industry: Famous Players and Paramount, 1912–1921" (PhD diss., University of Wisconsin–Madison, 1998), 170, 181–182.

2. *United States v. Motion Picture Patents Company*, 225 F. 800 (1915), 2036, 2147–2148, 2352, 2828–2829.

3. Howard T. Lewis, *The Motion Picture Industry* (New York: D. Van Nostrand Company, 1933), 8.

4. Quinn, "Early Feature Distribution," 8; Sheldon Hall and Steve Neale, *Epics, Spectacles, and Blockbusters* (Detroit: Wayne State University Press, 2010), 47.

5. Quinn, "Early Feature Distribution," 180–181.

6. See Quinn, "Early Feature Distribution," 207, for a description of Paramount's organization of its star series in 1917–1918.

7. Thomas S. Watson Papers, Wisconsin Historical Society, Box 8, Folder 20. All subsequent Watson correspondence comes from this collection. See https://digicoll.library.wisc.edu/cgi/f/findaid/findaid-idx?c=wiarchives;view=reslist;subview=standard;didno=uw-whs-mss00820. Although the listed name of the collection is the "Thomas S. Watson Papers," Watson's middle initial is "J" in the correspondence itself.

8. Letter from C. W. Eckhardt to Watson, undated letters (ca. spring 1922), Watson Papers, Box 9, Folder 1.

9. "To Wage War on Selznick at Convention Next Week," *Variety*, June 30, 1916, 16.

10. Quinn, "Early Feature Distribution," 176, 179. *Variety* announced Pickford, Zukor, and Lasky's establishment of the Pickford Film Corporation in the very same issue just two pages later: "Pickford Co. Incorporated," *Variety*, June 30, 1916, 18.

11. "To Wage War," 16.

12. "To Wage War," 16.

13. Quinn, "Early Feature Distribution," 306; Richard Koszarski, *An Evening's Entertainment: The Age of the Silent Feature Picture, 1915–1928* (Berkeley: University of California Press, 1990), 34.

14. "Selznick Shows Value of Open Booking," *Motography*, October 28, 1916, 989.

15. "Adolph Zukor Discusses 'Program System' Versus 'Open Booking' Method of Film Distribution," *New York Clipper*, August 5, 1916, 33; "Attacks the Open Booking System," *MPW*, August 12, 1916, 1088.

16. "Zukor Discusses," 33.

17. Karen Ward Mahar, "Women, Filmmaking, and the Gendering of the American Film Industry, 1896–1928" (PhD diss., University of Southern California, 1995), 290.

18. "Wildcatting Personality," *Photoplay*, December 1916, 63–64.

19. Koszarski, *An Evening's Entertainment*, 34–35.

20. "Alameda League Against Exhibitors' Star System," *MPN*, October 21, 1916, 2512.

21. Al Thornburg, "Open Booking or the Program—Which?—III," *MPN*, October 28, 1916, 2655.

22. John H. Kunsky, "Open Booking or the Program," 2655.

23. "Why Program Booking Is Imperative," *MPN*, December 30, 1916, 4178; "Open Booking or the Program—Which?—VI," *MPN*, December 9, 1916, 3611; William A. Brady, "Brady Talks on Program System," *Motography*, July 21, 1917, 138.

24. "Rothapfel Goes in for Open Booking at Rialto," *MPN*, December 23, 1916, 3983.

25. "Paramount and Triangle Adopt Open Market Plan," *Variety*, March 30, 1917, 21; "Triangle Makes Important Announcement," *Motography*, April 21, 1917, 807; "Triangle's New Booking Policy," *MPW*, April 21, 1917, 410.

26. "Adopt Open Market Plan," 21.

27. "Triangle Takes Steps Which Promise Tremendous Reforms," *Variety*, April 13, 1917, 17; "Triangle to Abolish Deposits; Will Bond Exhibitors," *MPN*, April 28, 1917, 2637; Kalton Lahue, *Dreams for Sale: The Rise and Fall of the Triangle Film Corporation* (South Brunswick, NJ: A. S. Barnes, 1971), 166–167.

28. "Triangle to Abolish 'Deposit' System," *MPW*, April 28, 1917, 588.

29. Koszarski, *An Evening's Entertainment*, 72–73; "Exhibitors Organize," *Variety*, April 27, 1917, 19; "Big Exhibitors Form Co-operative Association," *MPW*, April 28, 1917, 589.

30. Quinn, "Early Feature Distribution," 205–206; Koszarski, *An Evening's Entertainment*, 73–75; Mahar, "Women, Filmmaking, and the Gendering of the American Film Industry," 312–315.

31. "Big Exhibitors Form Co-Operative Association," 589.

32. Miles H. Alben, "History of First National Pictures Inc.," unpublished manuscript, n.d., 20, Folder 15494A, Warner Bros. Archives, School of Cinematic Arts, University of Southern California, Los Angeles.

33. Quinn, "Early Feature Distribution," 255.

34. Letter from William Fox to Sol Wurtzel, June 12, 1918, in *William Fox, Sol M. Wurtzel and the Early Fox Film Corporation, Letters, 1917–1923*, ed. Lillian Wurtzel Semenov and Carla Winter (Jefferson, NC: McFarland, 2001), 50; *Exhibitors Herald and Motography* (hereafter *EHM*), December 21, 1918, 50; "Fox Activities Reviewed for 1918," *MPN*, December 28, 1918, 3885.

35. Quinn, "Early Feature Distribution," 204–208.

36. "Fox for Open Bookings," *Variety*, May 11, 1917, 32.

37. "Paramount Declares for Open Booking," *MPW*, May 5, 1917, 770; "Metro Announces Plans," *Motography*, July 28, 1917, 197.

38. "Future Film Conditions," *Variety*, December 28, 1917, 228.

39. "The Program Question," *Motography*, January 27, 1917, 175.

40. "Booking Plans Changing," *Variety*, March 23, 1917, 17.

41. Quinn, "Early Feature Distribution," 144–145, 267. VLSE was a partnership between the Vitagraph, Lubin, Selig, and Essanay companies.

42. W. W. Hodkinson Corporation to Watson, September 15, 1921, Watson Papers, Box 9, Folder 8.

43. Leslie Midkiff Debauche, *Reel Patriotism* (Madison: University of Wisconsin Press, 1997), 140.

44. "Spring Crop of State Righters Bulling the Feature Market," *Variety*, March 2, 1917, 21.

45. Richard Allen Nelson, "Commercial Propaganda in the Silent Film: A Case Study of *A Mormon Maid*," *Film History* 1, no. 2 (1987): 157.

46. *Exhibitors Herald* (hereafter *EH*), September 15, 1917, 35–38; *EH*, July 6, 1918, 41–44.

47. "State Rights Department," *MPW*, May 26, 1917, 1305; "List of State Rights Pictures," *MPW*, July 21, 1917, 554.

48. Jacob Wilk, "The Open Market," *Variety*, December 31, 1917, 228.

49. "Screen Classics, Inc., Enlarges Its Scope," *EH*, May 11, 1918, 30.

50. William Paul, *When Movies Were Theater: Architecture, Exhibition, and the Evolution of American Film* (New York: Columbia University Press, 2016), 152–153.

51. Quinn, "Early Feature Distribution," 181–183.

52. For representative examples of specials being held over for extended runs, see "'The Crisis' Is Held Over," *MPW*, December 30, 1916, 1917; "Wisconsin Theater Notes," *MPW*, February 24, 1917, 1231; "Among State Rights Companies," *MPW*, March 31, 1917, 2144.

53. Paul, *When Movies Were Theater*, 136–137.

54. "Move to Abolish Daily Program Change Gains Nationally," *MPN*, February 3, 1917, 709.

55. "Making Longer Runs Possible," *MPN*, May 18, 1918, 2935.

56. "'Cleopatra' Claims a Chicago Record," *MPN*, July 27, 1918, 602; "'Cleopatra' Makes Chicago Hit," *MPN*, June 22, 1918, 3714; "Five Million See 'Cleopatra,'" *MPN*, August 17, 1918, 1063; "Fox Reports Phenomenal Business for 'Cleopatra,'" *MPW*, August 24, 1918, 1134.

57. "Fox Reports Phenomenal Business for 'Cleopatra.'" The general phe-

nomenon of the biggest specials being held over by exhibitors in their subsequent rental-basis runs was seen in the mid-1910s as well with films such as *Intolerance* and *Civilization*. See "Wisconsin Theater Notes," 1231; "Among State Rights Companies," 2144.

58. Letter from William Fox to Sol Wurtzel, March 4, 1918, in Semenov and Winter, *William Fox*, 38.

59. DeBauche, *Reel Patriotism*, 139.

60. "Cheese Cake" (Universal advertisement), *MPW*, January 1, 1916, 6; "Carl Laemmle Warns Exhibitors Day of the Program Has Passed," *EH*, June 29, 1918, 30.

61. See "The Diluted Picture," *MPW*, November 5, 1910, 1038; "The 'Change Daily' Abuse," *MPW*, November 12, 1910, 1104; "The Exhibitor's Opportunity," *MPW*, August 5, 1911, 269; "Long Runs," *Motography*, February 1912, 52; "Hodkinson—Conservative Iconoclast," *MPW*, February 14, 1914, 816.

62. William A. Johnston, "The Deadly Movie Fan," *MPN*, January 20, 1917, 375. See also "The Star and the Daily Change," *MPN*, January 27, 1917, 537; "Move to Abolish Daily Program Change," 709.

63. "Tendency to Longer Runs Is Growing," *MPN*, January 3, 1920, 401.

64. Koszarski, *An Evening's Entertainment*, 34–35.

65. "Tendency to Longer Runs Is Growing," 401.

66. "Letters from a Self-Made Exhibitor to His Son," *MPN*, April 27, 1918, 2500–2501.

67. "Letters from a Self-Made Exhibitor to His Son," 2501.

68. Robertson-Cole Distributing Corporation Open Booking Contract with Watson, January 25, 1921, Watson Papers, Box 10, Folder 9.

69. Letter from Watson to Fox Film Corporation, July 2, 1921, Watson Papers, Box 8, Folder 20.

70. *Humoresque* had premiered at Paramount's two-a-day "run house," the Criterion, that May. "What the Big Houses Say," *MPN*, survey of all issues between September 11, 1920, 2057, and December 18, 1920, 4575.

71. For representative examples, see "What the Big Houses Say," *MPN*, November 13, 1920, 3703, and December 4, 1920, 4231.

72. "What the Big Houses Say," *MPN*, December 18, 1920, 4576.

73. "What the Big Houses Say," *MPN*, November 20, 1920, 3881. Famous Players–Lasky films were frequently held over in their own presentation houses, the Rivoli and the Rialto.

74. "Who Started This Open Market, Anyway?" *MPN*, May 10, 1919, 3014.

75. Prices in the United States rose between 14 percent and 18 percent every year from 1917 through 1920, compared to an average historical rate of about 3 percent. See US Bureau of Labor Statistics, "Historical Consumer Price Index for All Urban Consumers," Table 24, *CPI Detailed Report*, July 2016, www.bls.gov /cpi/cpid1607.pdf.

76. Theaters already paid a seating tax, which had been assessed in the Revenue Act of 1916. DeBauche, *Reel Patriotism*, 101, 143.

77. Kia Afra, "Hollywood's Trade Organizations: How Competition and Collaboration Forged a Vertically-Integrated Oligopoly, 1915–1928" (PhD diss., Brown University, 2011), 190–198; "The War Tax on Theatres," *Variety*,

September 14, 1917, 7; "Tax Date Confuses Managers Working Out Payment Plan," *Variety*, October 12, 1917, 6; "War Tax Troubles Multiply in All Amusement Fields," *Variety*, October 26, 1917, 7.

78. Afra, "Hollywood's Trade Organizations," 195.

79. "House to Lay 5 Per Cent. Rental Tax," *MPW*, August 31, 1918, 1234; "Tax Law Passed by Congress Hits Theatres," *MPW*, March 1, 1919, 1192; "Burt," "Explanation of New Film Rental Tax," *EHM*, April 19, 1919, 24; "Film Rental Tax Effective May 1," *EHM*, April 26, 1919, 29.

80. "Effect of Tax Pleases Detroit Exhibitors," *MPW*, November 24, 1917, 1215; "Varying Reports from Firing Line on First Effects of Tax," *MPN*, November 17, 1917, 3420, 3424.

81. "Exhibitors Bare Teeth at Producers Who Pass Tax Along," *MPN*, November 17, 1917, 3421–3422; "Relay of Footage Tax Causes Big Controversy," *EH*, November 3, 1917, 15, 18.

82. "Special Productions and Longer Runs Used to Counteract Effects of War Tax," *EH*, December 29, 1917, 22.

83. DeBauche, *Reel Patriotism*, 101–102.

84. "Members of the M.P.E.L.A. . . . ," *MPW*, January 5, 1918, 63; "Government Enforces Lightless Night Rule," *Motography*, January 12, 1918, 1; "'Turn Out the Lights—Go to the Movies' Movement Started to Save Nation's Fuel," *EH*, February 9, 1918, 14; "Big Theatrical Business All Over the East Monday," *Variety*, January 25, 1917, 5; "Theatres, Dazed, Rally Quickly," *MPN*, February 2, 1918, 680.

85. "Exhibitors Must Settle for Tuesday, General Belief," *Variety*, January 25, 1918, 48.

86. "Griffith, Pickford, Fairbanks, Hart and Chaplin Organize to Release Direct," *Wid's Daily*, January 17, 1919, 1; "'Big Five' in Mammoth Combination," *MPN*, January 25, 1919; "Tremendous Money Interests Reported Backing Big Five," *Variety*, January 31, 1919, 1, 58, 54; "Star Combination Was Unexpected," *MPW*, February 1, 1919, 619.

87. Tino Balio, *United Artists: The Company Built by the Stars*, vol. 1, *1919–1950* (Madison: University of Wisconsin Press, 2009), 28.

88. "Griffith Explains," *Wid's Daily*, January 17, 1919, 1.

89. "'Co-operation Is Watchword of United,'" *MPN*, June 21, 1919, 4186.

90. "Press Praises Hodkinson Policy," *MPN*, April 26, 1919, 2642; "Hodkinson's Open Booking Meets Immediate Favor," *MPW*, May 3, 1919, 656.

91. "Dynamite!," advertisement for W. W. Hodkinson Corporation, *EHM*, April 26, 1919, 2; "Dead Cats!," advertisement for W. W. Hodkinson Corporation, *EHM*, May 3, 1919, 13; "Hodkinson Primes Some Dynamite," *MPW*, May 24, 1919, 1151. See also "'Murder Is a Crime, But I Won't Commit Any More Murders after September," advertisement for W. W. Hodkinson Corporation, *MPW*, June 14, 1919, 1573.

92. "Who Started This Open Market, Anyway?," 3014–3015.

93. "Famous Players–Lasky Expected to Adopt Open Booking in Fall," *EHM*, May 31, 1919, 22; "Famous Players–Lasky Chiefs Give Outline of Next Season's Plans," *MPW*, June 28, 1919, 1919–1920; "Metro Discloses Plans for New Season," July 5, 1919, 303; "Every Picture Strictly on Its Merit," *MPN*, July 12, 1919, 535; "Elaborate Productions to Back Merit Booking," *EHM*, July 19,

1919, 33; "Victory Near in Fight on Program System," *EHM*, April 26, 1919, 17; "This Fall Brings Wonderful New Era," *Wid's Daily*, May 18, 1919, 2–3; "Open Market Assured for 1920," *EHM*, May 10, 1919, 41–42.

94. "Fox Announces Extraordinary Schedule," *MPN*, July 19, 1919, 732; "Plain Words for Plain Men," *MPN*, August 2, 1919, 1012–1013; "'Exhibitor Wants Only Fair Play,'" *MPN*, July 12, 1919, 534.

95. "Universal Decides upon Releases for Star Series," *MPW*, March 1, 1919, 1236; "New Universal Policy Announced," *MPW*, May 31, 1919, 1323.

96. "Open Market Is 'Plain Bunk' Say Picture Exhibitors," *Variety*, July 11, 1919, 66.

97. "Exhibitors' Booking Pool to Oppose Open Market Plan," *Variety*, July 18, 1919, 48.

98. See Quinn, "Early Feature Distribution," 181.

99. "Open Market Is 'Plain Bunk' Say Picture Exhibitors," 66; "Exhibitors' Booking Pool to Oppose Open Market Plan," 48.

100. "Exhibitors' Booking Pool to Oppose Open Market Plan," 48.

101. Ben Singer, "1919—Movies and Righteous Americanism," in *American Cinema of the 1910s: Themes and Variations*, ed. Charlie Keil and Ben Singer (New Brunswick, NJ: Rutgers University Press, 2009), 228–229.

102. Benjamin B. Hampton, *A History of the Movies* (New York: Covici-Friede, 1931), 216–218.

103. Letter from Whitman Bennett to Charles Eyton, October 18, 1919, Adolph Zukor Correspondence, Margaret Herrick Library Digital Collections, http://digitalcollections.oscars.org/cdm/compoundobject/collection/p15759coll3/id/118/rec/64.

104. Semenov and Winter, *William Fox*, 133–134.

105. John W. McKay, "Money and Motion Pictures," *MacLean's Magazine* 34, no. 1 (January 1, 1921): 13, 42.

106. "Mayflower Launched Two Years Ago," *EH*, September 18, 1920, 59.

107. Matthew Bernstein, "Hollywood's Semi-Independent Production," *Cinema Journal* 32, no. 3 (Spring 1993): 41–54.

108. Jesse Lasky, "Specialized Production for the New Year," *MPW*, June 28, 1919, 1920. See also pp. 1919–1926.

109. "Eminent Authors Pictures Formed," *MPW*, June 7, 1919, 1469; "Goldwyn Talks of Writers' Plans," *MPW*, June 14, 1919, 1639.

110. "No Premium Now on Famous Authors So Far as Pictures Are Concerned," *Variety*, March 3, 1922, 45; "Art and Politics," *The Photodramatist*, October 1922, 26.

111. AFI Catalog Entries for Paramount and First National releases, 1919 and 1920.

112. *Film Daily Yearbook*, 1961, 233.

113. Letter from Whitman Bennett to Charles Eyton, October 18, 1919, Adolph Zukor Correspondence, http://digitalcollections.oscars.org/cdm/compoundobject/collection/p15759coll3/id/118/rec/64.

114. Letter from Whitman Bennett to Charles Eyton, October 18, 1919.

115. Afra, "Hollywood's Trade Organizations," 245–256.

116. Abridgment of Transcripts of Evidence, Part II—Evidence for the Respondents, *Federal Trade Commission v. Paramount Famous Lasky Corporation*, 1927, 619 (hereafter *FTC v. PFL*).

4 | SPACE: *From Franchising to Merchandising*

1. Michael Quinn, "Early Feature Distribution and the Development of the Motion Picture Industry: Famous Players and Paramount, 1912–1921" (PhD diss., University of Wisconsin–Madison, 1998).

2. Ben Singer, "Feature Films, Variety Programs, and the Crisis of the Small Exhibitor," in *American Cinema's Transitional Era,* ed. Charlie Keil and Shelley Stamp (Berkeley: University of California Press, 2004), 87.

3. Gregory Waller, "Mapping the Moving Picture World: Distribution in the United States circa 1915," in *Networks of Entertainment: Early Film Distribution, 1895–1915,* ed. Frank Kessler and Nanna Verhoeff (Bloomington: Indiana University Press, 2007), 98.

4. Maureen Rogers, "'Territory Going Fast!': State Rights Distribution and the Early Multi-Reel Feature Film," *Historical Journal of Film, Radio, and Television* 37, no. 4 (2017): 598–614.

5. Paulo Cherchi Usai, *Silent Cinema: An Introduction* (London: BFI, 2000), 10–11.

6. Thomas Dicke, "Franchising in the American Economy, 1840–1980" (PhD diss., Ohio State University, 1988), 2, 5.

7. Dicke, "Franchising in the American Economy," 5–6, 6–7, 2–3, 9–10.

8. Dicke, "Franchising in the American Economy," 27.

9. Max Alvarez, "The Origins of the Film Exchange," *Film History* 17, no. 4 (2005): 431–465.

10. Michael Quinn, "Distribution, the Transient Audience, and the Transition to the Feature Film," *Cinema Journal* 40, no. 2 (2001): 48; Rogers, "Territory Going Fast!," 602.

11. Ben Brewster, "Periodization of Early Cinema," in Keil and Stamp, *American Cinema's Transitional Era,* 67.

12. Sheldon Hall and Steve Neale, *Epics, Spectacles, and Blockbusters* (Detroit: Wayne State University Press, 2010), 24–25.

13. Quinn, "Early Feature Distribution," 116.

14. Letter from Western Import Company to Leading Features Company, November 10, 1914, Griffith Papers, Microfilm Edition, University Libraries (from originals held at the Museum of Modern Art in New York), Reel 2; Majestic Motion Picture Company Trial Balance, January 31, 1915, Aitken Papers, Wisconsin Historical Society, Box 33.

15. See ads for *At the Old Cross Roads, MPW,* August 29, 1914, 1283; W. H. Productions, *MPW,* January 5, 1918, 129; *The Haunted House, MPW,* September 21, 1918, 1666.

16. Quinn, "Early Feature Distribution," 120–123.

17. Quinn, "Early Feature Distribution," 123, 131.

18. Rogers, "Territory Going Fast!," 608.

19. Quinn, "Early Feature Distribution," 133.

20. Quinn, "Early Feature Distribution," 175–178.

21. Rob King, *The Fun Factory: The Keystone Film Company and the Emergence of Mass Culture* (Berkeley: University of California Press, 2008), 150–155. Triangle was directly interested in only three of these theaters, in New York, Chicago, and Philadelphia, and only through subleases.

22. Kalton Lahue, *Dreams for Sale: The Rise and Fall of the Triangle Film Corporation* (South Brunswick, NJ: A. S. Barnes, 1971), 150, 50.

23. "Brooklyn Pays $750,000 for Triangle Plays," *MPN*, October 23, 1915, 13; "More Wise Men in the Triangle Garden," *MPN*, October 30, 1915, 18; "Triangle Spells Dollars to These Men," *MPN*, November 6, 1915, 21.

24. Hall and Neale, *Epics, Spectacles, and Blockbusters*, 24; Tino Balio, ed., *The American Film Industry* (Madison: University of Wisconsin Press, 1985), 110–111; William Paul, *When Movies Were Theater: Architecture, Exhibition, and the Evolution of American Film* (New York: Columbia University Press, 2016), 122–123.

25. Quinn, "Early Feature Distribution," 306.

26. Contract between Triangle Film Corporation and H. I. Garson and P. P. Craft, November 17, 1915, Aitken Papers, Box 11.

27. Contract between Triangle Film Corporation and Big "T" Film Corporation, February 21, 1916, Aitken Papers, Box 11. By 1916, Kemble was a state rights distributor, handling various propaganda films. "Kemble to Handle Big Features," *Motography*, August 19, 1916, 447. The Big "T" Film Corporation would go completely bankrupt in early 1917, angering exhibitors who had already paid their deposits for Triangle service. "Exchange Fails—Ties Up Deposits," *MPW*, March 10, 1917, 1542; Lahue, *Dreams for Sale*, 164–165.

28. Contract between Triangle Film Corporation and Southwestern Triangle, October 4, 1915, Aitken Papers, Box 11.

29. Contract between Triangle Film Corporation and Ernest A. Fenton, December 27, 1915, Aitken Papers, Box 11.

30. "81st Street Gets Triangle," *Variety*, October 8, 1915, 18.

31. "H. Schwalbe Secures Local Triangle Rights," *MPW*, December 18, 1915, 2217.

32. "Christmas Spirit Much in Evidence in Quaker City Film Circles," *MPN*, January 15, 1916, 220.

33. "Duplex Enjoined from Using Triangle Films," *Detroit Free Press*, January 5, 1916, 9. See also "Crafts [*sic*] No Longer a Franchise Holder in Detroit," *MPN*, April 22, 1916, 2351; "Local Triangle Office Closed," *MPW*, April 8, 1916, 297; "Triangle's New Plans for State of Michigan," *MPW*, May 6, 1916, 1005.

34. "W. S. Hart Stops Over," *MPW*, June 16, 1917, 1823.

35. Contract between Triangle and Garson and Craft.

36. Contract between Triangle and Garson and Craft.

37. Quinn, "Early Feature Distribution," 188, 306.

38. King, *The Fun Factory*, 143–179.

39. Quinn, "Early Feature Distribution," 76.

40. This contradicts Lahue's claim that Triangle producers were reimbursed for their negative costs and then shared in receipts through a 65/35 arrangement. Unlike Paramount's arrangement with its producers, this lump sum payment was a reimbursement, not an advance. See Lahue, *Dreams for Sale*, 49; Quinn, "Early Feature Distribution," 138.

41. "Triangle Plans to Change Its Distributing Scheme," *MPN*, October 14, 1916, 2347; "New Triangle Exchange Proposition," *MPW*, October 14, 1916, 214.

42. Lahue, *Dreams for Sale*, 150.

43. Lahue, *Dreams for Sale*, 133.

44. *United States v. Motion Picture Patents Company*, 225 F. 800 (1915), 3203–3204.

45. "New Triangle Exchange Proposition," 214.

46. Quinn, "Early Feature Distribution," 125–126.

47. These numbers are based on Fine Arts production records for the 4500 Sunset Boulevard studios, held on microfilm reels 7 and 18 of the Aitken Collection, with supplementary data from Majestic's inventory files held in Box 33 of the same.

48. Lahue, *Dreams for Sale*, 177.

49. King, *The Fun Factory*, 157–158; Lahue, *Dreams for Sale*, 149–150.

50. Lahue, *Dreams for Sale*, 161, 165; King, *The Fun Factory*, 26–27.

51. "Aitken's Novel Scheme to Market 2,000 Old Triangles," *Variety*, January 12, 1923, 39.

52. Lahue, *Dreams for Sale*, 167.

53. Quinn, "Early Feature Distribution," 250–251.

54. Lahue, *Dreams for Sale*, 171, 182; "Lynch Purchase by Famous Clears Paramount Franchises," *Variety*, January 12, 1923, 39.

55. Eric Hoyt, *Hollywood Vault: Film Libraries before Home Video* (Berkeley: University of California Press, 2014), 47.

56. Contract between Triangle and Hyman Winik and Henry Brock, December 27, 1915, Aitken Papers, Box 11.

57. Robert Read, "A Squalid-Looking Place: Poverty Row Films of the 1930s" (PhD diss., McGill University, 2010), 80–85.

58. Susan Strasser, *Satisfaction Guaranteed: The Making of the American Mass Market* (Washington, DC: Smithsonian Books, 1989), 87.

59. Alfred D. Chandler Jr., *The Visible Hand: The Managerial Revolution in American Business* (Cambridge, MA: Harvard University Press, 1977), 215–222.

60. Chandler, *The Visible Hand*, 223–233.

61. Strasser, *Satisfaction Guaranteed*, 58–59.

62. Douglas Gomery, "U.S. Film Exhibition: The Formation of a Big Business," in Balio, *The American Film Industry*, 218–228.

63. Janet Staiger, "Announcing Wares, Winning Patrons, Voicing Ideals: Thinking about the History and Theory of Film Advertising," *Cinema Journal* 29, no. 3 (Spring 1990): 4–6.

64. Famous Players–Lasky claimed that for every member of the sales staff employed at its local exchanges, twenty-one others enacted the physical and logistical work of distribution. *The Story of the Famous Players–Lasky Corporation* (New York: Famous Players–Lasky Corporation, 1919), 31.

65. *The Story of the Famous Players–Lasky Corporation*, 27.

66. *The Story of the Famous Players–Lasky Corporation*, 29.

67. Quinn, "Early Feature Distribution," 139–140.

68. *The Story of the Famous Players–Lasky Corporation*, 29.

69. *The Story of the Famous Players–Lasky Corporation*, 29, 30.

70. Elinor Hayes, "The Employees' Publication," *University Journal of Business* 1, no. 1 (1922): 81.

71. JoAnne Yates, *Control through Communication: The Rise of System in American Management* (Baltimore: Johns Hopkins University Press, 1993), 65. Representative how-to guides include George Frederick Wilson, *The House*

Organ: How to Make It Produce Results (Milwaukee: Washington Park Publishing Company, 1915), and Robert E. Ramsay, *Effective House Organs* (New York: D. Appleton and Company, 1920).

72. Ramsay, *Effective House Organs*, 295; "States Rights House Organ," *Motography*, October 6, 1917, 727; advertisement for *The Parentage Messenger*, *MPN*, September 1, 1917, 1409; "*Parentage* Producer Urges Courtesy as Asset," *MPN*, September 1, 1917, 1441; "*Parentage* House Organ Brings Inquiries," *MPN*, October 6, 1917, 2354.

73. *The Studio Skeleton*, August 23, 1919, 2.

74. Yates, *Control through Communication*, 75–77.

75. Wilson, *The House Organ*, 13.

76. Wilson, *The House Organ*, 162.

77. "How One Smiling Selznick Lass Keeps Her Health," *Brain Exchange* (hereafter *BE*), May 31, 1922, 2. All issues of the magazine cited here were accessed at the Harry Ransom Center at the University of Texas at Austin. The issues are collected in three folders within an uncatalogued portion of the Myron Selznick material ("L. J. Selznick Miscellaneous") in the David O. Selznick Collection: BK 216 ("List of Creditors thru Misc.—Papers").

78. "Saphead Complaints," *BE*, May 6, 1921, 4.

79. "How the Honor Lists Are Calculated," *BE*, August 25, 1922, 4.

80. Wilson, *The House Organ*, 164.

81. Wilson, *The House Organ*, 163–164.

82. "$5,000 in Prize Money for Ten Selznick Managers Who Win 1921 Collections Contest," *BE*, March 29, 1921, 1.

83. "Selznick News Standings," *BE*, September 1, 1922, 4.

84. Wilson, *The House Organ*, 159.

85. "Hot Shots from Kansas City," *BE*, May 24, 1922, 4.

86. "What's Happened to Manager Fox?," *BE*, March 29, 1921, 1.

87. "Salesmen's Race Speeds Up," *BE*, March 22, 1921, 10.

88. *BE*, June 2, 1920, 10.

89. "St. Louis Staff Sends in Unique Cooperation Manifesto," *BE*, April 5, 1921, 1.

90. "Should Forward Ideas to Home Office," *BE*, November 20, 1920, 7.

91. For representative examples, see *BE*, January 30, 1922, 6; May 31, 1922, 3–4; July 13, 1922, 3; August 25, 1922, 2; October 21, 1922, 8; October 28, 1922, 4.

92. The Barter Column, *BE*, June 13, 1922, 3.

93. "Development of Merchandising Sense a Noticeable Trend in Picture Industry," *BE*, August 22, 1921, 3.

5. | TIME: *The Battle for Playdates*

1. William Paul, *When Movies Were Theater: Architecture, Exhibition, and the Evolution of American Film* (New York: Columbia University Press, 2016), 152–153.

2. Watson Papers, Wisconsin Historical Society, http://digital.library.wisc.edu/1711.dl/wiarchives.uw-whs-mss00820.

3. "Selznick Branches Out," *MPW*, April 8, 1916, 272.

4. The third clause of Metro's exhibition contract ca. 1921 is representative of the reservations most distributors had about the right to dictate playdates. Metro Pictures Corporation Rental Agreement with Watson, June 30, 1921, Watson Papers, Box 9, Folder 13.

5. Letter from C. W. Eckhardt to Watson, January 11, 1922, Watson Papers, Box 9, Folder 1.

6. Kia Afra, "Hollywood's Trade Organizations: How Competition and Collaboration Forged a Vertically-Integrated Oligopoly, 1915–1928" (PhD diss., Brown University, 2011), 170–177, 358–364. See also Richard Maltby, "The Standard Exhibition Contract and the Unwritten History of the Classical Hollywood Cinema," *Film History* 25, no. 1–2 (2013): 144.

7. Afra, "Hollywood's Trade Organizations," 364.

8. Maltby, "Standard Exhibition Contract," 138–153, citing Will H. Hays, *Arbitration in Business* (New York: Alexander Hamilton Institute, 1929), 22, http://mppda.flinders.edu.au/records/1490. Howard Lewis cited similar statistics given by Paramount at the FTC case. Howard T. Lewis, *The Motion Picture Industry* (New York: D. Van Nostrand Company, 1933), 263–265.

9. Evidence for the Respondents, *FTC v. PFL*, 624.

10. Abridgment of Transcripts of Evidence, Part I—Evidence for the Federal Trade Commission, *FTC v. PFL*, 190.

11. William A. Johnston, "Play Dates Are Pay Dates," *MPN*, July 15, 1922, 245; Martin Quigley, "Breaking Contracts," *EH*, August 5, 1922, 21.

12. Johnston, "Play Dates Are Pay Dates."

13. See "Loew Opposes Over-Booking," *EH*, July 16, 1921, 30; "Don't Over-Book!," *EH*, August 6, 1921, 29; "Sees an End of the Overbooking Evil," *Exhibitors Trade Review* (hereafter *ETR*), September 24, 1921, 1159.

14. J. D. Williams, "Where We Stand and Where We Get Off," *Associated First National Franchise*, August 1, 1921, 2.

15. *Associated First National Franchise*, November 15, 1921.

16. Martin J. Quigley, "Should Production Be Stopped?" *EH*, April 2, 1921, 27.

17. *Film Daily Yearbook*, 1961.

18. Richard Koszarski, *An Evening's Entertainment: The Age of the Silent Feature Picture, 1915–1928* (Berkeley: University of California Press, 1990), 34–35.

19. "Exhibitors Not for Hays," *Variety*, January 13, 1922, 43.

20. David Resha, "Strategies for Survival: The Little Exhibitor in the 1920s," *Quarterly Review of Film and Video* 29 (2012): 12–23.

21. Letter from Watson to W. W. Hodkinson Corp., November 3, 1922, Watson Papers, Box 9, Folder 8.

22. Letter from Robertson-Cole Chicago branch manager B. A. Lucas to Watson, November 11, 1920, Watson Papers, Box 10, Folder 9.

23. Letter from Associated Exhibitors to Watson, November 21, 1921, Watson Papers, Box 8, Folder 4. See also a similar letter from Fox to Watson, April 4, 1922, Watson Papers, Box 9, Folder 1.

24. Letter from Winfield Sheehan to Watson, February 5, 1923, Watson Papers, Box 9, Folder 1.

25. License Contract for Hodkinson Productions, March 7, 1920, Watson Papers, Box 9, Folder 8.

26. Letter from C. W. Eckhardt to Watson, undated (ca. 1921–1922), Watson Papers, Box 9, Folder 1.

27. For an example of a contract specifying a standard 25 percent deposit, see Robertson-Cole Distributing Corporation Open Booking Contract, January 25, 1921, Watson Papers, Box 10, Folder 9. See also Maltby, "Standard Exhibition Contract," 144.

28. License Contract for Hodkinson Productions, March 7, 1920, Watson Papers, Box 9, Folder 8.

29. Rental Agreement between Metro and Watson, June 14, 1921, Watson Papers, Box 9, Folder 13.

30. Martin L. Johnson, "*The Romance Promoter* with a *Deadline at 11*: Exhibitors, Urban Exchanges, and the Culture of Film Distribution in the United States, 1918–1925," *Historical Journal of Film, Radio, and Television* 41, no. 4 (2021): 672.

31. Letter from Watson to Fox, April 6, 1922, Watson Papers, Box 9, Folder 1.

32. "The Problem of 1920," *MPN*, April 10, 1920, 3257.

33. Letter from C. W. Eckhardt to Watson, March 11 and 23, 1922, Watson Papers, Box 9, Folder 1; Letter from Sidney Meyer to Watson, December 28, 1922, Watson Papers, Box 9, Folder 1.

34. "Exhibitors Not for Hays," 43.

35. "Inside Stuff on Pictures," *Variety*, May 19, 1922, 41.

36. Afra, "Hollywood's Trade Organizations," 360; *ETR*, February 17, 1923, 585–590. The Uniform Exhibition Contract would be amended in 1926 (when it was renamed the Standard Exhibition Contract) and again in 1928. Lewis, *The Motion Picture Industry*, 265–266.

37. Hays, *Arbitration in Business*, 12.

38. "Uniform Contract Ratified by N.Y. Exhibitor Groups," *ETR*, February 17, 1923, 577–588.

39. License Contract for Hodkinson Productions, March 7, 1920, Watson Papers, Box 9, Folder 8.

40. "Complete Text of Uniform Contract," *ETR*, February 17, 1923, 589; "Uniform Contract Is Adopted," *EH*, February 17, 1923, 35–38.

41. "Complete Text of Uniform Contract," 589.

42. "Concerning Playdates," *ETR*, February 10, 1923, 536.

43. See Martin Quigley, "The Uniform Contract," *EH*, February 17, 1923, 36; L. W. Boynton, "A Great Forward Step," February 18, 1923, 585–586; "Exhibitor Views on Uniform Contract," *ETR*, March 3, 1923, 687–689; "Breaking the Play Date Jam," February 19, 1923, 673; "Full Speed Ahead," March 31, 1923, 877; Robert E. Welsh, "The Editor's Views," *MPW*, May 19, 1923, 209.

44. "Uniform Contract Ratified and in Full Use Soon," *MPW*, February 17, 1923, 639.

45. "Uniform Contract Arouses Interest from Exhibitors," *EH*, March 3, 1923, 29–30; "M.P.T.O.A. Convention," *Variety*, May 24, 1923, 21.

46. "Theatre Owners Ask for Right of Preview," *ETR*, August 18, 1923, 493.

47. See Paramount lawyer Robert Swaine's questioning of Universal's southern exchange manager Ned Depinet, who claimed never to have heard the term "block booking" before the trial. Evidence for the Respondents, *FTC v. PFL*, 21.

48. For Paramount's argument that "block booking" was an extension of program shorts distribution, see Bruce Bromley's questioning of Selznick executive C. C. Ezell, Evidence for the Respondents, *FTC v. PFL*, 24–25.

49. See Kristin Thompson, *Exporting Entertainment* (London: BFI, 1985), 126–127. There are many examples of this particular usage of "block booking" in the trade press, but for a representative selection, see J. B. Sutcliffe, "British Notes," *MPW*, November 25, 1916, 1162; "Motion Pictures in the United Kingdom," *EH*, June 30, 1917, 45; "British Fear American 'Invasion,'" *New York Clipper*, July 23, 1919, 33; "After American Stars," *Wid's Daily*, December 3, 1919, 1, 3; Edward Godal, "British and Foreign Film Trade," *Variety*, December 19, 1919, 225; "Wanger Sees Death of Block Booking," *Film Daily* (hereafter *FD*), December 30, 1922, 1.

50. "Paramount Announces Seven Fall Productions for Block Booking," *MPW*, August 6, 1921, 624.

51. According to Kent, distributors distributed pictures "fairly evenly" throughout the season at a "regular rate per week or per month," with slight decreases in the hot summer months. Evidence for the Respondents, *FTC v. PFL*, 627.

52. That the first block of Group 4 was for 26 films was not an accident; this would have been exactly three months' worth of production from the old Paramount two-features-a-week program.

53. Evidence for the Respondents, *FTC v. PFL*, 608.

54. Quinn, "Early Feature Distribution," 265–266; Evidence for the Respondents, *FTC v. PFL*, 201–202.

55. Goldwyn advertisement, *MPW*, July 8, 1922, 72–73.

56. See "Letters from a Self-Made Exhibitor to His Son," *MPN*, April 27, 1918, 2500–2501; Contract between Triangle Film Corporation and H. I. Garson and P. P. Craft, November 17, 1915, Aitken Papers, Wisconsin Historical Society, Box 11.

57. Watson's June 1921 contract with Metro is a good example of this. Legal Copy of Metro Pictures Corporation Rental Agreement, June 14, 1921, Watson Papers, Box 9, Folder 13.

58. Fox advertisement, *EH*, September 3, 1921, 10.

59. Evidence for the Respondents, *FTC v. PFL*, 617–618.

60. Evidence for the Respondents, *FTC v. PFL*, 619, 600.

61. Evidence for the Respondents, *FTC v. PFL*, 119, 610, 620.

62. Evidence for the Respondents, *FTC v. PFL*, 77.

63. Metro Pictures Corporation Rental Agreement with Watson, June 30, 1921, Watson Papers, Box 9, Folder 13.

64. Goldwyn advertisement, *MPW*, July 8, 1922, 72–73.

65. For examples, see Paramount advertisement, *MPN*, June 30, 1923, 3031–3034; Goldwyn advertisement, "The Big Birds on the Horizon," *MPW*, September 2, 1922, inset between pages 2 and 3.

66. See Quinn, "Early Feature Distribution," 268–273.

67. "Realart Makes Rule to End Piling Up of Playing Dates," *Variety*, October 14, 921, 45.

68. Signed Order Blank between Frederick Jacoby and Watson, November 1, 1921, Watson Papers, Box 10, Folder 4.

69. "Realart Policies for 1921–22," *EH*, August 27, 1921, 53. Realart even referred to its exchanges as "service stations." See *MPN*, February 26, 1921, 1579–1581.

70. Quinn, "Early Feature Distribution," 272; Letter from Realart Pictures Corporation to Watson, April 7, 1922, Watson Papers, Box 10, Folder 4.

71. Payment a week in advance for individual titles remained standard until the Uniform Contract.

72. Metro Pictures Corporation Rental Agreement with Watson, June 30, 1921, Watson Papers, Box 9, Folder 13.

73. Evidence for the FTC, *FTC v. PFL*, 163.

74. Evidence for the Respondents, *FTC v. PFL*, 624.

75. The term "prerelease house" or "regular prerelease house" seems to have been used commonly enough to designate this type of theater as early as 1919. See "Pre-Release Showing for Talmadge Film," *MPN*, June 7, 1919, 3811; *Variety*, May 7, 1924, 24.

76. Paul, *When Movies Were Theater*, 153–154, 155–160, 160–171.

77. Paul, *When Movies Were Theater*, 142–143, 145.

78. "Pre-Release Showing for Talmadge Film," 3811.

79. Letter from C. W. Eckhardt to Watson, March 11 and 23, 1922, Watson Papers, Box 9, Folder 1; letter from Sidney Meyer to Watson, December 28, 1922, Watson Papers, Box 9, Folder 1.

80. Lea Jacobs and Andrea Comiskey, "Hollywood's Conception of Its Audience in the 1920s," in *The Classical Hollywood Reader*, ed. Steve Neale (New York: Routledge, 2012), 103.

81. "New Gotham Theatre Stages Extensive Exploitation Campaign," *MPN*, October 15, 1921, 1997; "Inside Stuff—Pictures," *Variety*, November 25, 1921, 41.

82. "Inside Stuff on Pictures," *Variety*, January 25, 1923, 45.

83. Jacobs and Comiskey, "Hollywood's Conception," 98.

84. Jack Poggi, *Theater in America* (Ithaca, NY: Cornell University Press, 1968), 24, 51.

85. "Inside Stuff on Legit," *Variety*, June 16, 1922, 14.

86. Despite its use of weekly changes, the Rivoli was noted as "a comparatively small capacity theater [2,200 seats] for a weekly change feature policy." "Inside Stuff on Legit," 14. As Paul, *When Movies Were Theater*, notes, the status of the Rivoli would be explicitly changed to that of a "run house" in 1926 (p. 153). See "Paramount's 3d Run House," *Variety*, June 23, 1926, 8.

87. "Kunsky Strong for Two-a-Day Theatres," *MPN*, January 19, 1924, 247.

88. "With Live Exhibitors," *ETR*, September 3, 1921, 992.

89. "Exhibitors Foresee a Higher Admission Era for Productions That Are Worth While," *MPW*, April 2, 1921, 480.

90. "Zukor's Remedy: Says Profit in Skillful Booking," *Variety*, October 7, 1921, 1, 32.

91. Paul, *When Movies Were Theater*, 153.

92. "Blood and Sand," *Variety*, August 11, 1922, 32; "Broadway's Big Week Gives Exhibitors Hope," *Variety*, August 18, 1922, 44.

93. "Exhibitors 400 Days Offer," *Variety*, August 18, 1922, 47.

94. "Extended Broadway Runs Tie Up Circuit Releases," *Variety*, August 25, 1922, 39.

95. Paul, *When Movies Were Theater*, 165–169.

96. Howard T. Lewis, *Harvard Business Reports*, vol. 8, *Cases on the Motion Picture Industry* (New York: McGraw-Hill, 1930), 189–195.

97. Evidence for the Respondents, *FTC v. PFL*, 201–202, 296, 594–630, 612–614.

98. Quinn, "Early Feature Distribution," 266.

99. Letter from Jesse L. Lasky to Adolph Zukor, July 2, 1921, Adolph Zukor Correspondence, Margaret Herrick Library Digital Collections, http://digitalcollections.oscars.org/cdm/ref/collection/p15759coll3/id/244. See also Richard Koszarski, *Hollywood on the Hudson* (New Brunswick, NJ: Rutgers University Press, 2008), 29–31; "Paramount to Force Production Costs Down 25 Percent," *MPN*, July 9, 1921, 323.

100. Letter from Lasky to Zukor, July 2, 1921.

101. "Book Lists Paramount Films," *MPN*, March 19, 1921, 2070.

102. Letter from Adolph Zukor to Jesse Lasky, July 11, 1921, Adolph Zukor Correspondence, http://digitalcollections.oscars.org/cdm/ref/collection/p15759coll3/id/256.

103. Letter from Jesse Lasky to Adolph Zukor, July 18, 1921, Adolph Zukor Correspondence, http://digitalcollections.oscars.org/cdm/ref/collection/p15759coll3/id/260.

104. Letter and memorandum from Morris Kohn to Adolph Zukor, December 14, 1921, Adolph Zukor Correspondence, http://digitalcollections.oscars.org/cdm/ref/collection/p15759coll3/id/280.

105. Letter from Adolph Zukor to Jesse Lasky, April 10, 1923, Adolph Zukor Correspondence, Box 1, Folder 6.

106. Lewis, *Harvard Business Reports*, 189–195.

107. "License for Exhibition of Paramount Pictures," *Variety*, May 26, 1922, 38.

108. "Famous Players' Newest Contract Is Setting Exhibitors Guessing," *Variety*, May 26, 1922, 39.

109. "Theatre Owners Ask for Right of Preview," 493.

110. "Paramount Line-Up Complete to February," *ETR*, May 27, 1922, 1881.

111. "'Your Contract for Paramount Pictures,'" *ETR*, May 27, 1922, 1889.

112. "Circulated," *MPW*, April 28, 1923, 928.

113. "Fifty Million People Will Read This Announcement!," *EH*, July 29, 1922, 10; Sidney R. Kent, "Box-Office Insurance for Exhibitors," *ETR*, May 27, 1922, 1885.

114. *EH*, June 2, 1923, 63.

115. "Box-Office Insurance for Exhibitors," 1885.

116. "Frank E. Woods Promoted," *MPN*, January 29, 1921, 1034.

117. "Victor H. Clarke Made Special Representative," *MPW*, May 28, 1921, 389; *MPW*, August 13, 1921, 728.

118. Record of meeting between representatives of the Producers branch and representatives of the Writers branch, Academy of Motion Picture Arts and Sciences, July 15, 1927, 54, https://mppda.flinders.edu.au/records/303.

119. Record of meeting between Producers and Writers, 57–58.

120. Benjamin Hampton, *A History of the Movies* (New York: Covici-Friede, 1931), 316–317.

121. Record of meeting between Producers and Directors, Academy of Motion Picture Arts and Sciences, July 22, 1927, 44, https://mppda.flinders.edu.au/records/306.

122. Record of meeting between Producers and Writers, 53.

123. "Six Months of Paramount Films," *EH*, May 27, 1922, 57.

124. David Bordwell, Janet Staiger, and Kristin Thompson, *The Classical Hollywood Cinema: Film Style and Mode of Production to 1960* (New York: Columbia University Press, 2016), 320.

125. Record of meeting between Producers and Writers, 54.

126. Evidence for the Respondents, *FTC v. PFL*, 478.

127. As late as December 1922, Paramount was implying a release date of March 19 for *The Covered Wagon*. "Semi-Annual Announcement," *MPN*, December 23, 1922, 3101.

128. "No More Program Productions Famous Players Telling Sales Force," *Variety*, May 3, 1923, 19.

129. "Exhibitors and 'Wagon' Cause Concern to F.P.-L.," *Variety*, August 23, 1923, 17.

130. "Famous Players Block Cut to Be Acted on by T.O.C.C.," *ETR*, October 10, 1925, 9.

131. Letter from Jesse Lasky to Adolph Zukor, April 10, 1923, Adolph Zukor Correspondence, Box 1, Folder 6.

132. Lewis, *Harvard Business Reports*, 189–195.

133. "Famous Expected to Materially Cut Production Schedule Next Season," *FD*, May 8, 1923, 1.

134. "Here Are the Stars, Directors, and Writers," *MPN*, June 2, 1923, 2579–2580.

135. Evidence for the Respondents, *FTC v. PFL*, 614; "The First 12—One a Week," *FD*, July 15, 1923, inside cover.

136. *MPN*, September 1, 1923, 3.

137. Evidence for the Respondents, *FTC v. PFL*, 614.

138. "Where We Leave the Old Road," *EH*, September 8, 1923, inside cover.

139. According to the AFI catalog, the films from that season with verified prereleases in cities other than New York were *Nice People* (Los Angeles, 1922), *The Siren Call* (Chicago, 1922), *The Cowboy and the Lady* (Cleveland, 1922), *Kick In* (Los Angeles, 1922), *The World's Applause* (Chicago, 1923), *Adam's Rib* (Los Angeles, 1923), and *Java Head* (Chicago, 1923).

140. "Paramount's New System," *Variety*, August 23, 1923, 17.

141. Evidence for the Respondents, *FTC v. PFL*, 48.

142. Evidence for the Respondents, *FTC v. PFL*, 9, 48–49, 50–51.

143. Evidence for the Respondents, *FTC v. PFL*, 566.

6 | PRICING: *What Price Sound?*

1. Lee Grieveson, *Cinema and the Wealth of Nations: Media, Capital, and the Liberal World System* (Oakland: University of California Press, 2018), 253–261.

2. The exhibition contract blanks for Shubert's roadshow of *The Life of Our Saviour* specified "____ per cent of the gross." Blank Memorandum of Agreement, 1914, Priest General Correspondence.

3. These were *Over the Hill to the Poorhouse* (Fox, 1920), *A Connecticut Yankee in King Arthur's Court* (Fox, 1921), *Queen of Sheba* (Fox, 1921), and *The Covered Wagon* (Paramount, 1923).

4. "Will Percentage Solve Distribution Problem?" *ETR*, November 17, 1923, 1137. The article's calculations are corroborated by tax collection figures from the US Treasury Department, reprinted in *Film Daily Yearbook 1922–23*, 352.

5. "Paramount's 3d Run House," *Variety*, June 23, 1926, 8; William Paul, *When Movies Were Theater: Architecture, Exhibition, and the Evolution of American Film* (New York: Columbia University Press, 2016), 153.

6. Population figure from *1940 Census of Population*, vol. 1, *Number of Inhabitants*, 919, www.census.gov/library/publications/1942/dec/population-vol -1.html.

7. Amended and Supplemental Complaint, *United States of America v Paramount Inc. et al.*, Equity No. 87-273 (1950), reprinted in *Film History* 4, no. 1 (1990): 20, 39 note 12.

8. Brian Taves, "The B Film: Hollywood's Other Half," in *Grand Design: Hollywood as a Modern Business Enterprise*, by Tino Balio (Berkeley: University of California Press, 1993), 316–318. See also Lea Jacobs, "The B Film and the Problem of Cultural Distinction," *Screen* 33, no. 1 (1992): 1–13.

9. F. Andrew Hanssen, "Revenue-Sharing in Movie Exhibition and the Arrival of Sound," *Economic Inquiry* 40, no. 3 (July 2002): 389–391.

10. Howard T. Lewis, *The Motion Picture Industry* (New York: D. Van Nostrand Company, 1933), 190–191.

11. Donald Crafton, *The Talkies: American Cinema's Transition to Sound, 1926–1931* (Berkeley: University of California Press, 1997), 111, 252.

12. Hanssen, "Revenue-Sharing," 380.

13. Hanssen, "Revenue-Sharing," 380, 388–389.

14. See *Film Daily Yearbook 1931*, 713. The seven predominantly percentage-paying houses surveyed on the document Hanssen references ranged in size from 873 to 1,800 seats. The smallest house on the list, the 873-seat Tivoli in Los Angeles, actually had the highest weekly revenue, at around $4,500/week.

15. *Film Daily Yearbook 1933*, 713.

16. "Get Ready for Percentage Bookings," *EHM*, May 31, 1919, 33.

17. "Film Rentals on Percentage Basis of F.P.-L. Sales Plan," *Variety*, May 23, 1919, 66.

18. "Picture Percentage Plan May Please Legitimate Houses," *Variety*, August 8, 1919, 3.

19. "Picture Percentage Plan May Please Legitimate Houses," 3.

20. "Why Not Percentage Booking?" *MPN*, September 27, 1919, 2566.

21. William A. Johnston, "Percentage Is Coming," *MPN*, November 15, 1919, 3573–3574; A. H. Blank, "Percentage Means Equity," *MPN*, December 6, 1919, 4057–4058.

22. J. P. Gruwell, "Percentage—Two Sides," *MPN*, January 3, 1920, 396, 400.

23. "Percentage?," *MPN*, December 13, 1919, 4236.

24. "Rubens' Views on Percentage," *EH*, April 3, 1920, 68.

25. Gruwell, "Percentage—Two Sides," 397, 402. (The question mark within parentheses appears in the original.)

26. "New York Exhibitors Rap Percentage, High Salaries, and Production Costs," *MPW*, February 14, 1920, 1025.

27. *MPW*, March 13, 1920, 1761; *MPN*, February 21, 1920, 1874.

28. "Metro Will Not Force 'Percentage,'" *EH*, April 17, 1920, 41.

29. "Paul Mooney Completes Tour," *MPN*, January 10, 1920, 642.

30. "Industry Needs Thorough Readjustment Along the Lines of Sanity and Justice," *MPW*, May 15, 1920, 923; "Cleveland Convention Dates Definitely Fixed June 8–11," *EH*, May 22, 1920, 41; "Resolutions Adopted at Cleveland by Exhibitors' Convention," *MPN*, June 26, 1920, 57.

31. "Exhibitors Form New Organization," *MPN*, February 28, 1920, 2097–2098. See also "Percentage Booking Arouses N.Y. Ire," *MPN*, February 14, 1920, 1649, 1652.

32. "B'Way Story," *Variety*, September 9, 1921, 36.

33. Telegram from F. J. Godsol to Lee Shubert, April 21, 1921, General Correspondence, 1910–1926, Shubert Archive, Box 411, Folder 2443.

34. Telegram from Lee Shubert to F. J. Godsol, April 22, 1921, General Correspondence, 1910–1926, Shubert Archive, Box 411, Folder 2443.

35. Letter from Lee Shubert to F. J. Godsol, April 23, 1921, General Correspondence, 1910–1926, Shubert Archive, Box 411, Folder 2443.

36. "Inside Stuff on Pictures," *Variety*, June 30, 1922, 34.

37. "Deals," *FD*, February 11, 1926, 1–2.

38. "Lynch Houses Book 1st National Features on 20–80 Basis," *Variety*, October 6, 1922, 46.

39. "Suit for $25,000 Filed by Famous Against Cooneys," *EH*, February 6, 1926, 31.

40. "Will Percentage Solve Distribution Problem?," 1137.

41. "Herald Readers Analyze Distribution," *EH*, multiple 1924 issues: January 19 (21–24), January 26 (29–31), February 2 (35–37), February 9 (33–35), February 16 (40).

42. "Sees Combines," *FD*, December 26, 1922, 1; "Percentage Booking System Inevitable, Says Hodkinson," *EH*, December 16, 1922, 35; "Rowland's Remedy," *FD*, October 3, 1923, 1; "Movement on Foot to Make Percentage Booking the Rule—Not the Exception," *EH*, April 11, 1925, 28.

43. "Mastbaum's Ideas," *FD*, October 21, 1923, 4; "Cleveland Opposes Percentage," *FD*, January 4, 1926, 1; *EH*, December 6, 1924, 64.

44. "Philadelphia," *EH*, January 30, 1926, 71.

45. Crafton, *The Talkies*, 111.

46. "Nine Big Specials," *MPW*, May 15, 1926, 212–213.

47. Crafton, *The Talkies*, 72.

48. *Variety*, April 6, 1927, 7; Sheldon Hall and Steve Neale, *Epics, Spectacles, and Blockbusters* (Detroit: Wayne State University Press, 2010), 80.

49. Crafton, *The Talkies*, 82.

50. Ross Melnick, *American Showman: Samuel "Roxy" Rothafel and the Birth of the Entertainment Industry, 1908–1935* (New York: Columbia University Press, 2012), 288.

51. "Chicago $53,000 with Ederle," *Variety*, February 13, 1927, 7.

52. Crafton, *The Talkies*, 70–76, 86, 104, 127–128.

53. *Variety*, September 14, 1927, 7.

54. Advertisement for *The Kid Brother*, *FD*, March 4, 1927, 2; "Percentage for Lloyd Pictures," *MPN*, May 6, 1927, 1661.

55. "Again—Percentage Bookings," *EH*, May 7, 1927, 22.

56. "Percentage," *FD*, November 10, 1927, 1.

57. The full exchange is available as MPPDA Digital Archive Record #1409, https://mppda.flinders.edu.au/records/1409.

58. Letter from Sidney Kent to Will Hays, April 20, 1927, MPPDA Digital Archive, https://mppda.flinders.edu.au/assets/Reels/Reel-3/03-2659.JPG.

59. Letter from Felix Feist to Gabriel Hess, August 12, 1927, MPPDA Digital Archive, https://mppda.flinders.edu.au/assets/Reels/Reel-3/03-2650.JPG.

60. Letter from Arthur Mayer to Gabriel Hess, July 22, 1927, 2, MPPDA Digital Archive, https://mppda.flinders.edu.au/assets/Reels/Reel-3/03-2652.JPG (through 2654.JPG).

61. Memorandum of Purchase, Famous Players–Lasky Corporation, April 12, 1926, MPPDA Digital Archive, https://mppda.flinders.edu.au/assets/Reels/Reel-3/03-2655.JPG.

62. Crafton, *The Talkies*, 130.

63. "New Uniform Contract Written," *Exhibitors Herald and Moving Picture World* (hereafter *EHMPW*), February 25, 1928, 13; *EHMPW*, March 3, 1928, 15–19, 30. See also Kia Afra, "Hollywood's Trade Organizations: How Competition and Collaboration Forged a Vertically-Integrated Oligopoly, 1915–1928" (PhD diss., Brown University, 2011), 236–237.

64. Examples of these riders are available at MPPDA Digital Archive, https://mppda.flinders.edu.au/records/1480, scans 05-1757 through 05-1818.

65. George Schiffer, "The Law and the Use of Music in Film," *Film Comment* 1, no. 6 (1963): 39.

66. Paramount Famous Lasky Exhibition Contract Blank, MPPDA Digital Archive, https://mppda.flinders.edu.au/assets/Reels/Reel-5/05-1802.JPG.

67. Universal Pictures Exhibition Contract Blank, MPPDA Digital Archive, https://mppda.flinders.edu.au/assets/Reels/Reel-7/07-2331.JPG.

68. Ernest A. Rovelstad, "Charge on Film and Score Making Small House Close, Declare Many Exhibitors," *Exhibitors Herald-World* (hereafter *EHW*), June 15, 1929, 89.

69. *Publix Theaters Corporation Theater Managers Accounting Manual*, p. 23, E. V. Richards Collection, Harry Ransom Center.

70. "Score Charge for Records Too Expensive, Say Exhibs," *Variety*, May 29, 1929, 22.

71. "J. C. Jenkins—His Colyum," *EHW*, June 1, 1929, 63.

72. "Sound Pictures Cause Upheaval in South," *FD*, July 5, 1929, 4.

73. "Buying Sound Films," *EHW*, June 22, 1929, 158.

74. Kia Afra, *The Hollywood Trust: Trade Associations and the Rise of the Studio System* (Lanham, MD: Rowman and Littlefield, 2016), 236–243.

75. Afra, *Hollywood Trust*, 251–252.

76. "Texas Unit Opposed," *FD*, July 5, 1929, 1, 6; "Writ Sound Against Deposits," *FD*, July 31, 1929, 1; "Allied States Declares War on Arbitration Method," *MPN*, August 3, 1929, 415.

77. "Percentage," *EHW*, May 25, 1929, 18; William A. Johnston, "Box Office Money," *MPN*, May 25, 1929, 1759.

78. "Sound Percentage Parley Is Set," *MPN*, July 6, 1929, 63, 117.

79. "Box Office Money," 1759.

80. Documents from these meetings are available at the MPPDA Digital Archive, Record #633, https://mppda.flinders.edu.au/records/633. A record of the meetings and attendees is available at https://mppda.flinders.edu.au/assets/Reels/Reel-7/07-1058.jpg (through 1061.jpg).

81. "Declaration of Policy of Distributors in Respect to the Problems of the Owners of Small, Independent Theaters," July 1929, MPPDA Digital Archive, https://mppda.flinders.edu.au/assets/Reels/Reel-7/07-1105.jpg.

82. "Declaration of Policy of Distributors in Respect to the Problems of the Owners of Small, Independent Theaters," July 1929, MPPDA Digital Archive, https://mppda.flinders.edu.au/assets/Reels/Reel-7/07-1111.jpg.

83. Telegram from Harry Warner to Will Hays, July 25, 1929, MPPDA Digital Archive, https://mppda.flinders.edu.au/assets/Reels/Reel-7/07-1080.jpg (to 1081.jpg).

84. Letter from C. C. Pettijohn to Sidney Kent, July 26, 1929, MPPDA Digital Archive, https://mppda.flinders.edu.au/assets/Reels/Reel-7/07-1075.jpg.

85. "Sound Picture Prices Reduced to Aid Theaters," *New York Herald Tribune*, July 27, 1929, 1, 6; "Pledge Immediate Relief," *FD*, July 27, 1929, 1.

86. "Myers Hits Adjustment Plan as All Wrong," *FD*, July 24, 1929, 1, 2.

87. Schiffer, "Law and the Use of Music," 39.

88. "Reciprocity Brings Progress," *EHW*, April 12, 1930, 23, 24.

89. "Percentage Evil Worse," *Variety*, May 14, 1930, 5.

90. "Percentage Cheaters," *Variety*, April 23, 1930, 5, 20.

91. "Distribs Claim Exhibs Kicking In on % Deals," *Variety*, December 22, 1931, 7.

92. "Inside Stuff—Pictures," *Variety*, May 17, 1932, 41.

93. Crafton, *The Talkies*, 250–253.

EPILOGUE

1. Cecilia Kang, "How Trump's Pick for Top Antitrust Cop May Shape Competition," *New York Times*, April 25, 2017, www.nytimes.com/2017/04/25/technology/how-trumps-pick-for-top-antitrust-cop-may-shape-competition.html.

2. "Federal Court Terminates Paramount Decrees," US Department of Justice, Office of Public Affairs, August 7, 2020, www.justice.gov/opa/pr/federal-court-terminates-paramount-consent-decrees.

3. "The Paramount Decrees," US Department of Justice, Antitrust Division, n.d., www.justice.gov/atr/paramount-decree-review.454

Bibliography

ARCHIVES

Harry Ransom Center, University of Texas at Austin.
Margaret Herrick Library, Academy of Motion Picture Arts and Sciences, Los Angeles.
Shubert Archive, Lyceum Theatre, New York.
Warner Bros. Archives, School of Cinematic Arts, University of Southern California, Los Angeles.
Wisconsin Historical Society, Madison.

GOVERNMENT AND LEGAL AND DOCUMENTS

Abridgment of Transcripts of Evidence, Part I—Evidence for the Federal Trade Commission. *Federal Trade Commission v. Paramount Famous Lasky Corporation*, 1927 (published March 17, 1931).
Abridgment of Transcripts of Evidence, Part II—Evidence for the Respondents. *Federal Trade Commission v. Paramount Famous Lasky Corporation*, 1927 (published March 17, 1931).
Amended and Supplemental Complaint, *United States of America v. Paramount Inc. et al.*, Equity No. 87-273 (1950). Reprinted in *Film History* 4, no. 1 (1990): 3–39.
"Federal Court Terminates Paramount Decrees." US Department of Justice, Office of Public Affairs, August 7, 2020, www.justice.gov/opa/pr/federal -court-terminates-paramount-consent-decrees.
Federal Trade Commission vs. Vaudeville Managers' Protective Association et al. [Stenographic transcript]. March 27, 1919. HathiTrust Digital Library, https://babel.hathitrust.org/cgi/pt?id=uc1.c3092502.
Historical Statistics of the United States, Colonial Times to 1970, Part I. Washington, DC: US Bureau of the Census, 1975.
1940 Census of Population. Vol. 1, *Number of Inhabitants*. US Bureau of the Census, www.census.gov/library/publications/1942/dec/population-vol-1.html.

"The Paramount Decrees." US Department of Justice, Antitrust Division, n.d., www.justice.gov/atr/paramount-decree-review.

United States House of Representatives, Committee on Interstate Commerce. *Motion-Picture Films (Compulsory Block Booking and Blind Selling)* (1940).

United States v. Motion Picture Patents Company, 225 F. 800 (1915).

BOOKS, JOURNAL ARTICLES, AND DISSERTATIONS

Abel, Richard. "Early Film Programs: An Overture, Five Acts, and an Interlude." In *A Companion to Early Cinema*, edited by Andre Gaudreault, Nicolas Dulac, and Santiago Hidalgo, 334–359. Oxford: Wiley, 2012.

Afra, Kia. "Hollywood's Trade Organizations: How Competition and Collaboration Forged a Vertically-Integrated Oligopoly, 1915–1928." PhD diss., Brown University, 2011.

Afra, Kia. *The Hollywood Trust: Trade Associations and the Rise of the Studio System*. Lanham, MD: Rowman and Littlefield, 2016.

Alben, Miles H. "History of First National Pictures Inc." Unpublished manuscript, n.d, folder 15494A. Warner Bros. Archives, School of Cinematic Arts, University of Southern California, Los Angeles.

Allen, Robert C. "The Movies in Vaudeville: Historical Context of the Movies as Popular Entertainment." In *The American Film Industry*, edited by Tino Balio, 57–82. Madison: University of Wisconsin Press, 1985.

Allen, Robert C. *Vaudeville and Film, 1895–1915: A Study in Media Interaction*. Dissertations on Film 1980. New York: Arno Press, 1980.

Allen, Robert C., and Douglas Gomery. *Film History: Theory and Practice*. New York: McGraw-Hill, 1985.

Alvarez, Max. "The Motion Picture Distributing and Sales Company." *Film History* 19, no. 3 (2007): 247–270.

Alvarez, Max. "The Origins of the Film Exchange." *Film History* 17, no. 4 (2005): 431–465.

Anderson, Mark Lynn. "The Historian Is Paramount." *Film History* 26, no. 2 (2014): 1–30.

Anderson, Robert. "The Motion Picture Patents Company: A Reevaluation." In *The American Film Industry*, edited by Tino Balio, 133–152. Madison: University of Wisconsin Press, 1985.

Backer, Samuel. "The Informational Economy of Vaudeville and the Business of American Entertainment." *Business History Review* 95, no. 3 (Autumn 2021): 423–446.

Bakker, Gerben. *Entertainment Industrialized: The Emergence of the International Film Industry, 1890–1940*. New York: Cambridge University Press, 2008.

Balio, Tino, ed. *The American Film Industry*. Madison: University of Wisconsin Press, 1985.

Balio, Tino. *Grand Design: Hollywood as a Modern Business Enterprise*. Berkeley: University of California Press, 1993.

Balio, Tino. *United Artists: The Company Built by the Stars*. Vol. 1, *1919–1950*. Madison: University of Wisconsin Press, 2009.

Bank, Rosemarie. "Antedating the Long Run: A Prolegomenon." *Nineteenth Century Theatre Research* 13, no. 1 (Summer 1985): 33–36.

Bank, Rosemarie. *Theatre Culture in America, 1825–1860*. Cambridge: Cambridge University Press, 1997.

Bernheim, Alfred. *The Business of the Theatre*. New York: Actors' Equity Association, 1932.

Bernstein, Matthew. "Hollywood's Semi-Independent Production." *Cinema Journal* 32, no. 3 (Spring 1993): 41–54.

Bordwell, David, Janet Staiger, and Kristin Thompson. *The Classical Hollywood Cinema: Film Style and Mode of Production to 1960*. New York: Columbia University Press, 1985.

Bowser, Eileen. *The Transformation of Cinema, 1907–1915*. Berkeley: University of California Press, 1990.

Brewster, Ben. "Periodization of Early Cinema." In *American Cinema's Transitional Era*, edited by Charlie Keil and Shelley Stamp, 66–75. Berkeley: University of California Press, 2004.

Brewster, Ben. "*Traffic in Souls*: An Experiment in Feature-Length Narrative Construction." *Cinema Journal* 31, no. 1 (Autumn 1991): 40–44.

Brewster, Ben, and Lea Jacobs. *Theater to Cinema: Stage Pictorialism and the Early Feature Film*. New York: Oxford University Press, 1997.

Caves, Richard. *American Industry: Structure, Conduct, Performance*. Englewood Cliffs, NJ: Prentice-Hall, 1972.

Chandler, Alfred D., Jr. *The Visible Hand: The Managerial Revolution in American Business*. Cambridge, MA: Harvard University Press, 1977.

Cherchi Usai, Paulo. *Silent Cinema: An Introduction*. London: BFI, 2000.

Cooper, Mark Garrett. *Universal Women: Filmmaking and Industrial Change in Early Hollywood*. Urbana: University of Illinois Press, 2010.

Crafton, Donald. *The Talkies: American Cinema's Transition to Sound, 1926–1931*. Berkeley: University of California Press, 1997.

Davis, Hartley. "The Business Side of Vaudeville." *Everybody's Magazine* 17 (October 1907): 527–537.

Debauche, Leslie Midkiff. *Reel Patriotism*. Madison: University of Wisconsin Press, 1997.

de Klerk, Nico. "Program Formats." In *Encyclopedia of Early Cinema*, edited by Richard Abel, 533–535. London: Routledge, 2005.

Dicke, Thomas. "Franchising in the American Economy, 1840–1980." PhD diss., Ohio State University, 1988.

DiMeglio, John. *Vaudeville, U.S.A.* Bowling Green, OH: Bowling Green University Popular Press, 1973.

Dorsten, Aimee-Marie. "'Thinking Dirty': Digging Up Three 'Matriarchs' of Communication Studies," *Communication Theory* 22 (2012): 25–47.

Economides, Nicholas. "Bundling and Tying." In *The Palgrave Encyclopedia of Strategic Management*, edited by Mie Augier and David J. Teece, 140–145. London: Palgrave Macmillan, 2018.

Frick, John. "A Changing Theatre: New York and Beyond." In *1870–1945*, edited by Don B. Wilmeth and Christopher Bigsby, 196–232. Vol. 2 of *The Cambridge History of American Theatre*. New York: Cambridge University Press, 1999.

Frykholm, Joel. *George Kleine and American Cinema: The Movie Business and Film Culture in the Silent Era*. London: Palgrave, 2015.

Gaisford, John. *The Drama in New Orleans*. New Orleans: J. B. Steel, 1849.

Gaudreault, André, and Philippe Gauthier. "De la nouveauté des Passions filmées du cinéma des premiers temps. Ou: comment faire du neuf avec du vieux . . ." In *Jésus en représentations: De la Belle Époque à la postmodernité*, edited by Alain Boillat, Jean Kaempfer, and Philippe Kaenel, 173–189. Gollion, Switzerland: Infolio, 2011.

Giraud, Jean. *Lexique française du cinéma des origines à 1930*. Paris: CNRS, 1958.

Gomery, Douglas. "U.S. Film Exhibition: The Formation of a Big Business." In *The American Film Industry*, edited by Tino Balio, 218–251. Madison: University of Wisconsin Press, 1985.

Grieveson, Lee. *Cinema and the Wealth of Nations: Media, Capital, and the Liberal World System*. Oakland: University of California Press, 2018.

Hall, Sheldon, and Steve Neale. *Epics, Spectacles, and Blockbusters*. Detroit: Wayne State University Press, 2010.

Hallam, Julia, and Les Roberts, eds. *Locating the Moving Image: New Approaches to Film and Place*. Bloomington: Indiana University Press, 2014.

Hampton, Benjamin B. *A History of the Movies*. New York: Covici-Friede, 1931.

Hanssen, F. Andrew. "Revenue-Sharing in Movie Exhibition and the Arrival of Sound." *Economic Inquiry* 40, no. 3 (July 2002): 380–402.

Hayes, Elinor. "The Employees' Publication." *University Journal of Business* 1, no. 1 (1922): 81–94.

Hays, Will H. *Arbitration in Business*. New York: Alexander Hamilton Institute, 1929.

Hewitt, Barnard. "'King Stephen' of the Park and Drury Lane." In *The Theatrical Manager in Britain and America: Player of a Perilous Game*, edited by Joseph W. Donohue Jr., 87–141. Princeton, NJ: Princeton University Press, 1971.

Hidalgo, Santiago, ed. *Technology and Film Scholarship: Experience, Study, Theory*. Amsterdam: Amsterdam University Press, 2018.

Hill, Erin. *Never Done: A History of Women's Work in Media Production*. New Brunswick, NJ: Rutgers University Press, 2016.

Hoyt, Eric. *Hollywood Vault: Film Libraries before Home Video*. Berkeley: University of California Press, 2014.

Hoyt, Eric, Derek Long, Kit Hughes, and Anthony Tran. "*Variety*'s Transformations: Digitizing and Analyzing the First 35 Years of the Canonical Trade Paper." *Film History* 27, no. 4 (2015): 76–105.

Huettig, Mae D. *Economic Control of the Motion Picture Industry*. Philadelphia: University of Pennsylvania Press, 1944.

Jacobs, Lea. "The B Film and the Problem of Cultural Distinction." *Screen* 33, no. 1 (Spring 1992): 1–13.

Jacobs, Lea, and Andrea Comiskey. "Hollywood's Conception of Its Audience in the 1920s." In *The Classical Hollywood Reader*, edited by Steve Neale, 94–109. New York: Routledge, 2012.

Johnson, Martin L. "*The Romance Promoter* with a *Deadline at 11*: Exhibitors, Urban Exchanges, and the Culture of Film Distribution in the United States, 1918–1925." *Historical Journal of Film, Radio, and Television* 41, no. 4 (2021): 665–684.

Kang, Cecilia. "How Trump's Pick for Top Antitrust Cop May Shape Competition." *New York Times*, April 25, 2017. www.nytimes.com/2017/04/25 /technology/how-trumps-pick-for-top-antitrust-cop-may-shape-competition .html.

Keil, Charlie, and Shelley Stamp, eds. *American Cinema's Transitional Era*. Berkeley: University of California Press, 2004.

Kessler, Frank, and Nanna Verhoeff, eds. *Networks of Entertainment: Early Film Distribution, 1895–1915*. Bloomington: University of Indiana Press, 2007.

Kinnard, Roy, and Tim Davis. *Divine Images: A History of Jesus on the Screen*. New York: Carol Publishing Group, 1992.

King, Rob. *The Fun Factory: The Keystone Film Company and the Emergence of Mass Culture*. Berkeley: University of California Press, 2008.

Koszarski, Richard. *An Evening's Entertainment: The Age of the Silent Feature Picture, 1915–1928*. Berkeley: University of California Press, 1990.

Koszarski, Richard. *Hollywood on the Hudson*. New Brunswick: Rutgers University Press, 2008.

Lahue, Kalton. *Dreams for Sale: The Rise and Fall of the Triangle Pictures Corporation*. South Brunswick, NJ: A. S. Barnes, 1971.

Lewis, Howard T. *Harvard Business Reports*. Vol. 8, *Cases on the Motion Picture Industry*. New York: McGraw-Hill, 1930.

Lewis, Howard T. *The Motion Picture Industry*. New York: D. Van Nostrand Company, 1933.

Lewis, Kevin. "A World across from Broadway: The Shuberts and the Movies." *Film History* 1, no. 1 (1987): 39–51.

Lloyd, Herbert. *Vaudeville Trails through the West*. Philadelphia, 1919.

Long, Derek. "From Program Shorts to Mutual Masterpictures: Cost Control as a Macroscale Production Strategy at 4500 Sunset Boulevard, 1914–15." *Film History* 29, no. 3 (2017): 76–104.

Mahar, Karen Ward. "Women, Filmmaking, and the Gendering of the American Film Industry, 1896–1928." PhD diss., University of Southern California, 1995.

Maltby, Richard. "The Standard Exhibition Contract and the Unwritten History of the Classical Hollywood Cinema." *Film History* 25, no. 1–2 (2013): 138–153.

Maltby, Richard, Daniel Biltereyst, and Philippe Meers, eds. *Explorations in New Cinema History: Approaches and Case Studies*. Malden: Wiley-Blackwell, 2011.

McConachie, Bruce. "American Theatre in Context, from the Beginnings to 1870." In *Beginnings to 1870*, edited by Don B. Wilmeth and Christopher Bigsby, 111–181. Vol. 1 of *The Cambridge History of American Theatre*. New York: Cambridge University Press, 1998.

McDermott, Douglas. "Structure and Management in the American Theatre." In *Beginnings to 1870*, edited by Don B. Wilmeth and Christopher Bigsby, 182–215. Vol. 1 of *The Cambridge History of American Theatre*. Cambridge: Cambridge University Press, 1998.

McNamara, Brooks. "Popular Entertainment." In *1870–1945*, edited by Don B. Wilmeth and Christopher Bigsby, 378–410. Vol. 2 of *The Cambridge History of American Theatre*. New York: Cambridge University Press, 1999.

McNamara, Brooks. *The Shuberts of Broadway*. New York: Oxford University Press, 1990.

Melnick, Ross. *American Showman: Samuel "Roxy" Rothafel and the Birth of the Entertainment Industry, 1908–1935*. New York: Columbia University Press, 2012.

Melnick, Ross. *Hollywood's Embassies: How Movie Theaters Projected American Power throughout the World*. New York: Columbia University Press, 2022.

Monod, David. *Vaudeville and the Making of Modern Entertainment, 1890–1925*. Chapel Hill: University of North Carolina Press, 2020.

Moore, Paul S. "'Bought, Sold, Exchanged, and Rented': The Early Film Exchange and the Market in Secondhand Films in *New York Clipper* Classified Ads." *Film History* 31, no. 2 (2019): 1–31.

Musser, Charles. "Another Look at the 'Chaser' Theory." *Studies in Visual Communication* 10, no. 4 (1984): 24–52.

Musser, Charles. *The Emergence of Cinema: The American Screen to 1907*. New York: Scribner's, 1990.

Musser, Charles, with Carol Nelson. *High-Class Moving Pictures: Lyman H. Howe and the Forgotten Era of Traveling Exhibition, 1880–1920*. Princeton, NJ: Princeton University Press, 1991.

Nasaw, David. *Going Out: The Rise and Fall of Public Amusements*. New York: Basic Books, 1993.

Nelson, Richard Allen. "Commercial Propaganda in the Silent Film: A Case Study of *A Mormon Maid*." *Film History* 1, no. 2 (1987): 149–162.

Page, Brett. *Writing for Vaudeville*. Springfield, MA: Home Correspondence School, 1915.

Paul, William. *When Movies Were Theater: Architecture, Exhibition, and the Evolution of American Film*. New York: Columbia University Press, 2016.

Phillips, Wyatt D. "'A Maze of Intricate Relationships': Mae D. Huettig and Early Forays into Film Industry Studies." *Film History* 27, no. 1 (2015): 135–163.

Poggi, Jack. *Theater in America*. Ithaca, NY: Cornell University Press, 1968.

Pritner, Calvin L. "William Warren's Financial Arrangements with Travelling Stars, 1805–1829." *Theatre Survey* 6, no. 2 (November 1965): 84–85.

Quinn, Michael. "Distribution, the Transient Audience, and the Transition to the Feature Film." *Cinema Journal* 40, no. 2 (2001): 35–56.

Quinn, Michael. "Early Feature Distribution and the Development of the Motion Picture Industry: Famous Players and Paramount, 1912–1921." PhD diss., University of Wisconsin–Madison, 1998.

Ramsay, Robert E. *Effective House Organs*. New York: D. Appleton and Company, 1920.

Read, Robert. "A Squalid-Looking Place: Poverty Row Films of the 1930s." PhD diss., McGill University, 2010.

Resha, David. "Strategies for Survival: The Little Exhibitor in the 1920s." *Quarterly Review of Film and Video* 29 (2012): 12–23.

Rogers, Maureen. "'Territory Going Fast!': State Rights Distribution and the Early Multi-Reel Feature Film." *Historical Journal of Film, Radio, and Television* 37, no. 4 (2017): 598–614.

Schatz, Thomas. *The Genius of the System: Hollywood Filmmaking in the Studio Era*. New York: Henry Holt and Company, 1988.

Schiffer, George. "The Law and the Use of Music in Film." *Film Comment* 1, no. 6 (1963): 39–43.

Schweitzer, Marlis. *When Broadway Was the Runway*. Philadelphia: University of Pennsylvania Press, 2009.

Semenov, Lillian Wurtzel, and Carla Winter, eds. *William Fox, Sol M. Wurtzel and the Early Fox Film Corporation: Letters, 1917–1923*. Jefferson, NC: McFarland, 2001.

Singer, Ben. "Feature Films, Variety Programs, and the Crisis of the Small Exhibitor." In *American Cinema's Transitional Era*, edited by Charlie Keil and Shelley Stamp, 76–100. Berkeley: University of California Press, 2004.

Singer, Ben. "1919: Movies and Righteous Americanism." In *American Cinema of the 1910s: Themes and Variations*, edited by Charlie Keil and Ben Singer, 225–248. New Brunswick, NJ: Rutgers University Press, 2009.

Smoodin, Eric. "As the Archive Turned: Writing Film Histories without Films." *The Moving Image* 14, no. 2 (Fall 2014): 96–100.

Snyder, Robert. *The Voice of the City: Vaudeville and Popular Culture in New York*. New York: Oxford University Press, 1989.

Spitzer, Marian. "The Business of Vaudeville." *Saturday Evening Post* 196, no. 47 (May 24, 1924): 18–19, 125, 129–130, 133.

Staiger, Janet. "Announcing Wares, Winning Patrons, Voicing Ideals: Thinking about the History and Theory of Film Advertising." *Cinema Journal* 29, no. 3 (Spring 1990): 3–31.

Staiger, Janet. "The Hollywood Mode of Production to 1930." In *The Classical Hollywood Cinema: Film Style and Mode of Production to 1960*, by David Bordwell, Janet Staiger, and Kristin Thompson, 85–153. New York: Columbia University Press, 1985.

Stamp, Shelley. *Lois Weber in Early Hollywood*. Oakland: University of California Press, 2015.

The Story of the Famous Players–Lasky Corporation. New York: Famous Players–Lasky Corporation, 1919.

Strasser, Susan. *Satisfaction Guaranteed: The Making of the American Mass Market*. Washington, DC: Smithsonian Institution Press, 1989.

Streible, Dan. *Fight Pictures: A History of Boxing and Early Cinema*. Berkeley: University of California Press, 2008.

Taves, Brian. "The B Film: Hollywood's Other Half." In *Grand Design: Hollywood as a Modern Business Enterprise*, by Tino Balio, 313–350. Berkeley: University of California Press, 1993.

Thompson, Kristin. *Exporting Entertainment*. London: BFI, 1985.

Troubridge, St. Vincent. *The Benefit System in the British Theatre*. London: Society for Theatre Research, 1967.

Waller, Gregory. *Main Street Amusements: Movies and Commercial Entertainment in a Southern City, 1896–1930*. Washington, DC: Smithsonian Institution Press, 1995.

Waller, Gregory. "Mapping the Moving Picture World: Distribution in the United States circa 1915." In *Networks of Entertainment: Early Film Distribution, 1895–1915*, edited by Frank Kessler and Nina Verhoeff, 94–102. Bloomington: Indiana University Press, 2007.

Wasko, Janet. *Movies and Money: Financing the American Film Industry.* Norwood, NJ: Ablex, 1982.

Wertheim, Arthur Frank. *Vaudeville Wars: How the Keith-Albee and Orpheum Circuits Controlled the Big-Time and Its Performers.* New York: Palgrave Macmillan, 2006.

Wilmeth, Don B. *Variety Entertainment and Outdoor Amusements: A Reference Guide.* Westport, CT: Greenwood Press, 1982.

Wilson, George Frederick. *The House Organ: How to Make It Produce Results.* Milwaukee: Washington Park Publishing Company, 1915.

Yates, JoAnne. *Control through Communication: The Rise of System in American Management.* Baltimore: Johns Hopkins University Press, 1993.

FILM AND ENTERTAINMENT INDUSTRY TRADE PAPERS AND HOUSE ORGANS

Associated First National Franchise
The Brain Exchange
Exhibitors Herald
Exhibitors Herald and Motography
Exhibitors Herald and Moving Picture World
Exhibitors Herald-World
Exhibitors Trade Review
Film Daily Yearbook
Motion Picture News
Motography
Moving Picture World
The Photodramatist
Picture-Play Magazine
Reel Life
Studio Skeleton
Variety
Wid's Daily

NEWSPAPERS AND MAGAZINES

MacLean's Magazine
New York Clipper
New York Herald Tribune
New York Times
Saturday Evening Post

WEB RESOURCES

Lantern Search Engine, lantern.mediahist.org
Margaret Herrick Library Digital Collections, digitalcollections.oscars.org
Media History Digital Library, mediahistoryproject.org
MPPDA Digital Archive, mppda.flinders.edu.au

Index

Note: page numbers in *italics* refer to figures.